IMAGES
of America

FONTANA

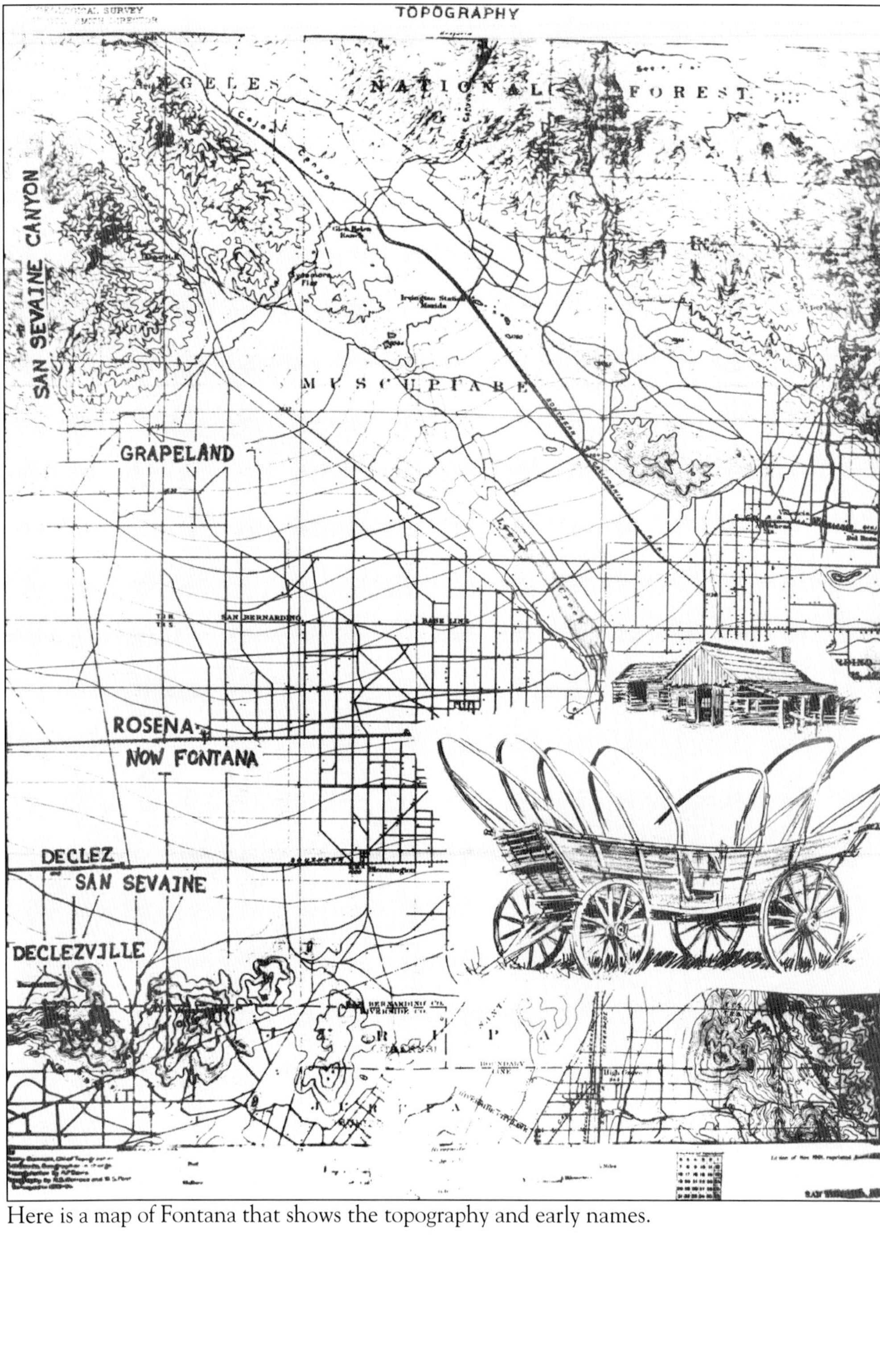

Here is a map of Fontana that shows the topography and early names.

IMAGES of America

FONTANA

John Charles Anicic Jr.

ARCADIA PUBLISHING

ISBN 978-0-7385-2900-4

Published by Arcadia Publishing
Charleston, South Carolina

Printed in the United States of America

Library of Congress Catalog Card Number: 2004104888

For all general information contact Arcadia Publishing at:
Telephone 843-853-2070
Fax 843-853-0044
E-mail sales@arcadiapublishing.com
For customer service and orders:
Toll-Free 1-888-313-2665

Visit us on the Internet at www.arcadiapublishing.com

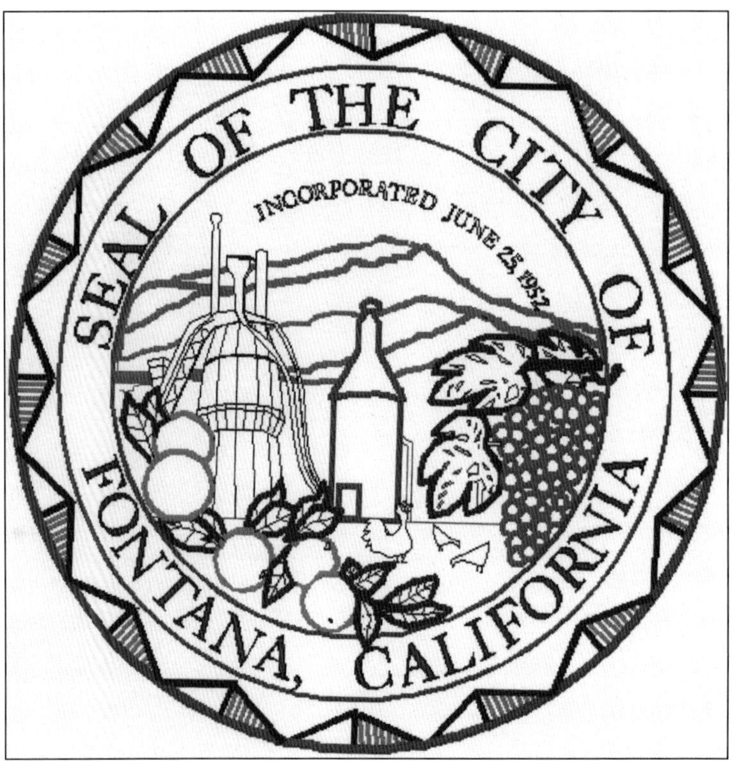

A.W.S. Austin's 1952 design for the seal of the city pays homage to Kaiser Steel, the area's grape, citrus, and poultry industries, and the mountains.

Contents

ACKNOWLEDGMENTS

Many people important to the history and preservation of Fontana have donated their time, money, and artifacts to this cause. They have helped me research and learn the chronicles of our wonderful city of Fontana. I have been compiling the history and photographs of Fontana since the 1970s, but I never imagined I would do a book. The names below should be mentioned, even though I know I will forget someone. Please forgive me.

Thank you to A.B. Miller and family; Cornelius DeBackey and his son Alex; Dr. Ernest Cadwell; Charles McLaughlin; Joe McKamie; the Roy Dowd family; the Olsen family; Judith Boyle McOmie; the Ingolds; John F. Comstock; Mildred Hilton Crawford; Mr. and Mrs. William Janka; Patricia Murray; Kay Williams Vandenberg; Emmy Lou Williams; Mr. and Mrs. Bill Perdew; John Perdew; John Spurlock; Robert Hickcox; and the *Herald News*.

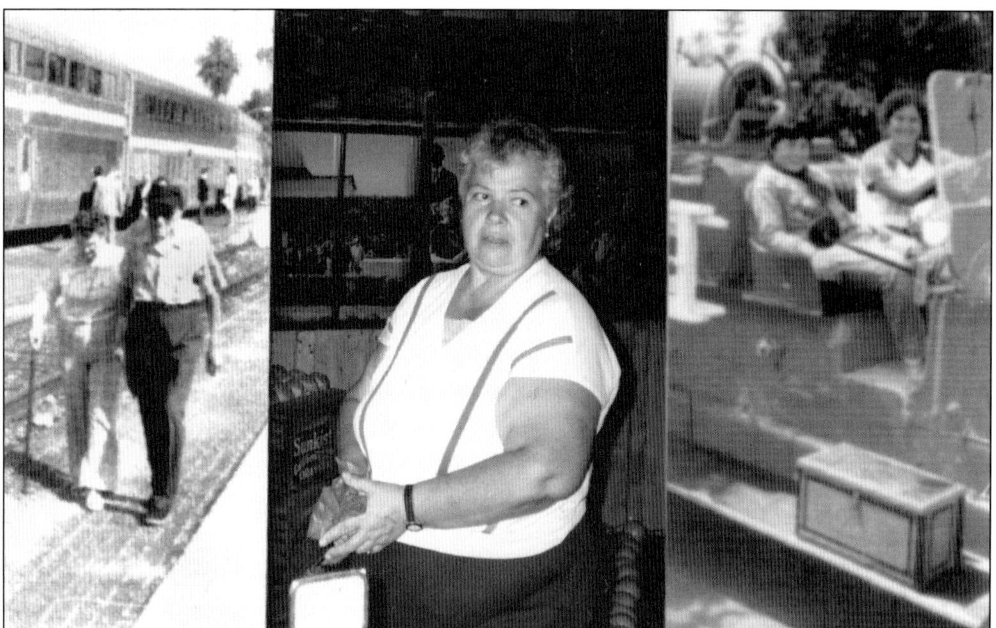

The Anicic family has been involved with the Fontana Historical Society for many years. Katherine and John Anicic Sr. helped restore the Pepper Street House (Camp No. 1); Rae Ellen Anicic, my wife, has supported me and helped with displays; Marie Therese (Smith) Anicic and John Anicic III helped with mixing mortar and pulling weeds, among other things. They have all been my support group for all I was able to do for the preservation of Fontana's past for the sake of future generations.

INTRODUCTION

This brief overview of Fontana's history will hopefully shed some light on the city's beginnings in the Inland Empire of San Bernardino County. John McGroarty, the famous poet of California, in his dedication speech at the Fontana Woman's Club House, had this to say:

> *It must have been near here, somewhere near Fontana, where old Don Antonio Maria Lugo lived on his 1813 land grant. The Don and his sons received a second grant in 1842 to the Rancho de San Bernardino. The ranch began at the Mountain of the Arrowhead in San Bernardino and ended at the Bay of Santa Monica.*

The ranch consisted of 137,700 acres set aside for Jose Maria Lugo, Jose Del Carmen Lugo, Vincent Lugo, and all the sons of Antonio Maria Lugo and Diego Sepulveda. In 1851, the Lugos sold the land grant to the Mormons, who colonized the San Bernardino Valley until they were called back to Salt Lake City in 1857. The area now includes San Bernardino, Rialto, Bloomington, and Fontana. In 1870, Andrew J. Pope received a patent from the U.S. government to this area. The Semi-Tropic Land and Water Company gained control of the Rancho's areas, but active development did not start until the early 1900s.

In 1875, the Southern Pacific Railroad came to the Valley, and in 1887 the Santa Fe Railroad built a track toward Los Angeles, naming the stop in Fontana "Rosena." Several families came to this area between 1892 and 1895. In 1901, Fontana Development Company bought the land.

A.B. Miller came to Rosena in 1905 to work the area before he bought the land in 1906. About 25 families lived in the area. In 1909, the town site was laid out and extensive crops were planted and grown.

The Fontana Company was organized in 1912. On June 7, 1913, the town site was dedicated with a special train from Los Angeles, a circus tent barbeque, and the selling of land. From 1915 to 1920 there was enlargement of farms on a continuously grand scale. In 1918, the Fontana Farms Company was organized, and by 1927, 399 families had bought land in Fontana. In 1929, the township was created. In 1925, A.B. Miller made a silent film of five rolls of Fontana to show at offices in Los Angeles. He also sent the films around the world, including India and Europe as well as within the U.S.

The area was built into a diversified agricultural area, with citrus, grains, grapes, poultry, cattle, and swine as its leading commodities. Mr. Miller also played a key role in the development of agriculture in California. The governor appointed him to the first agricultural board of California, which included helping to organize the state fair. He was in charge of California's display at the Chicago World's Fair and served on the advisory board of the Los Angeles County Fair. Mr. Miller died at his home of lymphosarcoma on Easter Sunday, April 18, 1941. He is buried at the Mountain View Cemetery in San Bernardino next to his mother and brother. R.E. Boyle took over the company as president.

In 1942, Fontana faced change. With World War II raging, a steel plant had to be built on the West Coast. Once selected, Fontana soon became the leading steel producer on the West Coast. The plant, Fontana Kaiser Steel, produced steel from 1942 to 1984 before it was closed. California Steel acquired the property and is still there today. The city now covers 56 square miles with a population of approximately 175,000 people. The area is also a center for shipping and trucking, and the California Speedway occupies part of the Kaiser site.

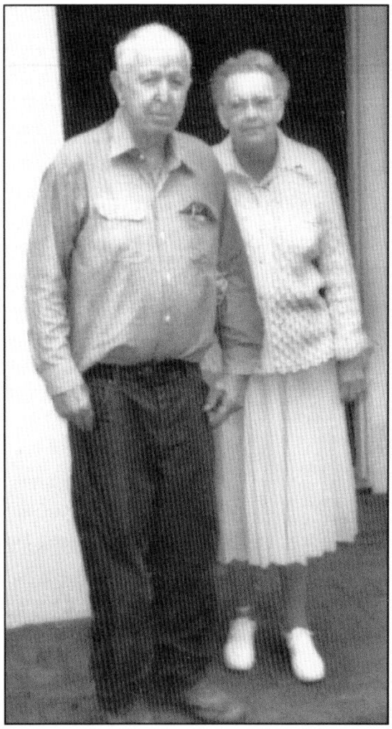

Pictured here are Judith Boyle McOmie and her husband, Lorenzo, of Santa Barbara. She was the daughter of Catherine and Richard Edward Boyle—the right-hand man to A.B. Miller. She graduated from Chaffey High School in 1930 and Stanford University in 1937. She was married in Redlands in 1946 and died on July 5, 1984, during a heart operation. She donated many items to the Fontana Historical Society, helped me with research and many long hours on the phone. She directed my research into areas not known by many on the historical society.

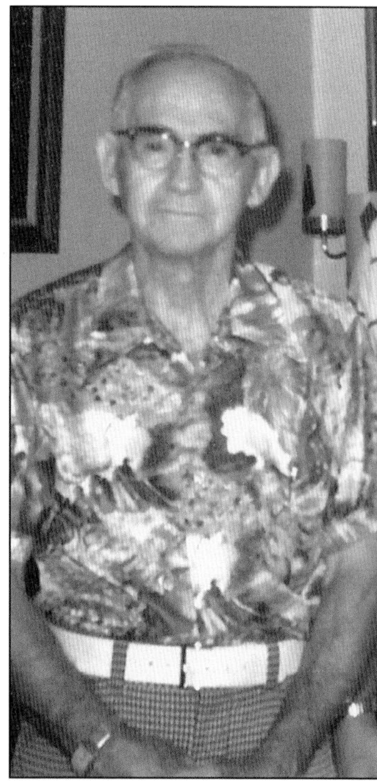

Joe McKamie was a worker with his brother Jim at the Camp No. 1 ranch site in the early 1900s. He notified the society about the location of the foreman's ranch house of the Fontana Farms Company in the 1970s, told many delightful stories about ranch life, and donated photographs. The society was able to save the house and make it a museum with the help of Mary Vagle and Hazel Putnam.

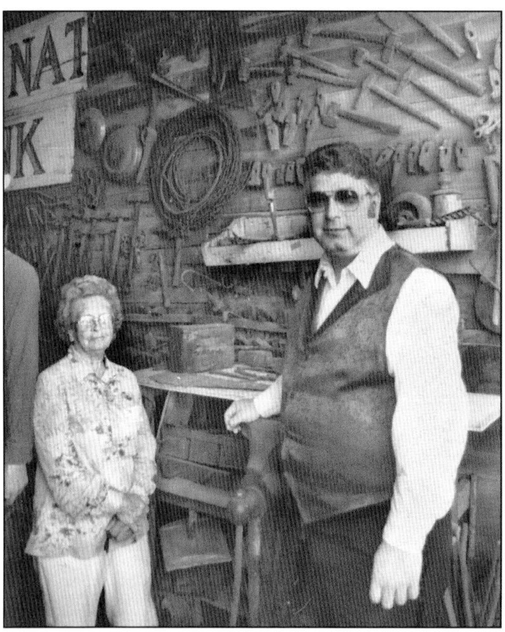

Hazel Putnam is the 96-year-old founder of the Fontana Historical Society, which was created in 1974. She has spent more than 30 years working to preserve the history of Fontana and has helped to restore several historical sites in the city. A historic section of downtown was recently named Hazel Putnam Plaza in her honor She has been an inspiration to me. We were very close through the years; she was like a grandmother to me.

One

Lytle Creek Water

A Lifeline

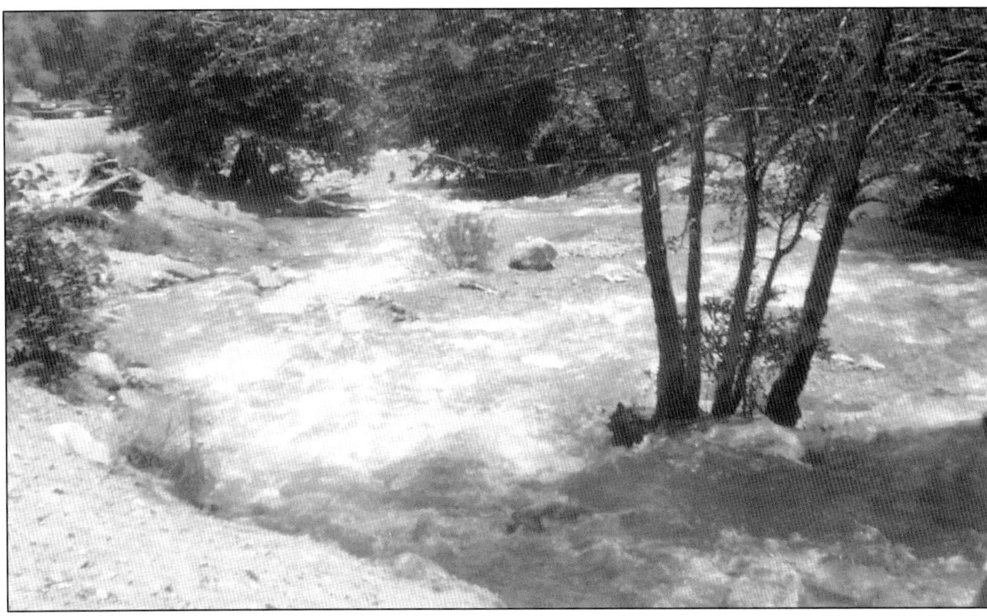

The San Gabriel Mountains run west to east across North Fontana to Cajon Pass. The watershed of Mount Baldy flows through Lytle Creek and other small creeks to canyons along the foothills in the south. In earlier days, open dirt ditches brought down the water. Later it was channeled through pipes and concrete ditches. The local water companies in charge of this watershed were Lytle Creek Water Company, Semi-Tropic Land and Water Company, Lytle Creek Water and Improvement Company, Fontana Development Company, Fontana Water Company, Fontana Union Water Company, Fontana Domestic Water Company, and now the San Gabriel Water Company The waterways and ditches were Grapeland Irrigation District ditches (west and east), Rialto Ditch (1888–1940), Carnaigre Ditch (1897–1930), the Grapeland west ditch (1892–present), and east ditch (1892–1937). Another water source was the Crawford Canyon Mutual Water Company, which supplied about 40 homes in the Grapeland area of North Fontana. The canyon citizens also use the water as it runs through the area towards Fontana waterworks at the mouth of the canyon. The canyon is a beautiful place to picnic and enjoy nature.

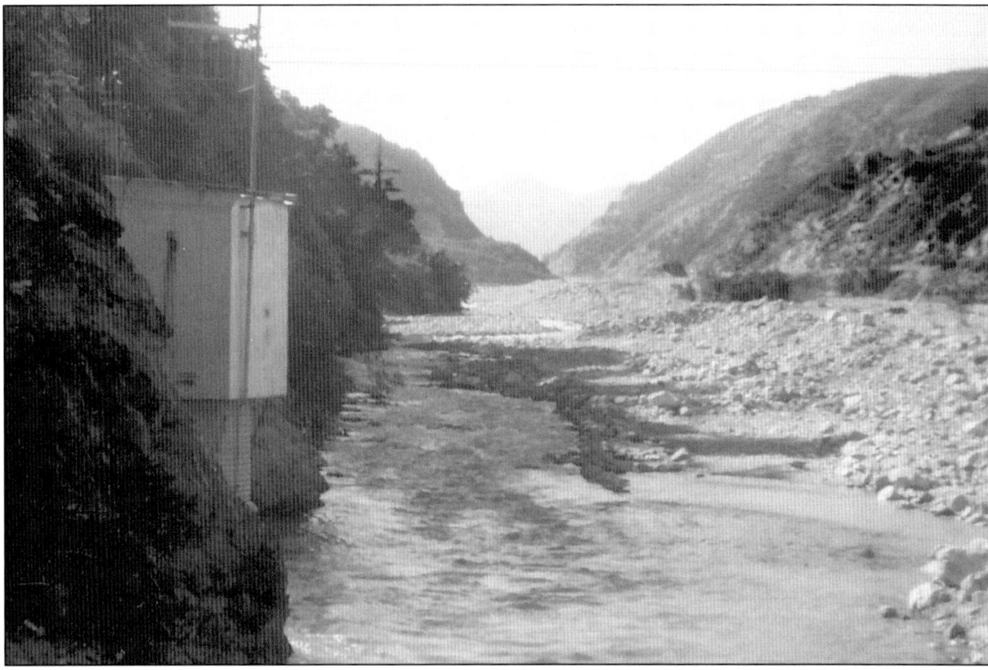

As the creek flows toward the mouth of the canyon, the water is above ground in the streambed, but the main flow travels through an underground tunnel built in the 1890s by the Grapeland Irrigation District. To the left of this photo is the tunnel entrance. If you stand on the south side of the road by this building, you can hear the water running under you below a metal grate.

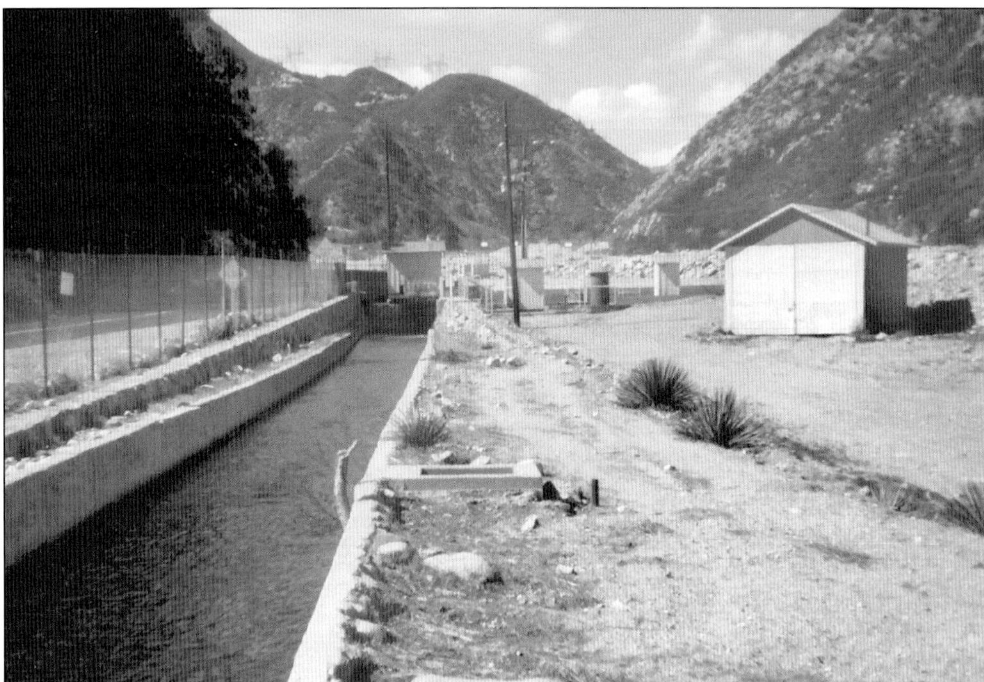

The concrete ditches along the east side of Lytle Creek Road as you go up the canyon road are the property and responsibility of Fontana Water Works.

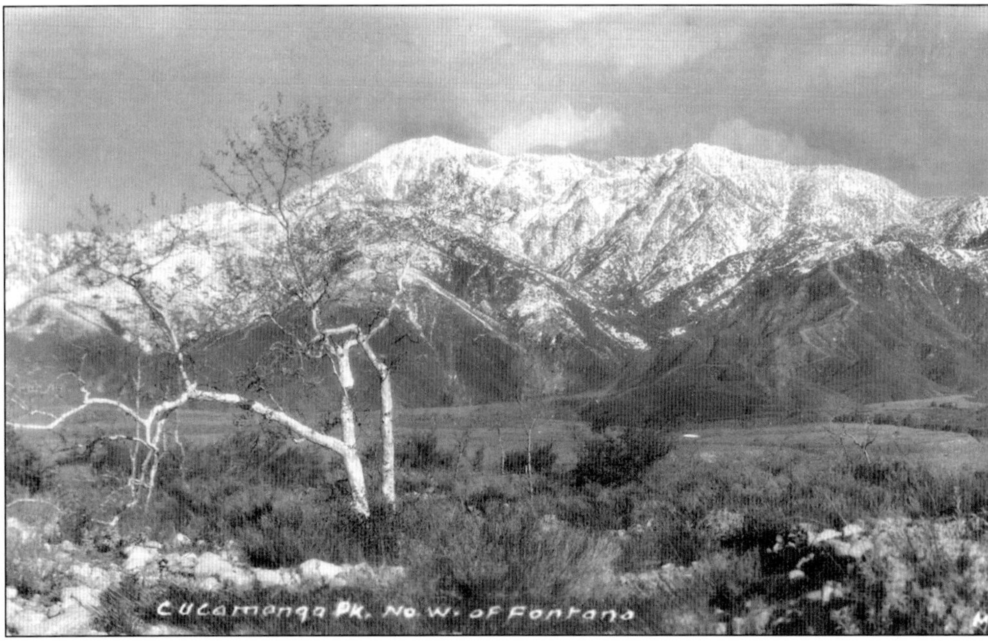

Cucamonga Peak in the San Gabriel Mountains has a watershed that joins Mount Baldy's to flow down canyons and into the Lytle Creek drainage area to supply Fontana.

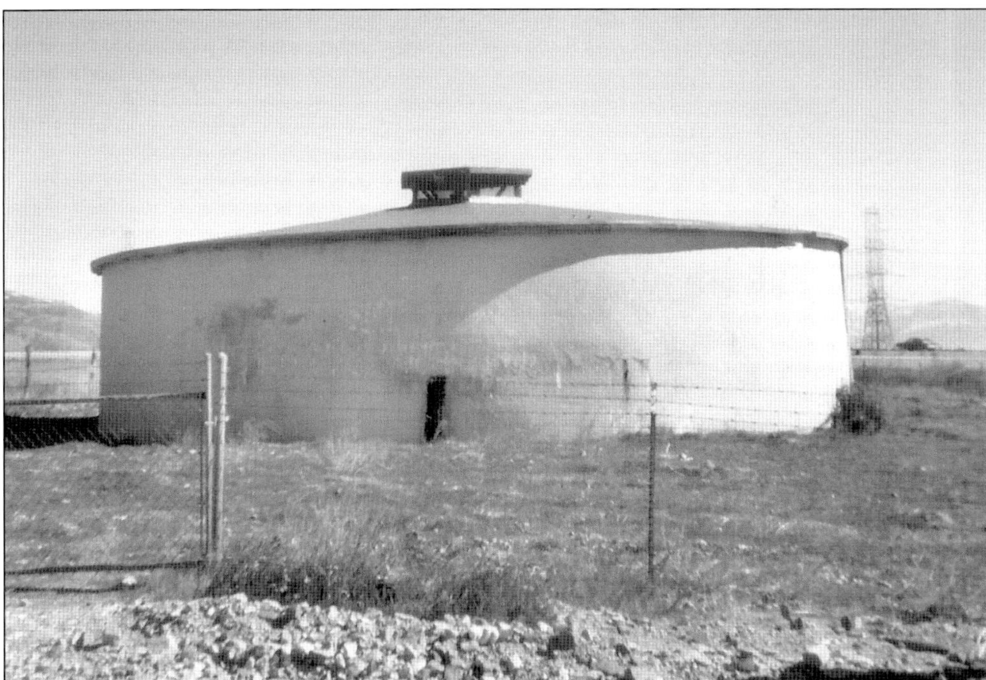
The water tank seen here is for the Crawford Canyon Mutual Water Company on the south side of Lytle Creek Road, next to the I-15 Freeway. The canyon on the side of the foothills supplies the tank via a small dam and pipes.

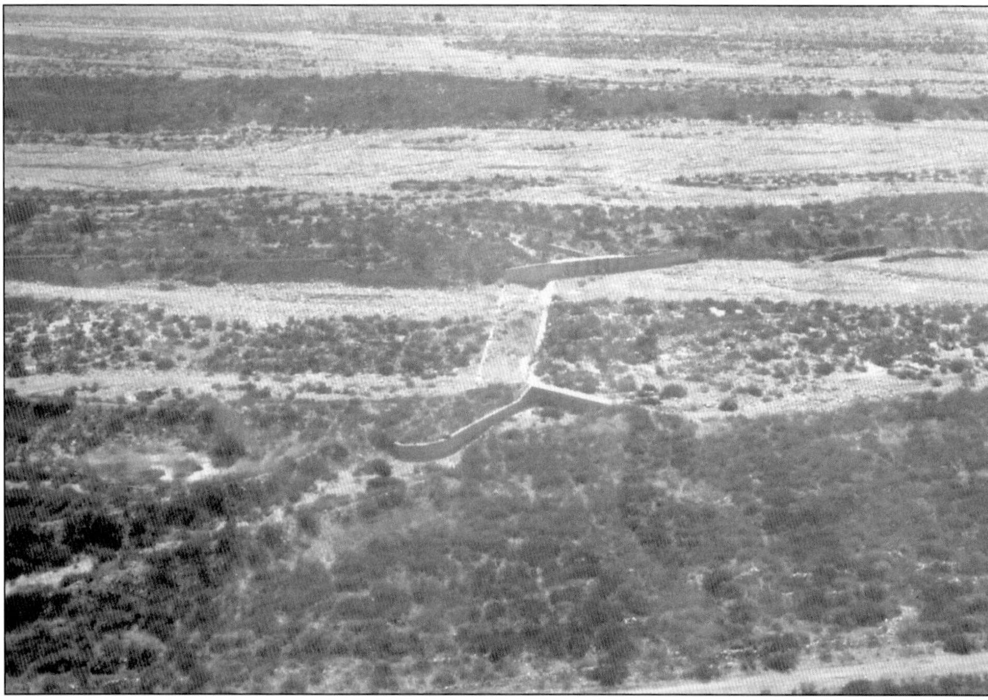

This 1930s aerial shot looks east at the 1930s dam area and gateways in Lytle Creek that were never completed. The plan was to stop the flow so it would go into the ground water table, but funds ran dry and the 1938 floods signaled the need for a different approach. The uncompleted dam is located just south of the I-15 Freeway, east of Sierra Avenue and Riverside Avenue.

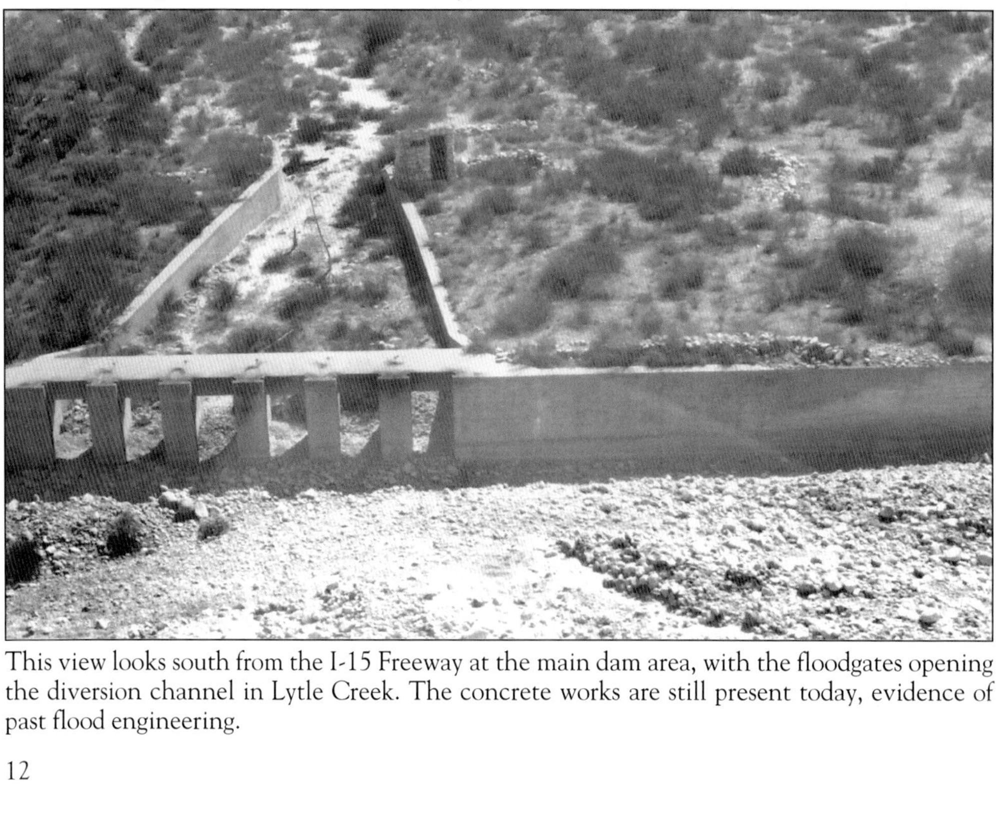

This view looks south from the I-15 Freeway at the main dam area, with the floodgates opening the diversion channel in Lytle Creek. The concrete works are still present today, evidence of past flood engineering.

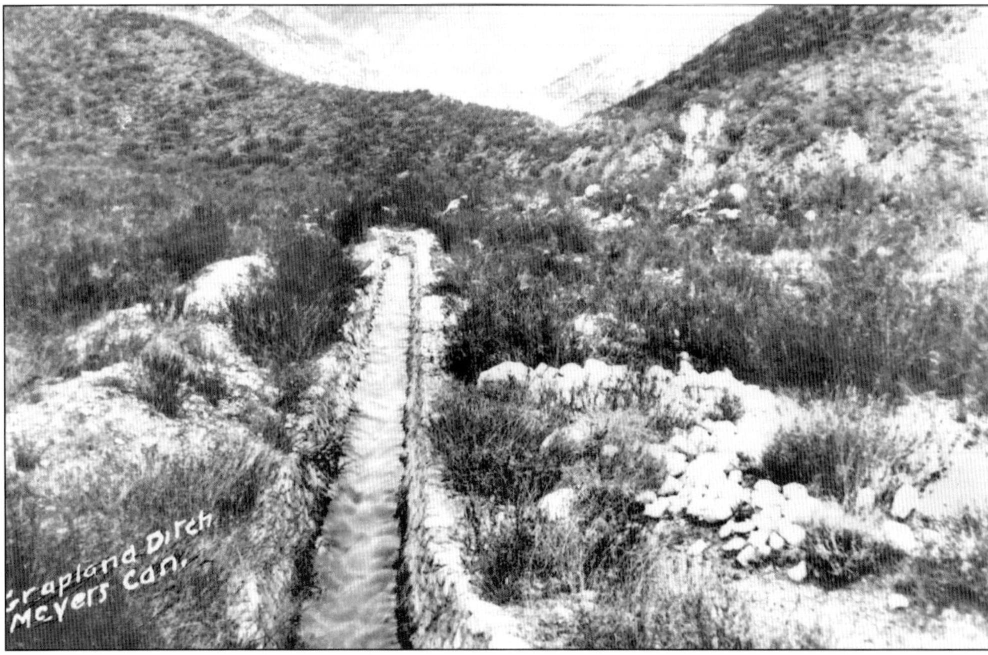

This 1870s photo shows the Water Ditch (actually mostly a dirt ditch) exiting the canyon to the Grapeland area.

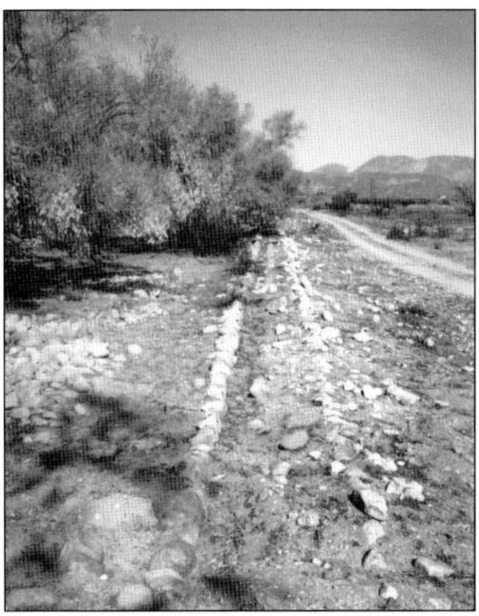

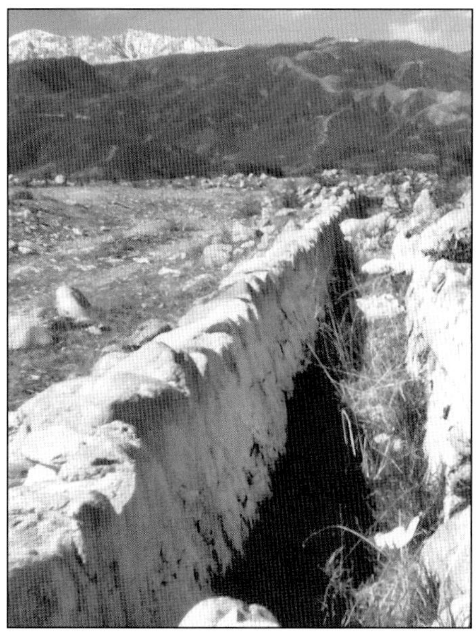

The photo on the left shows the western branch of the Grapeland Ditch (1892–1930) west of Sierra Avenue. Before it was redeveloped, the ditch ran for two miles to near Highland Avenue, half a mile west of Sierra Avenue, where Sierra Lakes is today. This photo was taken in the 1980s. The eastern branch was also lost to development in Rialto. The photo on the right shows the eastern branch of the Canaigre Ditch (1897–1930) looking northwest to the east of Riverside Avenue. Its concrete lining was mixed with stones and cement. The western branch still exists, but will be lost to development like the eastern portion was in Rialto. Fontana has the western branch.

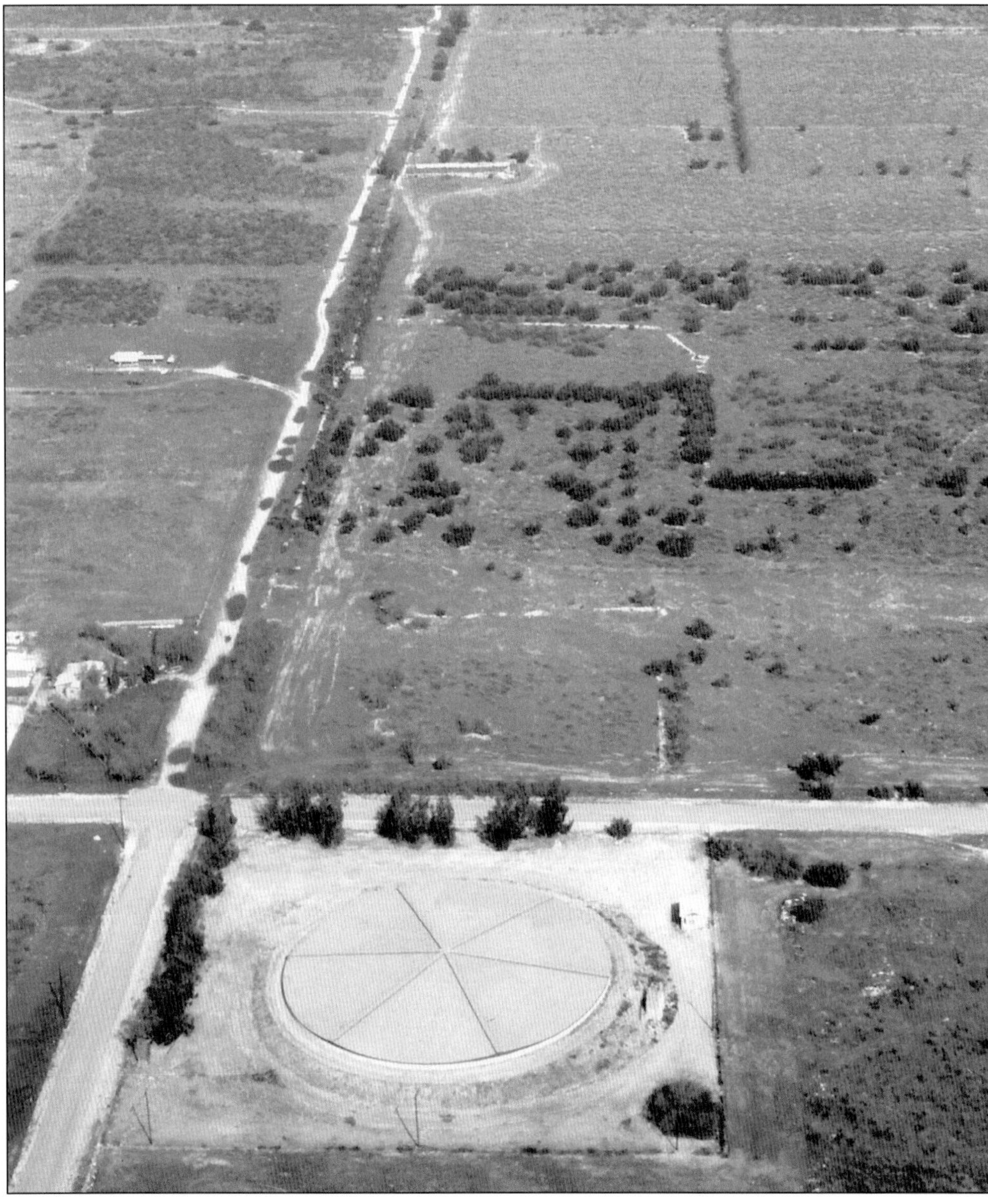

This aerial view shows the main Grapeland Irrigation District that ran along Summit Avenue, which was a dirt road at the time. The ditch (at about center left) had a concrete pipe inside to carry water to the aqueduct that ran east to west on the diagonal roadway (from top of photo to the reservoir at lower right, off Summit Avenue). The water came through a tunnel 90 feet below the creek in a tunnel 3,600 feet long with 20 shafts to collect water into gravels that were a natural subterranean reservoir. The four-by-six-foot tunnel was made of concrete. The round reservoir at the bottom was the 1887 Scofield Reservoir—the largest in the area. The diameter at the top was 210 feet, at the bottom 198 feet. It had a vertical slope of 7 feet, a depth of 14 feet, and a capacity of 3.6 million gallons. The Scofields owned 1,520 acres of flat land. The reservoir is now covered and in use. Pictured on page 15 is the aqueduct that runs on the right side of Summit Avenue to the large, rectangular reservoir in the upper center of this photo. The Scott site is just above the reservoir, and the white lines are aqueducts.

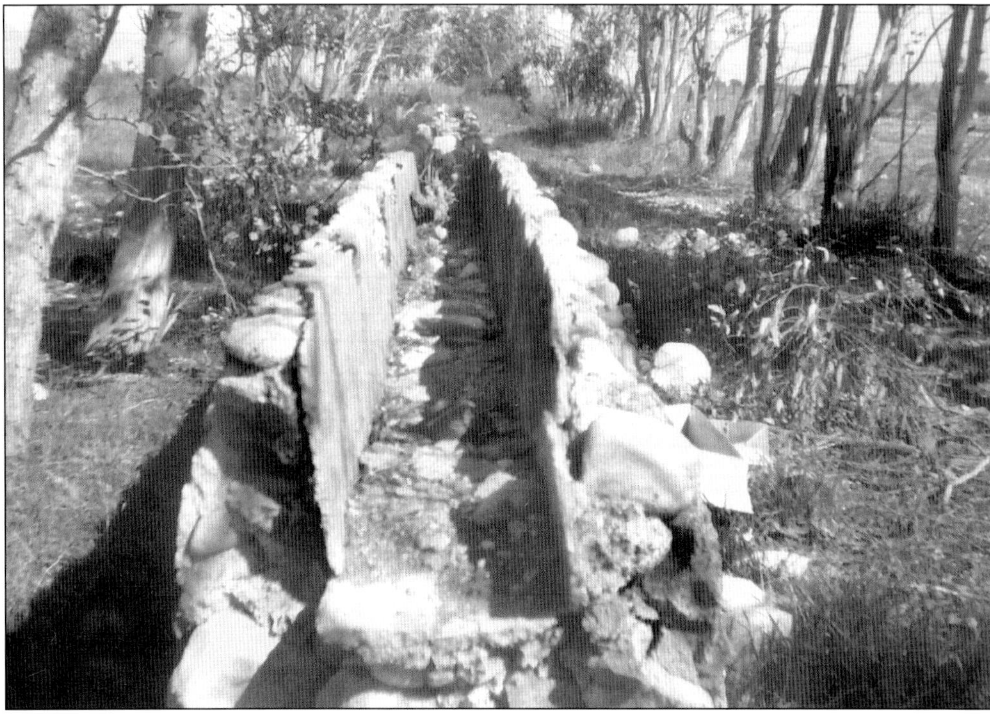

The aqueduct ran from ground level to more than three feet high into the large rock and huge cement reservoir. The water from the ditch came into the reservoir via an elaborate system, then ran west towards the large round reservoir through several smaller reservoirs on two Grapeland homesteads, and finally traveled into the main one.

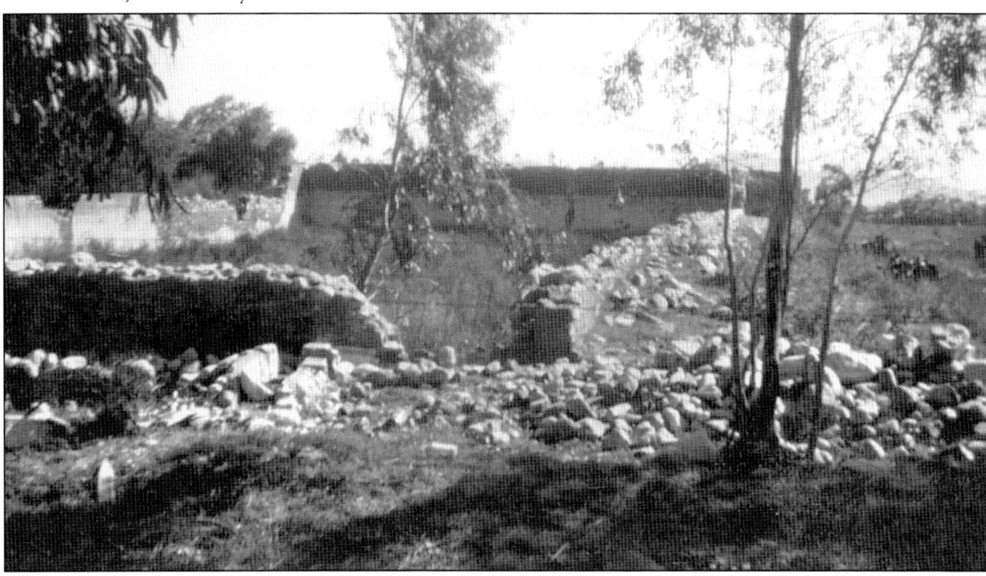

The large rectangular reservoir of rock and cement is shown here. It had a concrete floor and a large tall back at the south end. It was 30 feet wide and more than 90 feet to the south end. It was about 10 feet deep. Olive trees surrounded it on the east end as well as other trees gracing the full length of the aqueduct. Everything is gone now due to development. Only a tiny park remains.

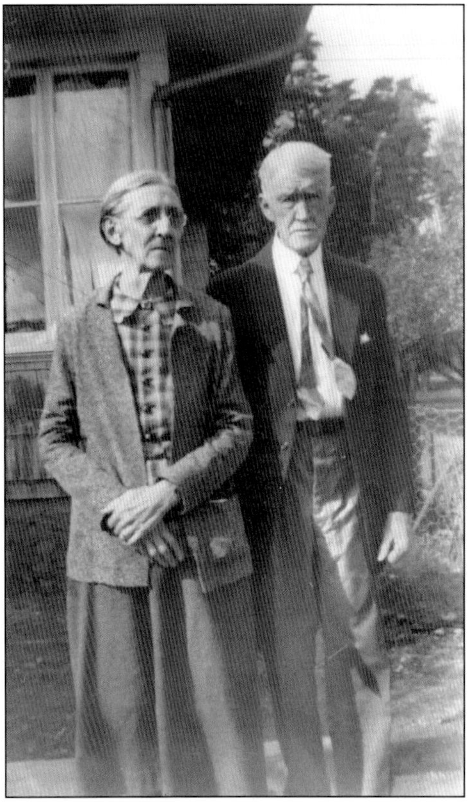

Mr. and Mrs. E.T. Myers are pictured outside their Grapeland home. They kept a daily log of all the happenings in Grapeland from the time they arrived till they left. They had journals of their travels to the area, and saved all of the paperwork of Grapeland and items of importance.

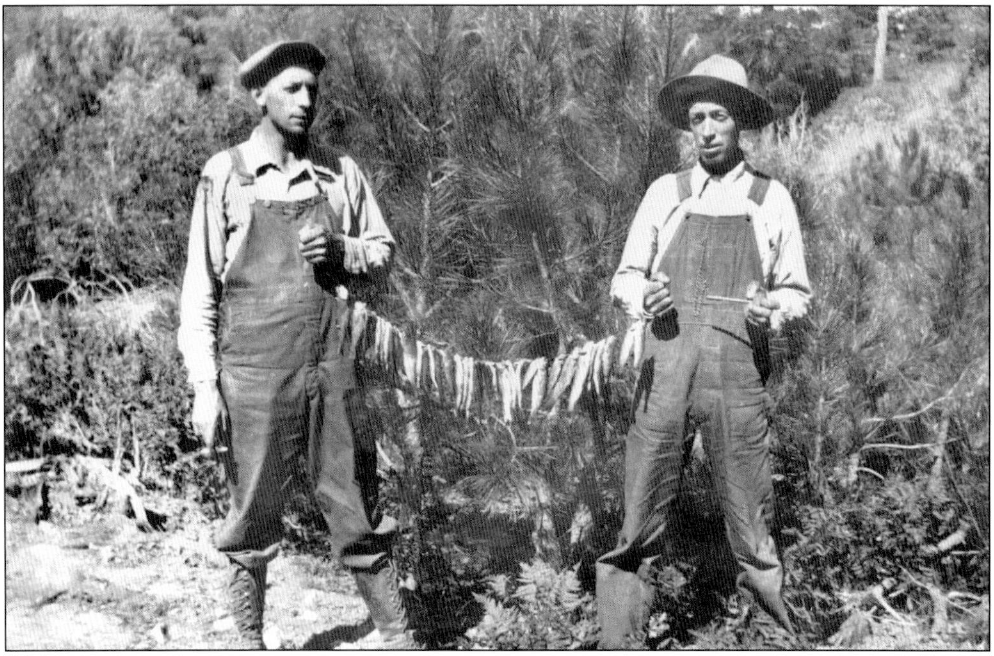

James and Arthur, the sons of E.T. Myers, are pictured here. They had been fishing in Lytle Creek, a short walk from their home. These two later brought their parents' archives from their barn loft in Hemet to Fontana to be shared with the community.

Two

Grapeland 1860s–1900

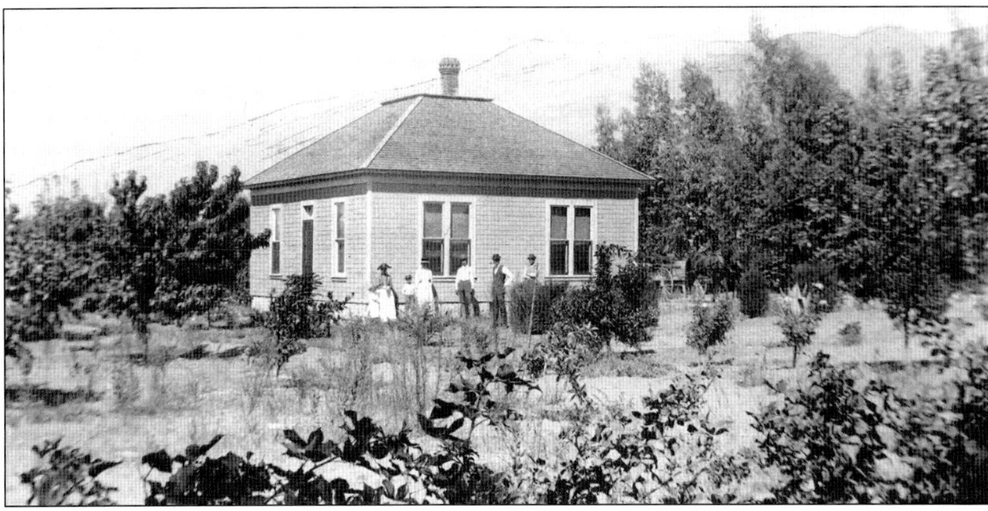

Alexander and Sarah Perdew settled the Grapeland area's original 10,600 acres in 1866. For 38 years, they lived on their property just north of what is now the I-15 Freeway. The Grapeland Irrigation District is situated west of Lytle Creek and north of Baseline Avenue, and is bounded as follows: on the east to Riverside Avenue by Rialto; on the west by the Etiwanda Colony; on the north by the San Gabriel Mountains; and on the northeast and east by the Muscapiabe Rancho. The Mojave Trail went through the northern part of Grapeland where there was a stage stop at the foot of the canyons. Most of the early settlers came after the Civil War by wagon. The Perdews came, settled, and brought water by ditches from the creek. G.F.R.B. Perdew built a home and grew 25 acres of peaches from seed. In 1890, net profit was $150 per acre—a huge success. The area was the highest producer in San Bernardino Valley. E.T. Myers was secretary of the district and saved the records from the 1890s. The Taylor Home, part of the Lytle Creek Winery, still exists on Lytle Creek Road and Duncan Canyon Road, and the J.D. Gebhart family still owns land in the area. They built all the waterworks in the creek and on the land. This photo of the E.T. Myers Grapeland home, which also served as the post office of the new community, was taken on September 19, 1892. The lumber for the house came from Big Bear. The two palms in the photo still exist today in the Edison Electric right-of-way. The house was square-shaped, with four rooms and a kitchen added on. The house faced north and had wood siding on the outside with plaster and lathe inside. The roof was a simple hip and ridge of wood shingles. The front door had a mail slot for its use as the post office.

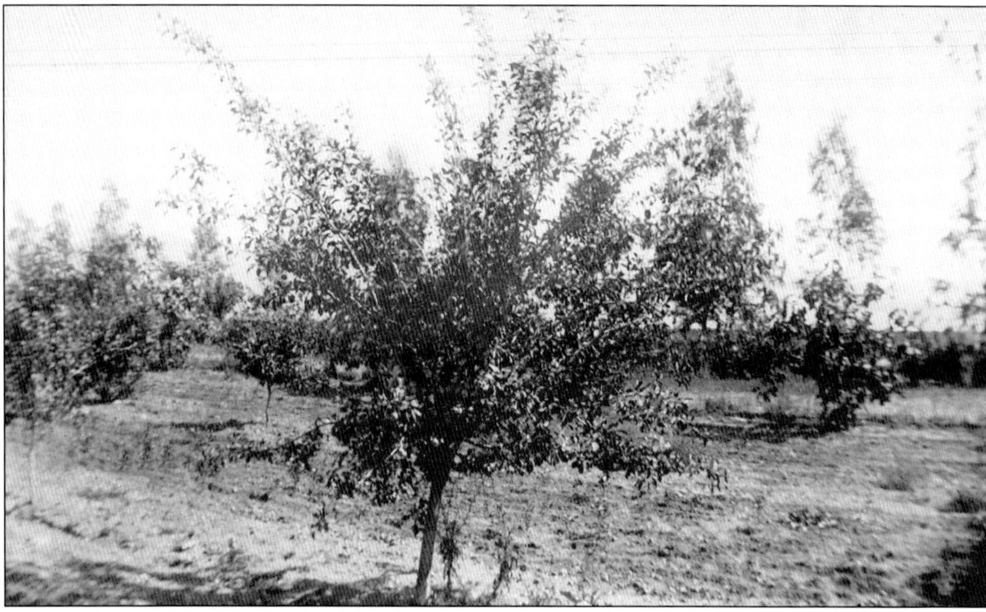

The Grapeland prune orchard of E.T. Myers is pictured here. He had also planted 5½ acres of grape cuttings and succeeded in raising a vineyard without water for several years, with more area added each year.

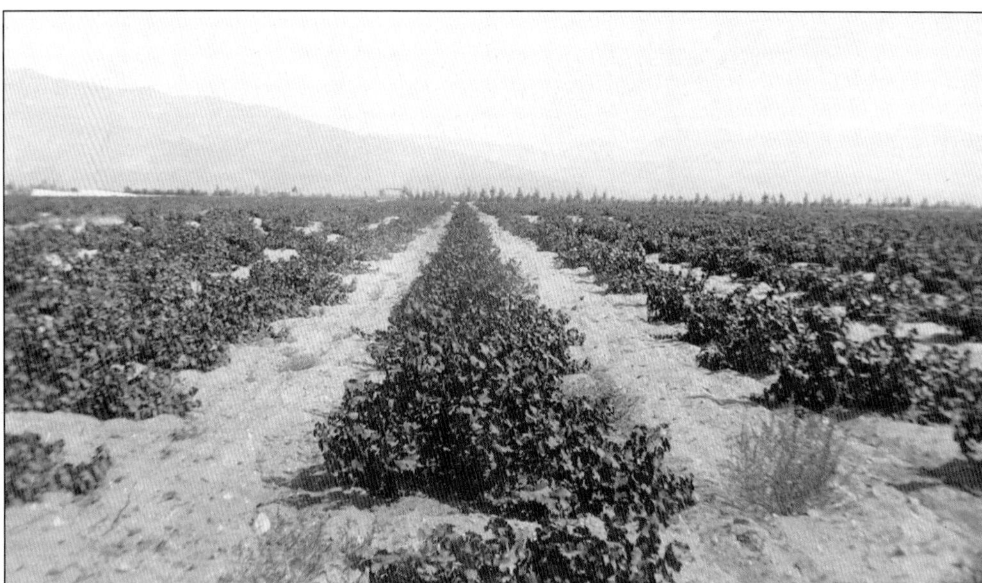

This raisin vineyard belonged to J.A. Scott in Grapeland.

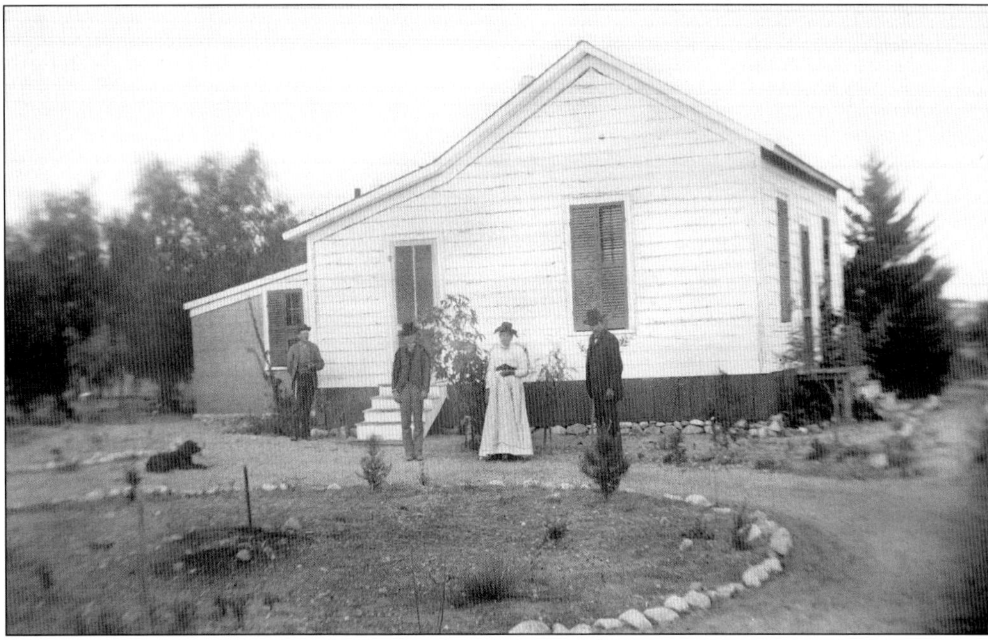

The Grapeland home of J.A. Scott is shown here. The site was on the southeast corner of Summit and Citrus Avenues. Some of the rocks from this site were used for the 75th-anniversary monument in front of city hall. The property once had aqueducts and a small reservoir, but everything has disappeared now because of development.

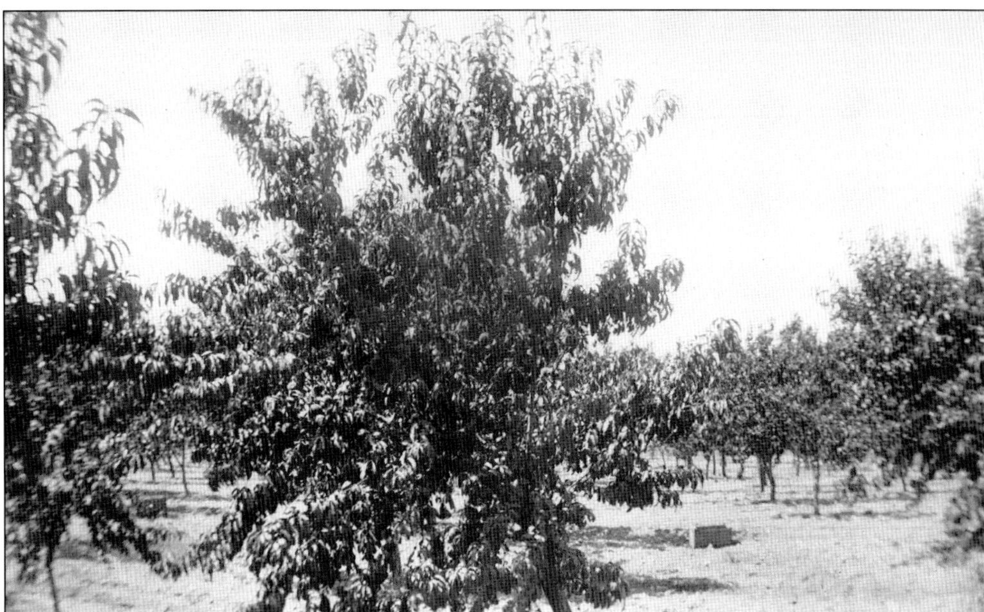

The peach orchard of G.F.R.B. Perdew in Grapeland is on display in this photo. Perdew was the first settler of Grapeland and had a great success with his orchards. The family still lives in the Etiwanda area.

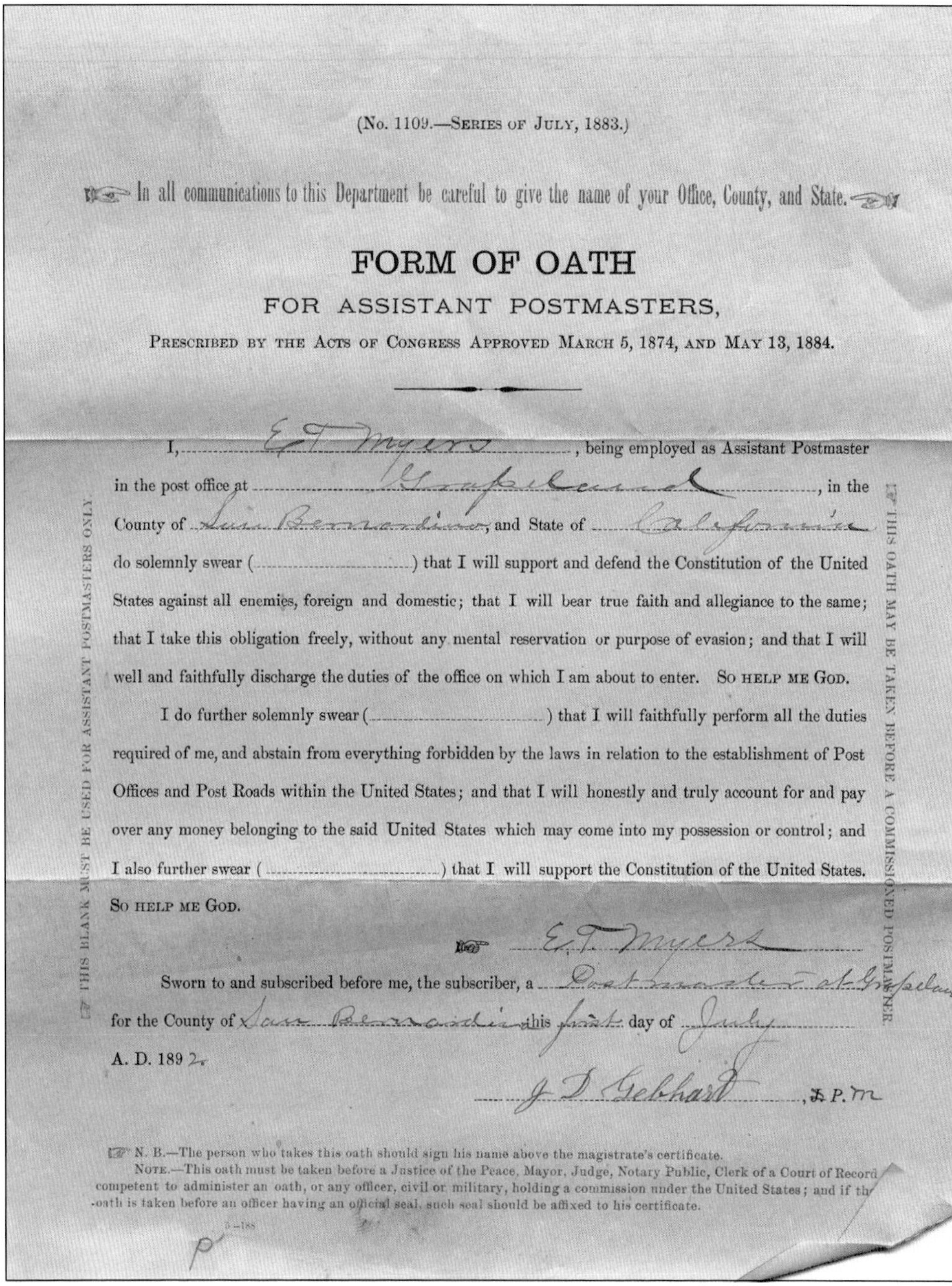
(No. 1109.—Series of July, 1883.)

In all communications to this Department be careful to give the name of your Office, County, and State.

FORM OF OATH

FOR ASSISTANT POSTMASTERS,

Prescribed by the Acts of Congress Approved March 5, 1874, and May 13, 1884.

I, E.T. Myers, being employed as Assistant Postmaster in the post office at Grapeland, in the County of San Bernardino, and State of California do solemnly swear (..........) that I will support and defend the Constitution of the United States against all enemies, foreign and domestic; that I will bear true faith and allegiance to the same; that I take this obligation freely, without any mental reservation or purpose of evasion; and that I will well and faithfully discharge the duties of the office on which I am about to enter. So help me God.

I do further solemnly swear (..........) that I will faithfully perform all the duties required of me, and abstain from everything forbidden by the laws in relation to the establishment of Post Offices and Post Roads within the United States; and that I will honestly and truly account for and pay over any money belonging to the said United States which may come into my possession or control; and I also further swear (..........) that I will support the Constitution of the United States. So help me God.

E.T. Myers

Sworn to and subscribed before me, the subscriber, a Postmaster at Grapeland for the County of San Bernardino this first day of July A. D. 1892.

J D Gebhart, P.M.

N. B.—The person who takes this oath should sign his name above the magistrate's certificate.

Note.—This oath must be taken before a Justice of the Peace, Mayor, Judge, Notary Public, Clerk of a Court of Record competent to administer an oath, or any officer, civil or military, holding a commission under the United States; and if the oath is taken before an officer having an official seal, such seal should be affixed to his certificate.

This Blank must be used for Assistant Postmasters only.

This oath may be taken before a commissioned postmaster.

This is a copy of the original oath sheet of Grapeland postmaster E.T. Myers, dated July 1, 1892.

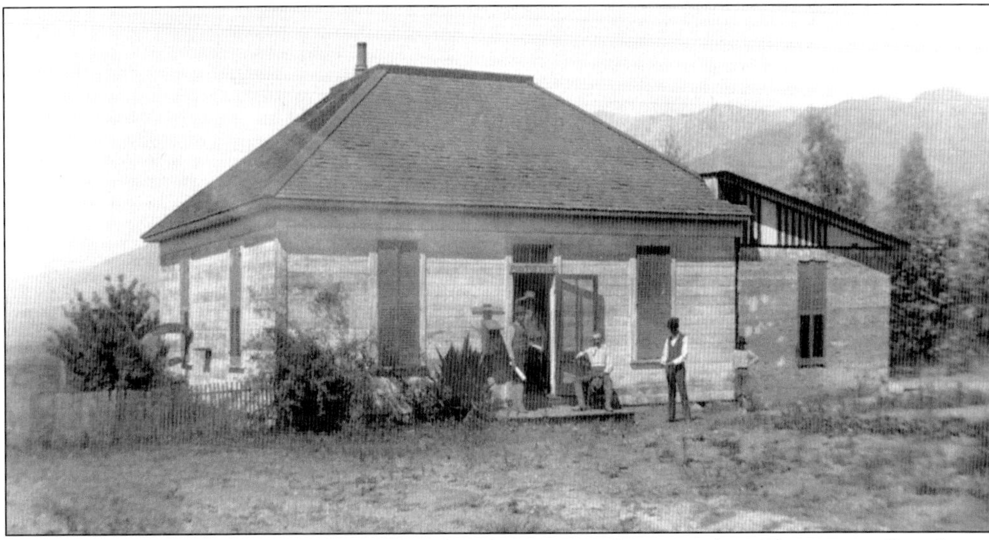

The area of Grapeland was called first by the name of Hesperides. The post office lasted from December 12, 1888, to February 2, 1889 and was on the corner of Duncan Canyon Road and Citrus Avenue. The residence of Greenberry F.R.B. Perdew was the probable site, since he was the first postmaster. The Myers home remained the post office from 1900 to 1904. The four postmasters of Grapeland were Perdew (February 8, 1889), Jacob Gebhardt (September 5, 1891), Francis A. Myers (October 23,1900) and John B. Brown Jr. (January 19, 1904). Mail after 1905 went to Etiwanda.

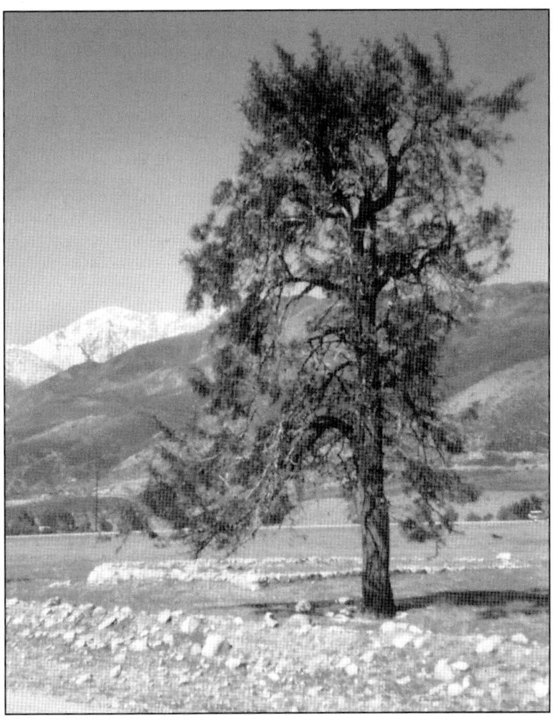

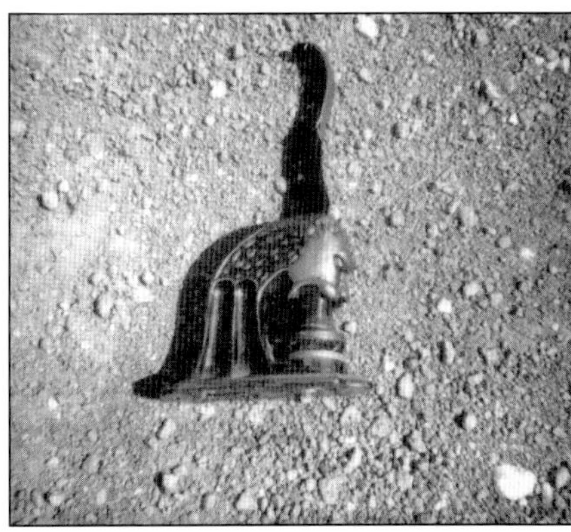

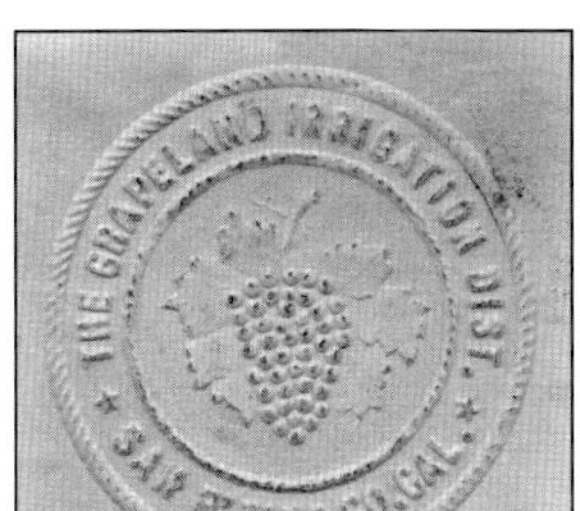

Pictured at left is the rock foundation of Grapeland's Perdew School site as it is today. At right are the original hand seal of Grapeland from the 1880s and an embossed copy, saved by the Myers family.

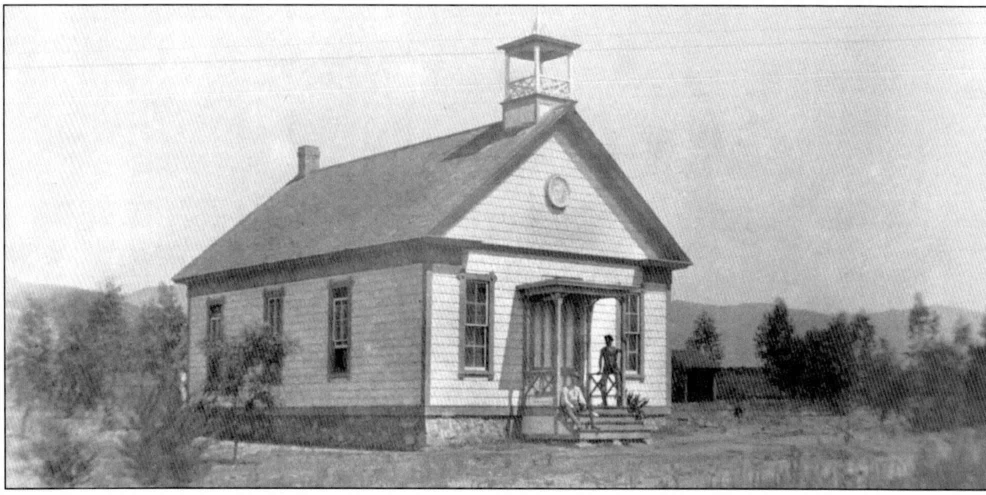

The Grapeland School also served as a church and meeting hall. It sat on the north side of Duncan Canyon Road and just east of Lytle Creek Road on property donated by the Perdew family. In the 1870 census, Alexander Glenn Perdew was listed as a farmer—and penmanship teacher. His son Joseph Edward Perdew was born in Grapeland on Oct. 4, 1864, and married Nettie Henderson on January 16, 1890. The couple lived about where the I-15 Freeway sits. Their old entrance is to the east of the school site, about 15 to 20 feet away. Joseph and Nettie raised corn, grapes, and nursery stock. He died on April 16, 1894, and Mrs. Perdew later moved to San Bernardino in 1902 and raised six children. She died on March 6, 1914. The foundation is still there, with one tree on the west side. The foundation was two feet wide, built with handset rocks. It was 36 feet by 25 feet. It is over 100 years old.

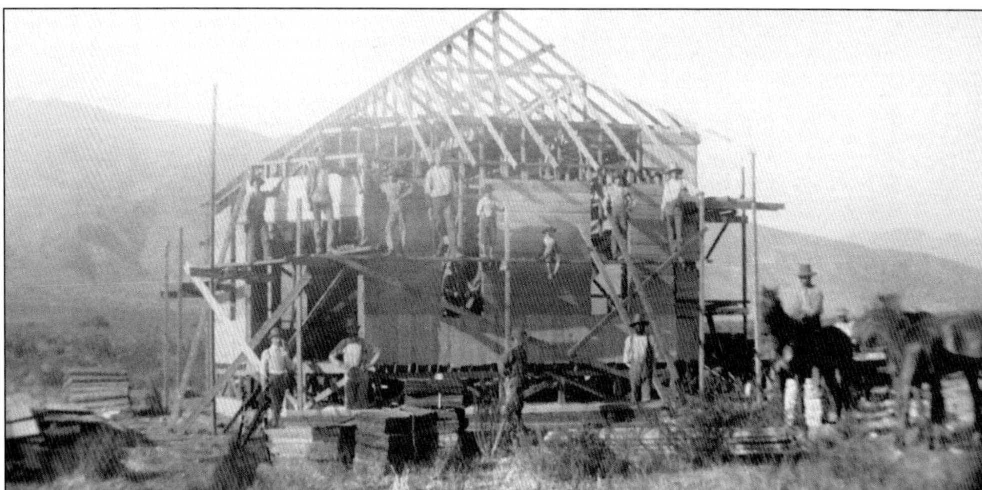

This shot depicts the Lower Perdew School House in Grapeland. In 1880, they petitioned for the formation of a school district. By 1885, the census showed an enrollment of 43 children in the district between the ages of 4 and 17. The school was a tidy, one-room structure, furnished with homemade and commercial desks. They had no playground equipment, and Mrs. S.A. Myers, a former student of the school, said they wanted a baseball so badly she got hold of a hard rubber ball and wrapped string around it until it achieved baseball size. In 1899, the Perdew School District combined with the Grapeland School District, and the school was moved to the corner of Summit and San Sevaine. Its closing was a blow to the community.

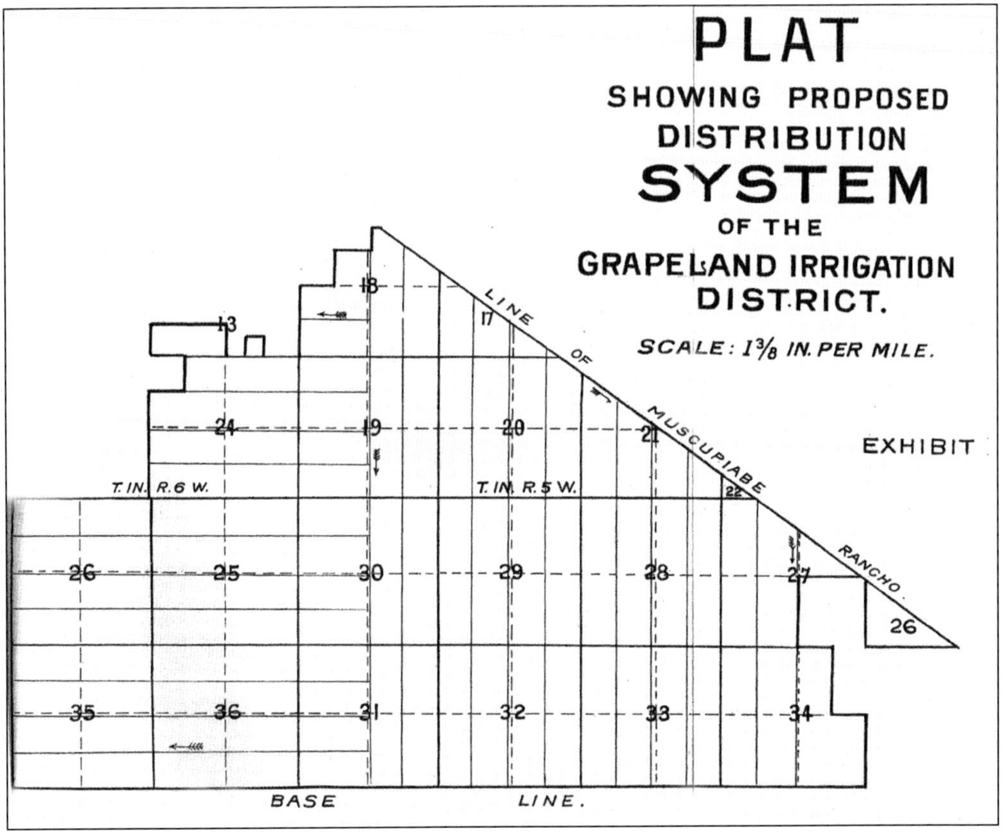

The plot sheet of Grapeland is shown in this image.

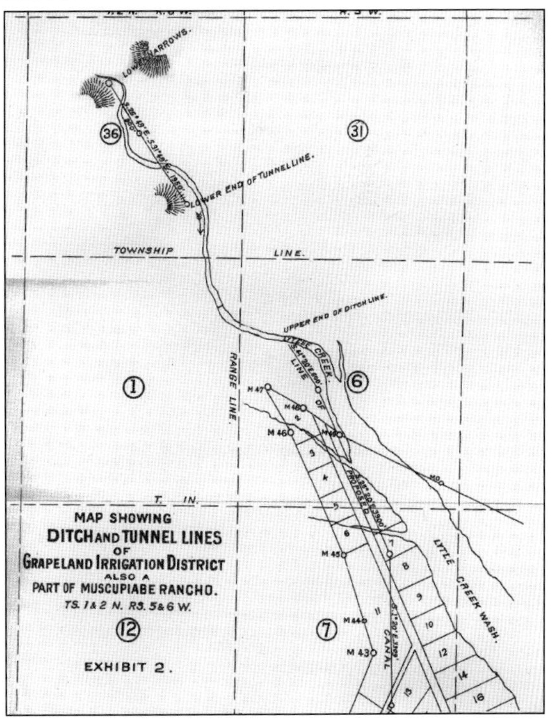

Pictured are tunnel sketch drawings of Grapeland in the Lytle Creek.

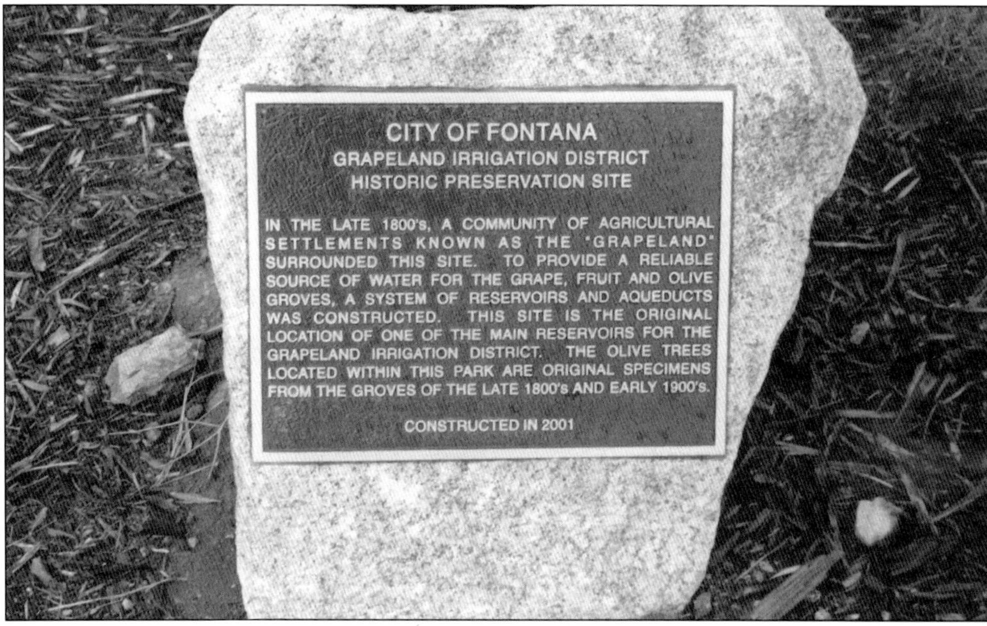

This plaque is all that is left on the land that was owned by Conrock. The La Questa development wanted to buy the land that was home to four Grapeland families, but a new development called Sierra Lakes took over and saved the olive groves for the sites, which had been sent to the Palm Springs area in the 1930s and 1940s. The four homes were named State of California historical points of interest, but they were not saved.

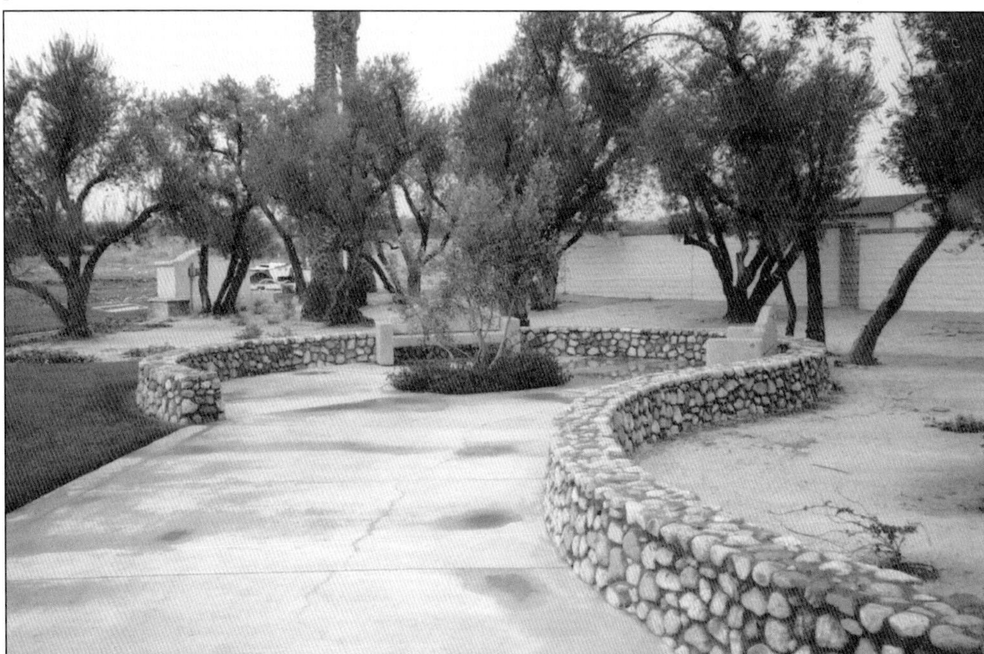

Shown here is the rock wall with a plaque area and the olive trees from around the large rectangular reservoir. This little park is at the north end of the Sierra Lakes housing area on Summit Avenue, home of the original reservoir.

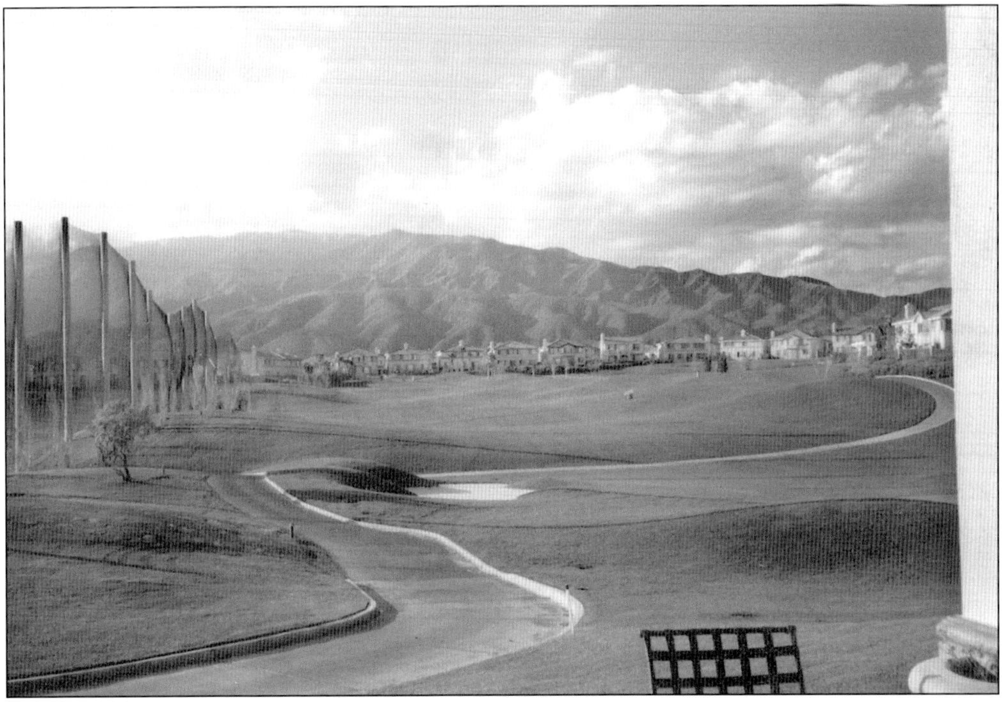

Built on the homesteads of four settlers from the 1880s, the Sierra Lakes Golf Course is shown here with homes along its border. This area is near the main clubhouse, which has beautiful views of the mountains and the city.

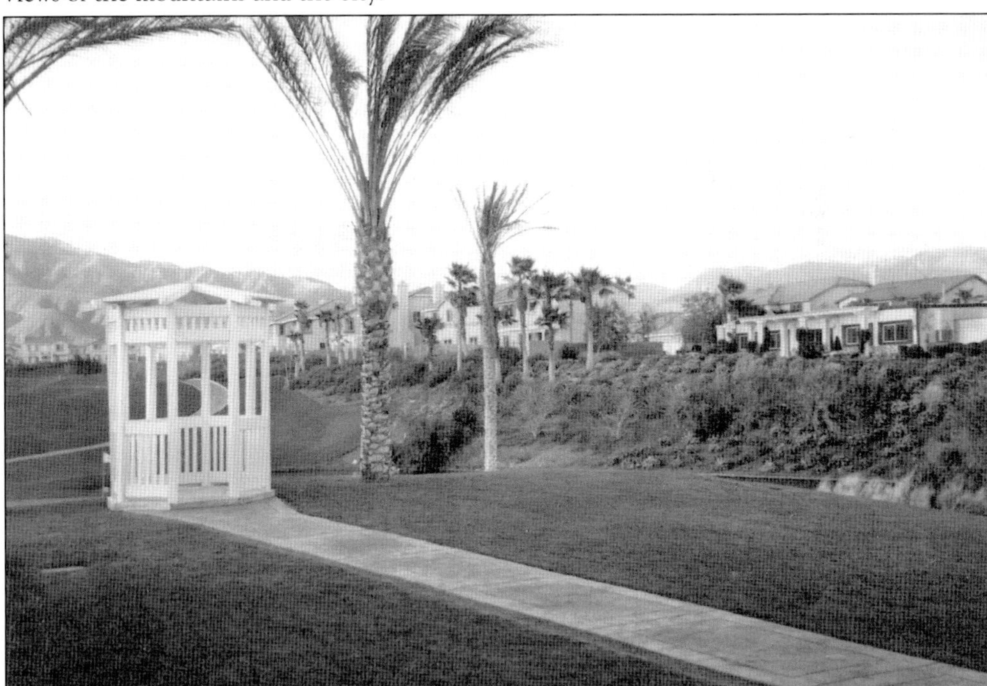

This is close up of the area next to the clubhouse, with a seating area, palms, and several lakefront homes.

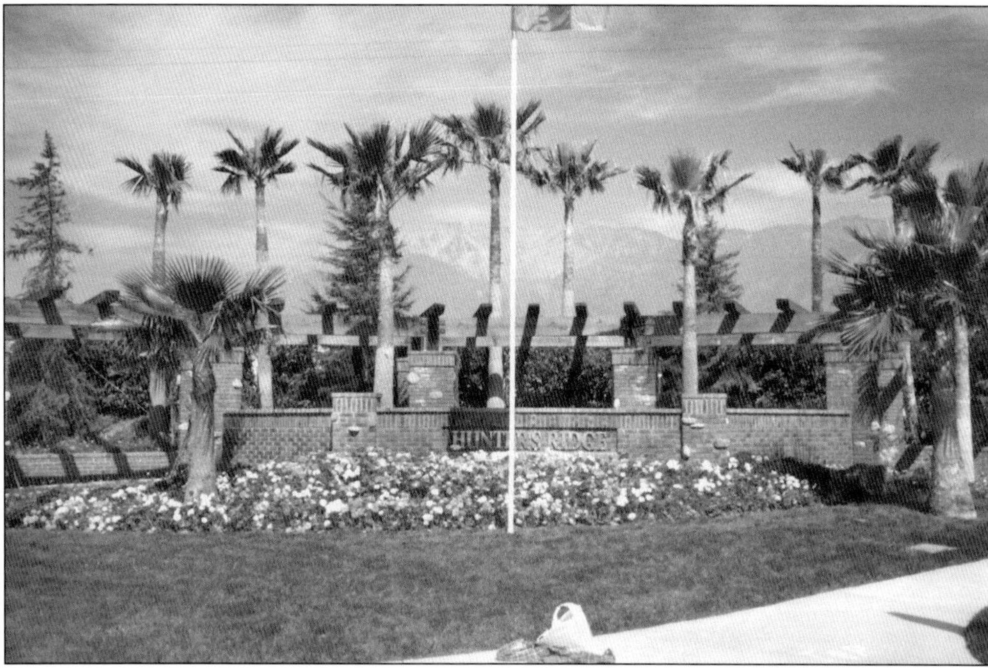

This is the entrance to the development of Hunter's Ridge in north Fontana. Named after the hunt club that used to be on the land, it was also home to the Bullock Ranch, owned by the family that started Bullocks department stores. The last area to be developed is the canyon above the lower homes. This area still has the original waterworks, and the rock kilns up on the hill were used to make lime for the cement of the winery/house that is now gone.

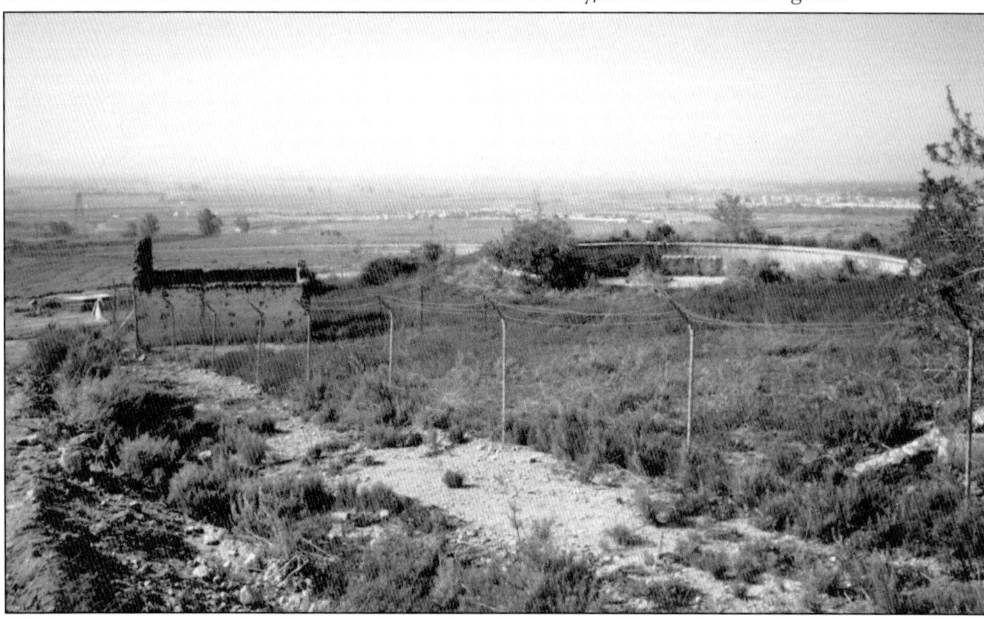

This the site of the winery/house stage stop that has a small smokehouse and large round reservoir with a house above it, built by the San Sevaine brothers. They had a vineyard, and supposedly the first champagne in California was made here. There were two reservoirs on the property that had water lines fed by gravity.

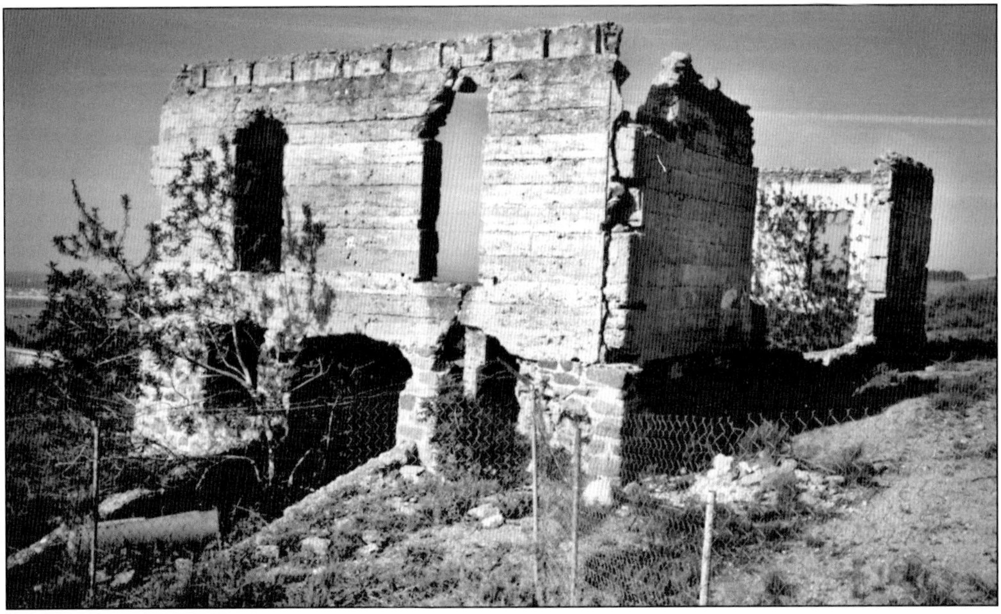

These are the ruins of the 1860s San Sevaine home/winery. It sat in the Edison Line right-of-way, but should have been saved. The winery was in the cellar with wagon access on east side that you can see in the photo. The home was above with a porch along the south side. Many artifacts were saved from the sites, as there were two other ruins of a sawmill with the water wheel to run the saw. In the roadway to the new development, the blacksmith shop was found under the dirt.

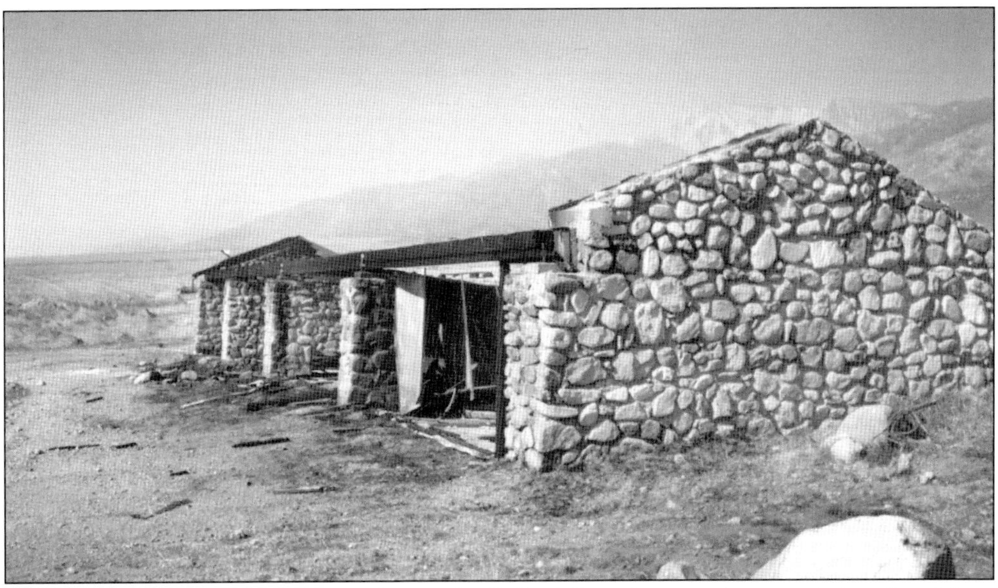

This is a look at the four-car garage during the Bullock Ranch era; unfortunately it suffered from a case of arson during the development of the area. The ranch had a fountain as well as main gate-entrance rockwork. The area also had 100-year-old trees, a surfaced parking area, landscaping with citrus trees, and water to the caretaker's home. The McGoverns were the caretakers for over 40 years, as they raised their family up on the mountain. They saved the house from wild fires several times and maintained the ranch through the years until development started.

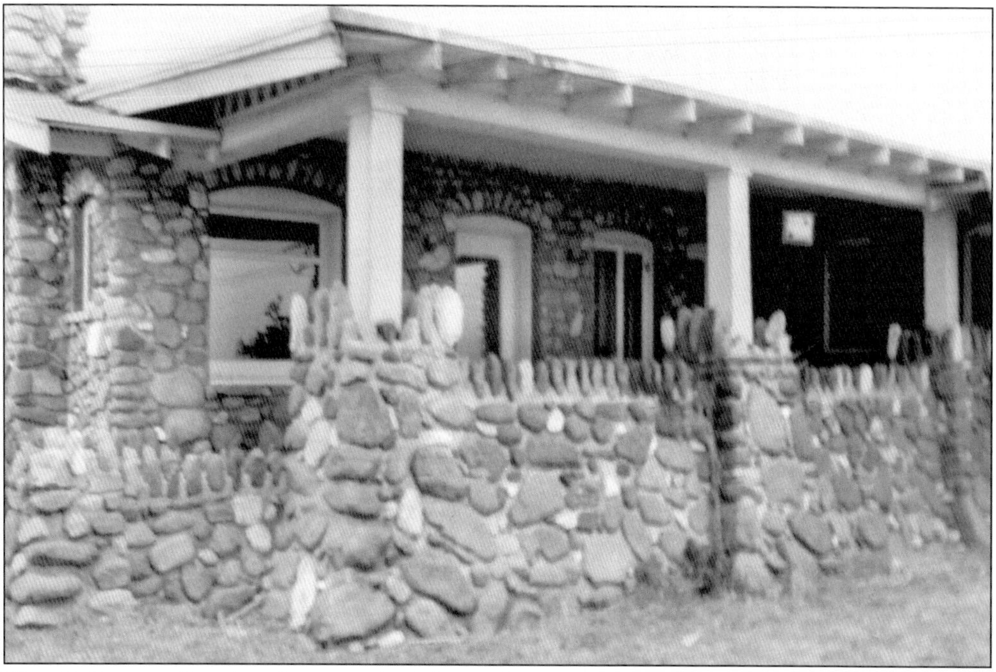

The McGoverns lived in the caretaker's home for years and took excellent care of the house. It had a summer porch on the north side and a kitchen with a cellar below. The living/dining room had a beautiful fireplace and a little office room at the west end with its own door. There were two bedrooms and a bathroom, and hardwood floors and cabinets built-in on either side of the fireplace. French doors graced the front porch, with a view of the whole valley.

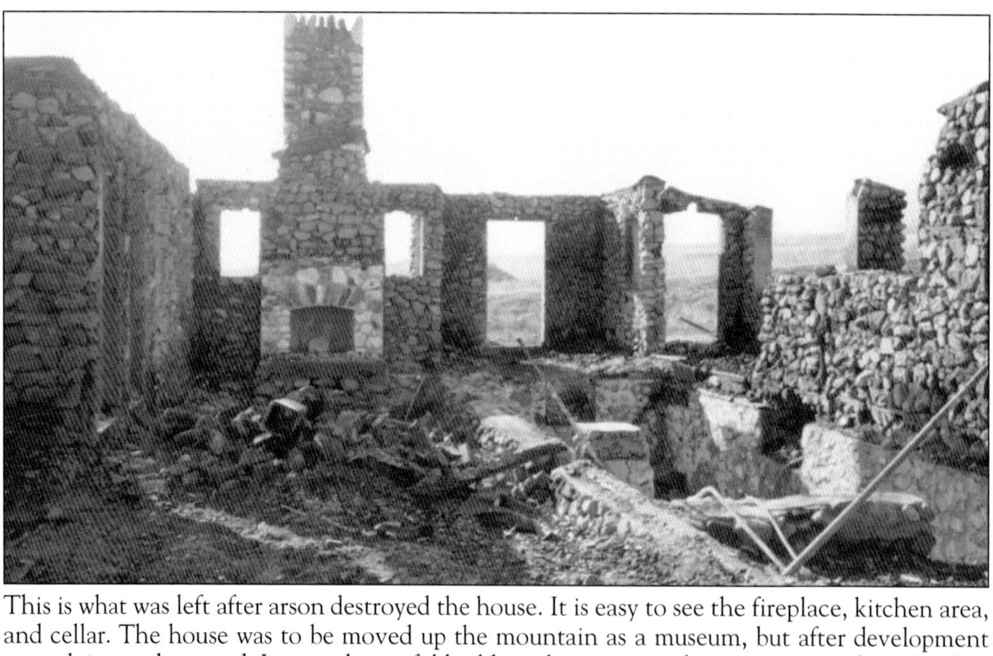

This is what was left after arson destroyed the house. It is easy to see the fireplace, kitchen area, and cellar. The house was to be moved up the mountain as a museum, but after development started, it was destroyed. It was a beautiful building that was saved so many times from fire, but unfortunately not every time. All that is left are these photos.

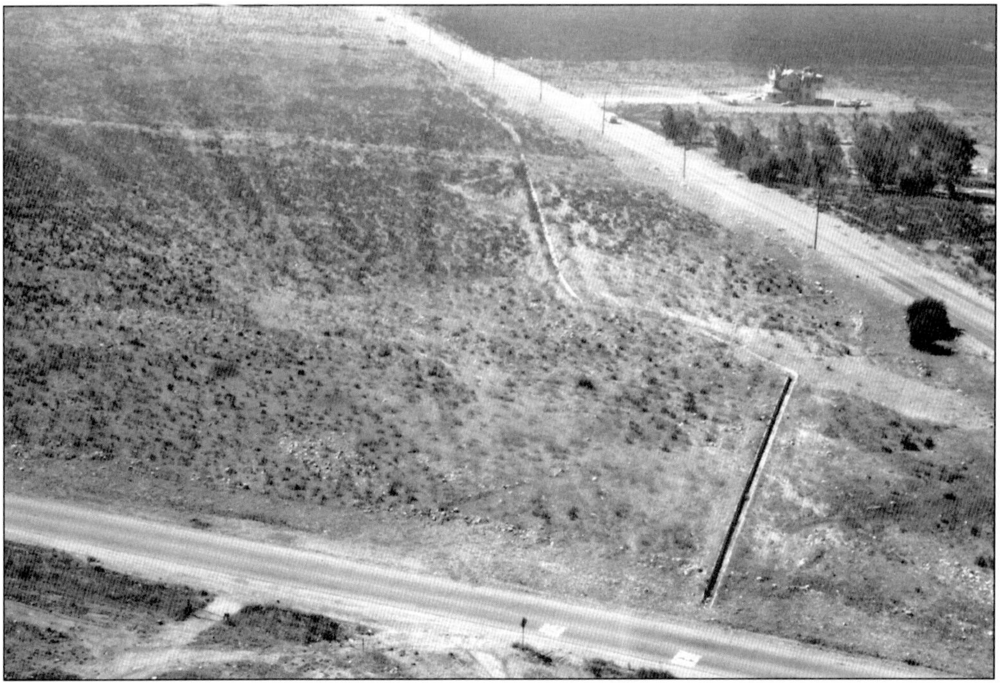

Depicted here is the Anglo-American Canaigre Company Ditch in North Fontana along Sierra Avenue. It was part of the Chicala Water Company of Iowa. The eastern part was destroyed when Rialto built the Northwest Specific Plan. It also took out many ruins of the Grapeland area. The ditch runs from Riverside Avenue towards Sierra Avenue. The two-story Victorian home from Redlands, moved in two pieces, was restored by Dr. Green of San Bernardino.

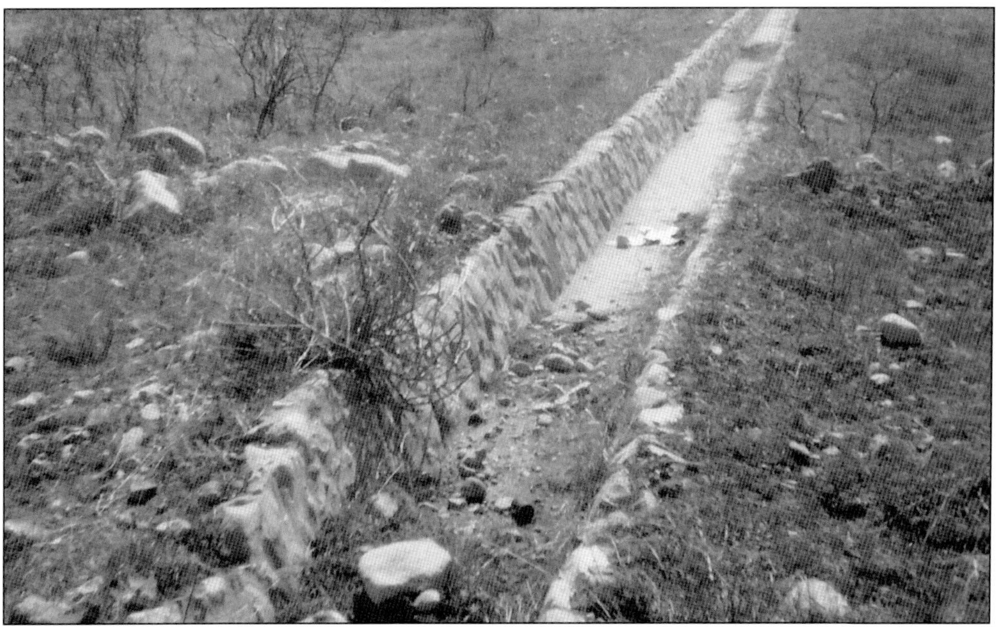

This image shows a close up of the ditch. It is in excellent condition after so many years. The trees in the photo above are where a house once stood that was burned down by the last wild fire to rage through Grapeland area a few years ago.

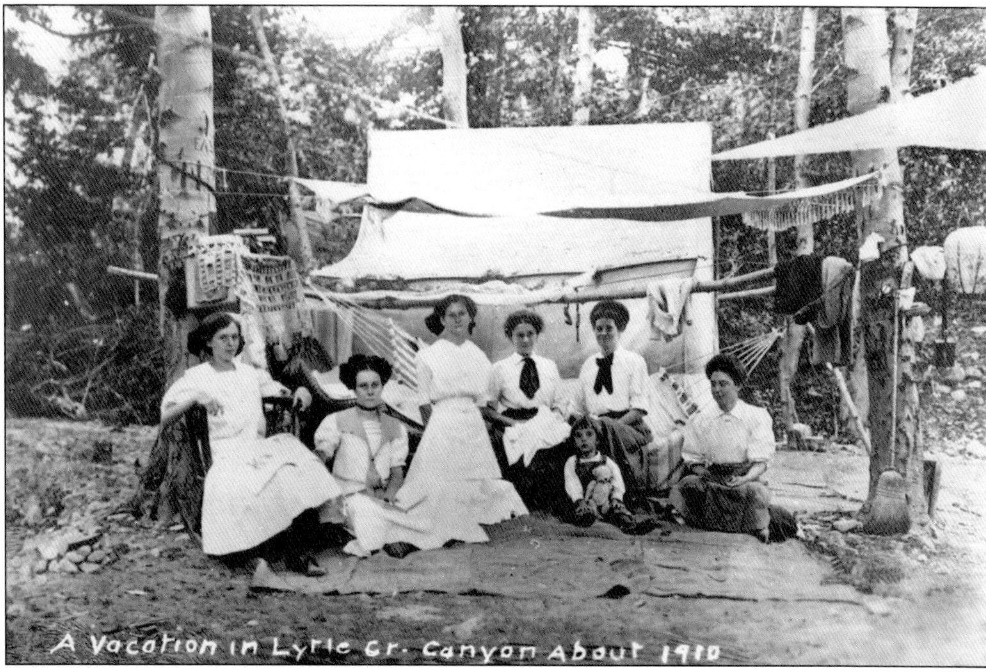

These visitors enjoy a vacation in Lytle Creek Canyon, *c.* 1910.

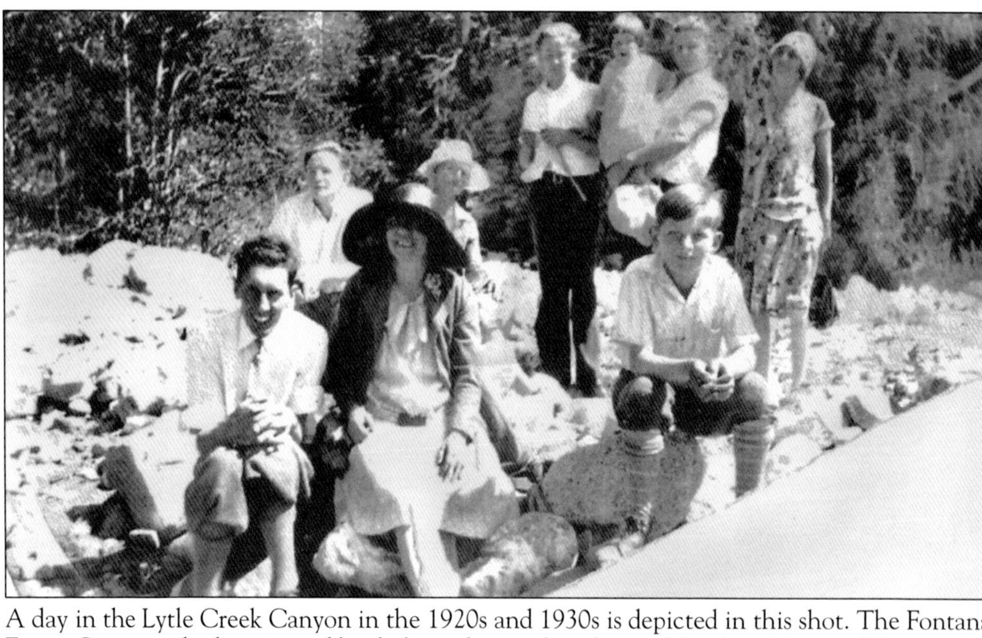

A day in the Lytle Creek Canyon in the 1920s and 1930s is depicted in this shot. The Fontana Farms Company had a piece of land along the creek to be used by the citizens of Fontana for picnics and fun.

Three

ROSENA 1890s–1912

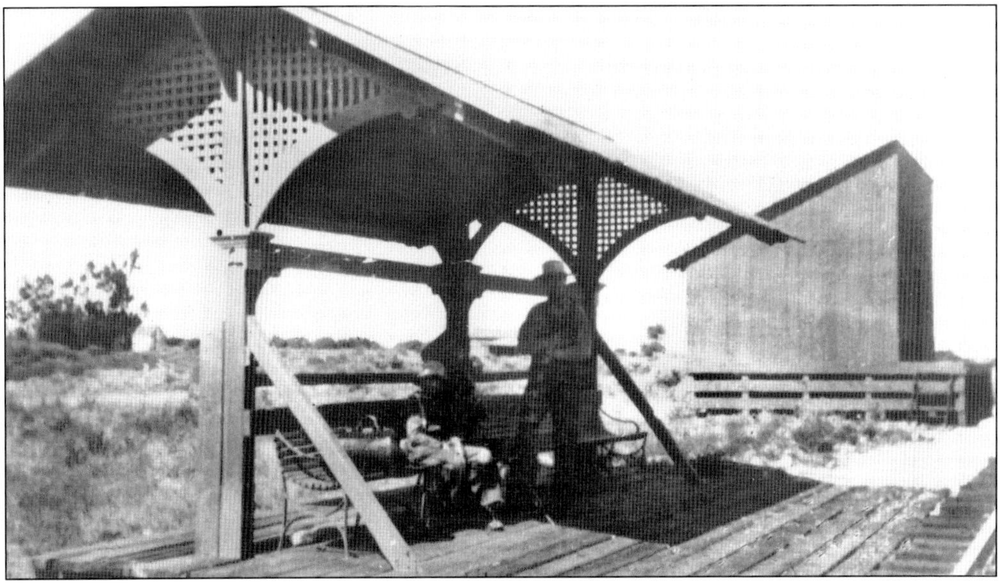

In 1887, the Santa Fe Railroad acquired the land to lay a new stretch of track from San Bernardino west to Los Angeles. After the railroad named its proposed towns along the track, Rosena finally had a stop. The Semi-Tropic Land and Water Improvement Company and the Lytle Creek Water and Improvement Company were also organized this same year. In 1889, the land boom burst and San Sevaine disappeared off the map, yet Rosena remained. In 1892, John Burdick bought land from Mr. Fountain, where the name "Fontana" was on the land deed. In 1895, 10 families lived around Rosena. Mr. Burdick planted crops that did not do well, due to a lack of water. In 1897, his family arrived. In 1900, the first settlement of 12 homes used the dry-farming method. In 1905, A.B. Miller obtained a lease to work the Rosena area land in 1906. He bought the land from the Fontana Development Company to form a ranch/farm and a new city. The Rosena Post Office was to the south of the Grapeland area. It operated from 1895 through 1901. The postmasters were: Catherine Showalter, April 9, 1895; Henry Holinger, July 28, 1895; Maggie Hill, March 10, 1896; and John Nicholson, November 17, 1896. In September 1901, everyone in the Rosena area had to go to Rialto for mail. The post-office system did not come back to the Fontana area for 10 years. Shown here in 1890 is the Santa Fe Railroad station stop at Rosena, which was west of Juniper Avenue and north of the Camp No. 1 ranch site.

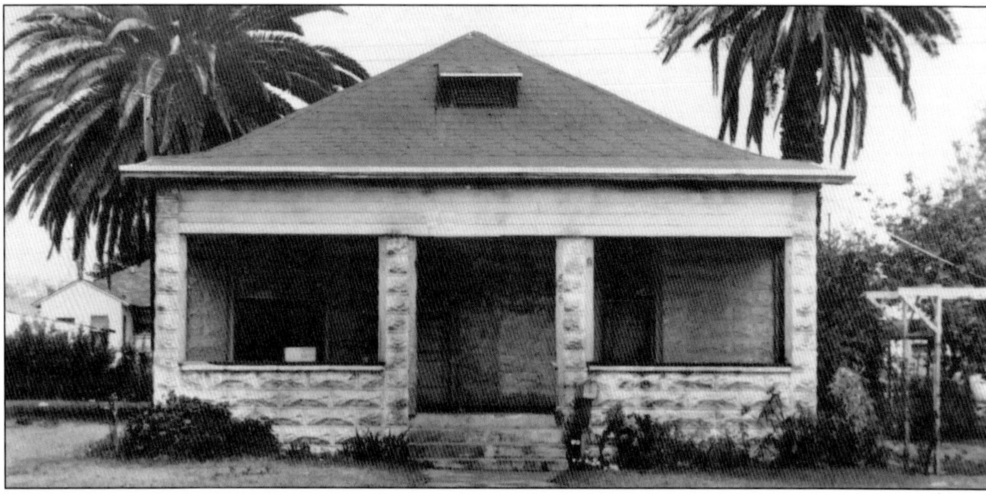

In March 1905, A.B. Miller arrived in Rosena. The first encampment was in a little clearing in the brush just south of the station called Rosena on the Santa Fe, near what is called Camp No. 1 now. He arrived with his farming and grading equipment, scrapers, and plows that had been used in the Imperial Valley, as well as tents and 200 head of horses and mules. No sooner had the teams been unhitched than a heavy downpour started. A hasty corral had been constructed the day before, livestock were turned out, and a ditch was dug to divert the water for the animals. The mess tent was raised and the making of a permanent camp started. Speaking of the rain later, Mr. Miller said: "To many it may have seemed a dreary start, but to a Californian a good rain is always a most glorious occasion, so our start was a very auspicious one." After the storm cleared, some people in the area came to swap horses and otherwise look over the "outfit." Their opinion, when they heard of the plan to farm the huge estate, was that the whole affair would "blow away in six months." This was the start of the Fontana Farms Company Camp No. 1 ranch site at what is now 8863 Pepper Street.

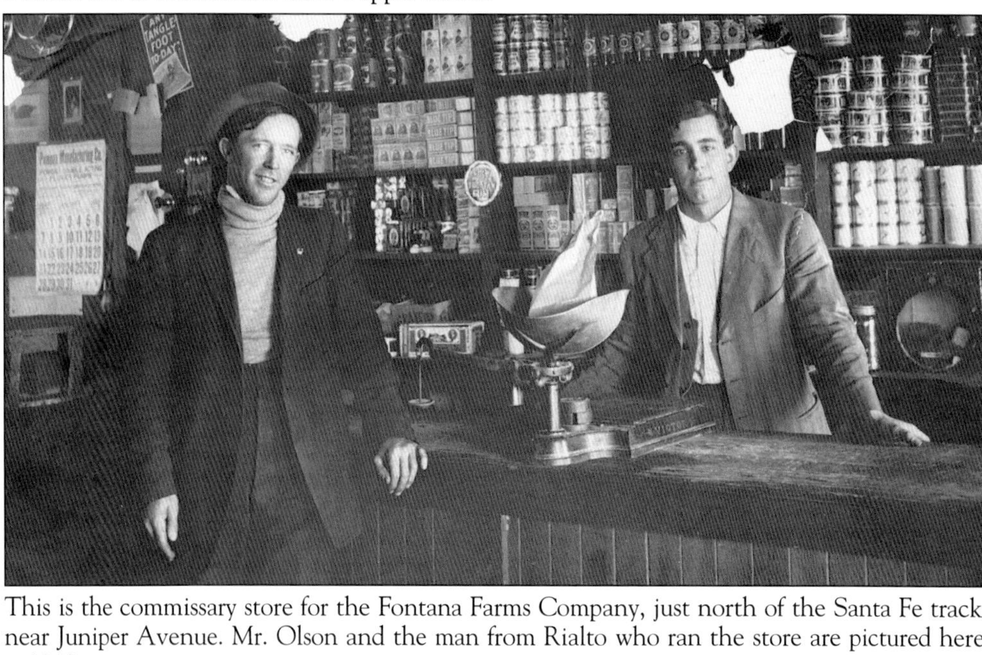

This is the commissary store for the Fontana Farms Company, just north of the Santa Fe tracks near Juniper Avenue. Mr. Olson and the man from Rialto who ran the store are pictured here, c. 1919.

In 1906, the area's cash crop was grain. Just before the harvest, the very dry fields caught fire. While the flames raged, the San Francisco earthquake of 1906 struck, and the bank that held insurance on the crop was in San Francisco. Their building burned, but they honored the policy and the Fontana Farms Company received the money needed to continue building the area.

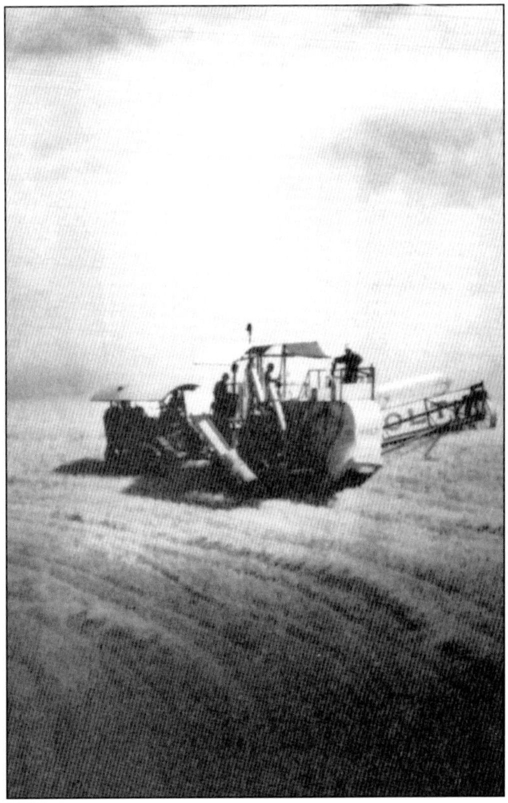

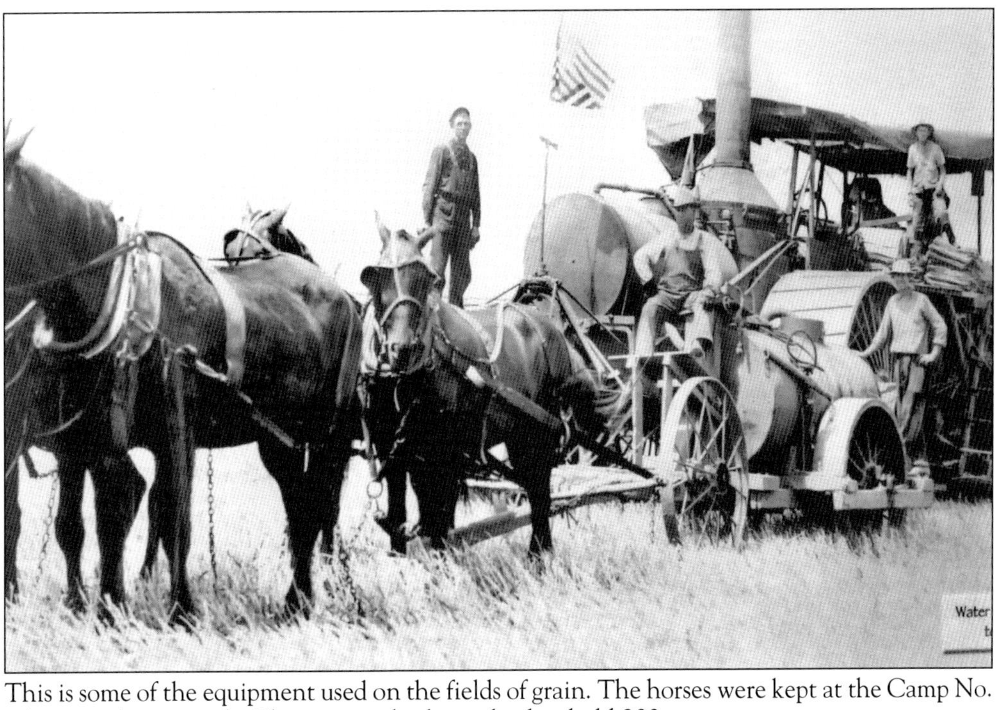

This is some of the equipment used on the fields of grain. The horses were kept at the Camp No. 1 barns with its corrals. There were also barracks that held 200 men.

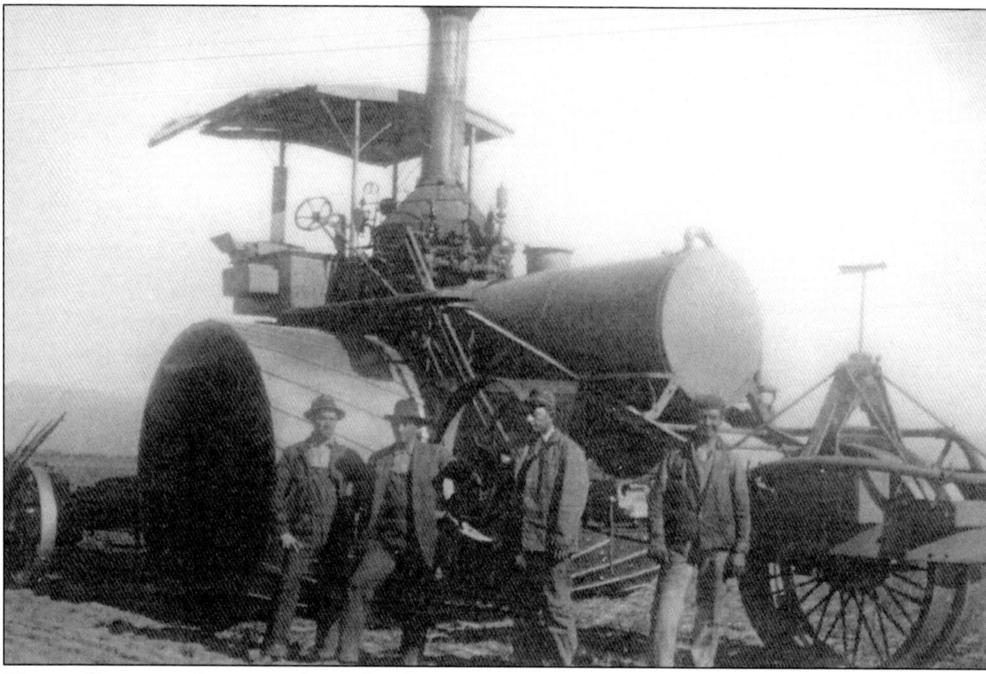

Shown here is a large combine for harvesting the grain fields. When the Fontana Farms Company closed in the 1940s, rumor has it that these big pieces of equipment were driven into the city dump and buried.

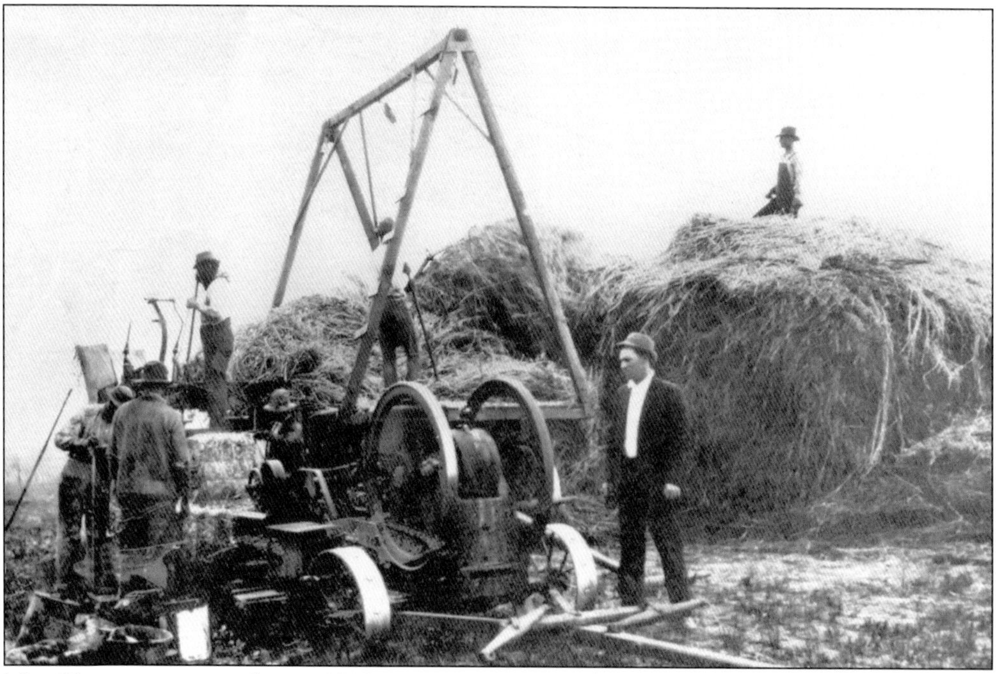

Mr. Olson is seen in this c. 1919 image overseeing the bailing of hay for animals at the Camp No. 1 area, where concrete pipe was also made for the water system laid out by Mr. Hasbrouck.

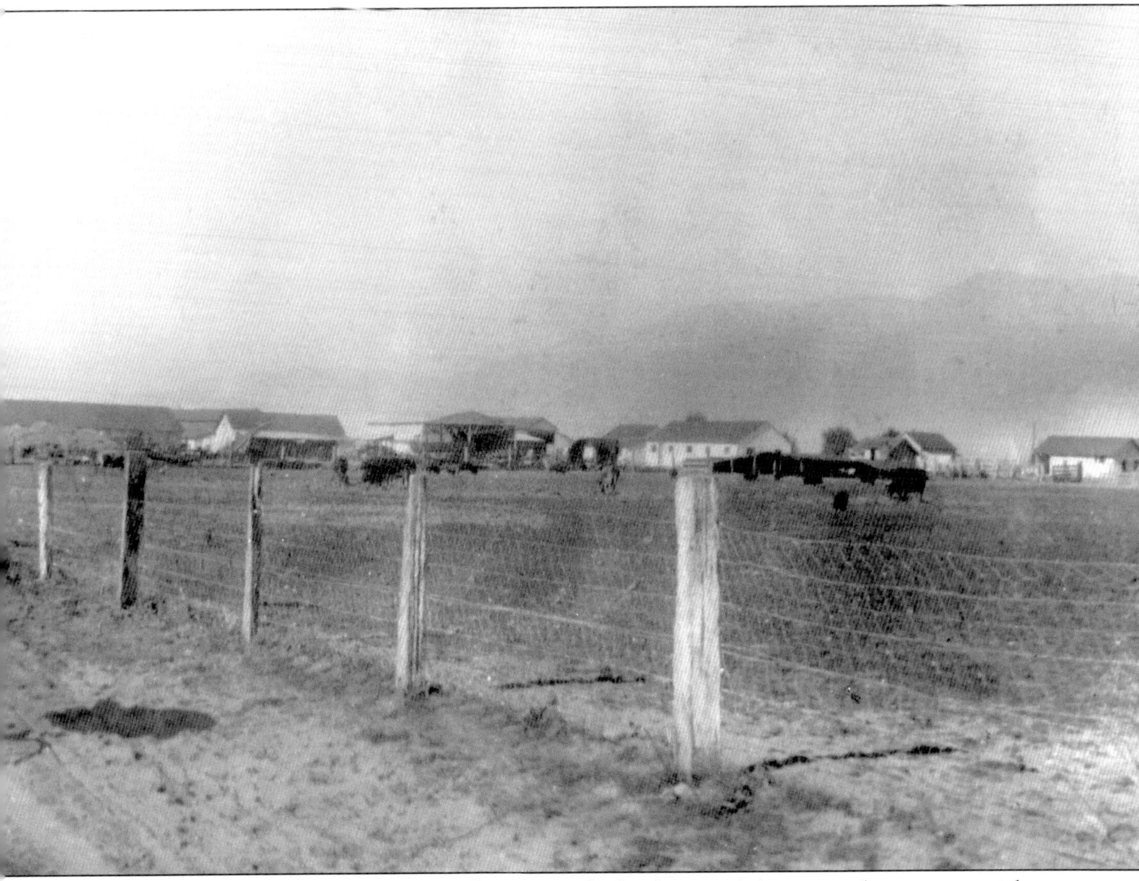

This is a photo of the Camp No. 1 ranch area, with the foreman's house at the extreme right. The compound consisted of barns and barracks for 200 men, as well as sheds, stables and pens, corrals, and the foreman's house. It took five years to clear 14,000 acres of brush that included 3,000 acres of barley. Twenty labor camps were established and the payroll was $30,000 to 40,000 monthly for 300 men who were mostly of Japanese and Mexican descent. When Miller bought the ranch area, he had 20,000 acres of land and used 75 percent of Lytle Creek water. The men lived at the camps near their work to save on transportation costs.

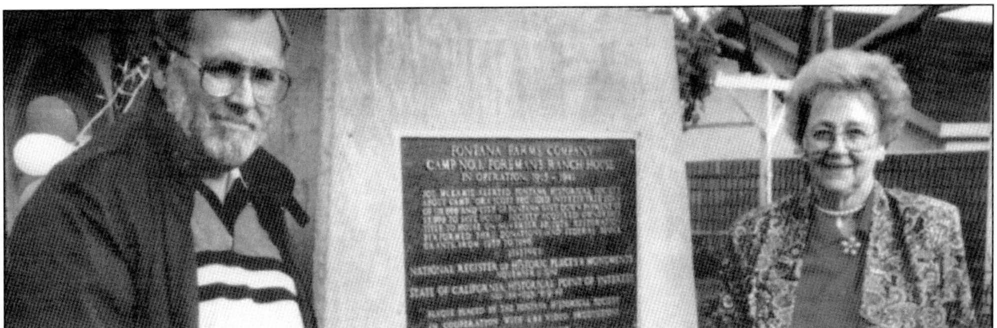

Pictured are Bea and Larry Watson, who donated the money to make the official State of California brass plaques for the Fontana Farms Company, Camp No. 1, Foreman's Ranch House Museum.

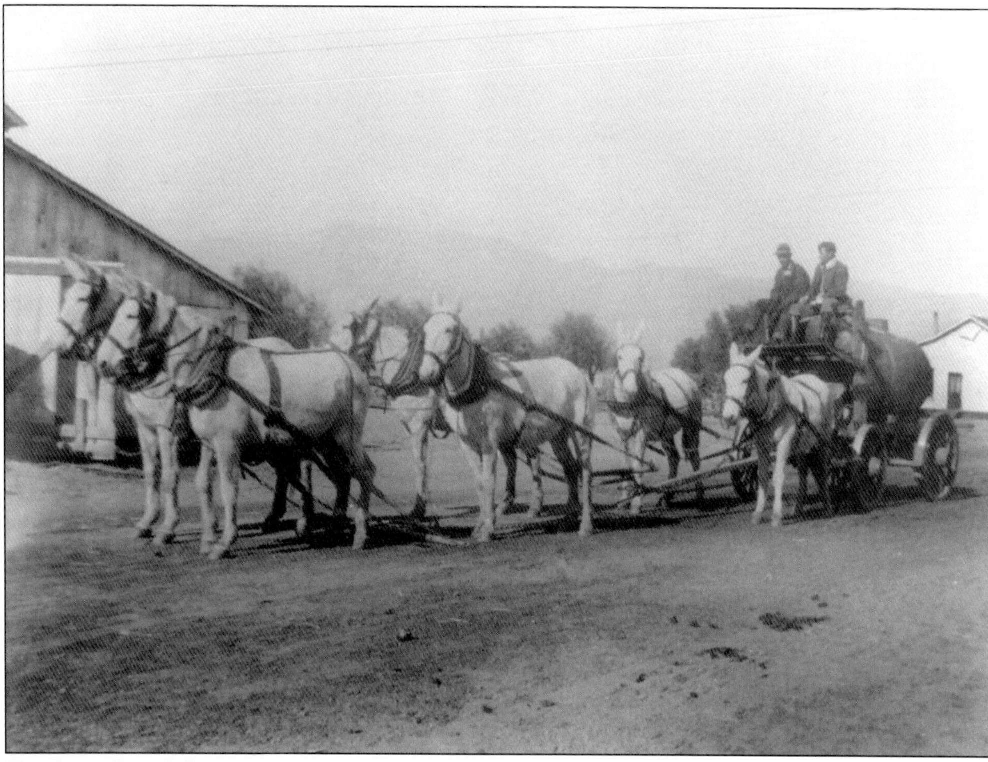

To the right of this water wagon is Camp No. 1's cookhouse, which burned to the ground in 1910.

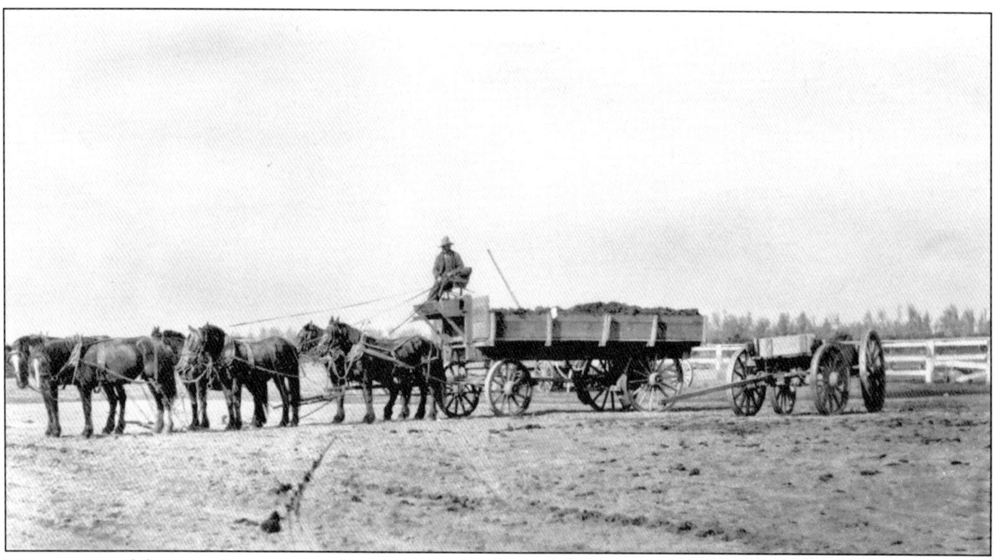

Wagons and horses line up at the Camp No. 1 ranch site near Merrill Avenue and Juniper Avenue, *c.* 1919.

Four

FONTANA 1913

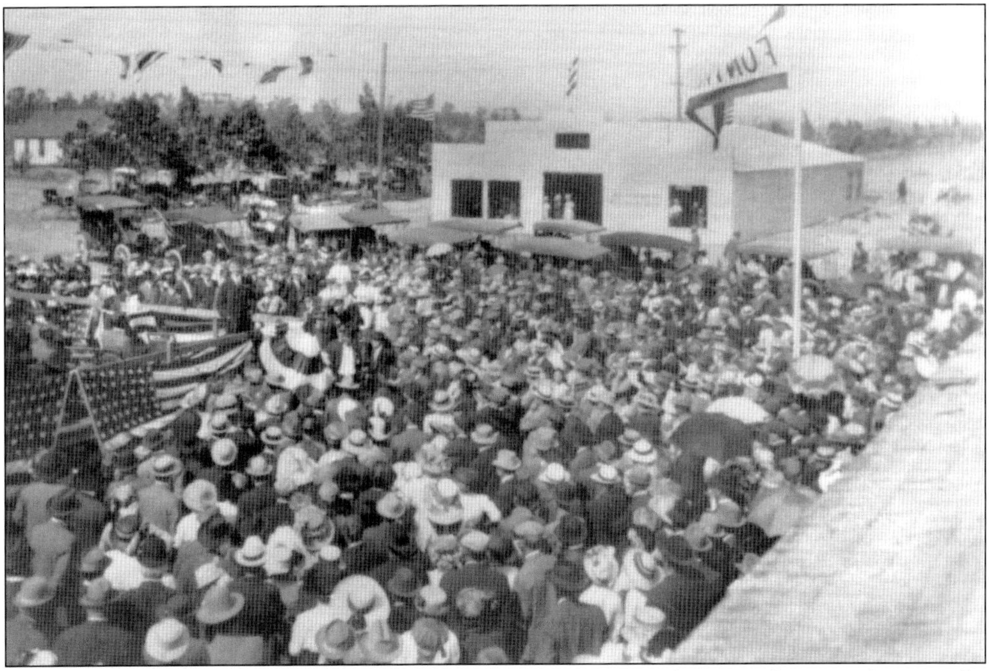

This crowd assembled on the southeast corner of Arrow Highway and Sierra Avenue for Fontana's dedication. Agents of the Fontana Company were busy all day selling town lots and acreage. Property was sold at $225 to $300 per acre, including water rights. All buyers had to pay one-quarter of the price at purchase, and sales totaled $59,125 for the day. Festivities concluded with a ballgame, fireworks, and a dance in the new garage. The day was such a success that it is now a yearly event called "Fontana Days." In 1910, the first building constructed at Camp No. 1, the cookhouse, burned to the ground. In 1912, the Fontana Union Water Company was incorporated, as was the Fontana Company. The first buildings completed on Wheeler Street included a garage, a restaurant, a lodge, three bungalows, and the Fontana Company tract office. More than 4,000 people from Los Angeles, San Bernardino, and surrounding areas attended the dedication on Saturday, June 7, 1913. The special train from Los Angeles was an hour late to the festivities due to a wreck. Mrs. Eliza Blanchard Miller, the mother of A.B. Miller, said "I christen thee Fontana," and struck the base of the flagpole with a bottle of Fontana's own grape juice as a band played. Judge Bledsoe was in charge of the event, and Paul Shoup, president of the Pacific Electric Railroad Company, moved the first dirt for the tracks that would link San Bernardino west to San Gabriel.

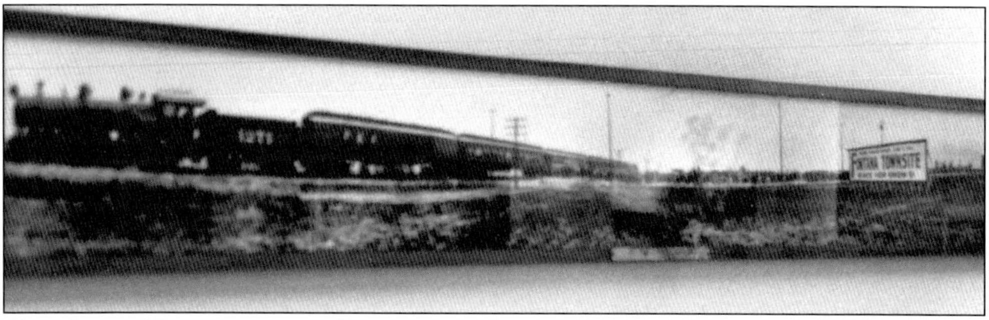

This photo of the train, coming from Los Angeles on the Santa Fe Railroad tracks, was donated to city hall in 1961 for its dedication. There had been a wreck on the tracks earlier, so the train arrived late and parked on the tracks near where the Metrolink station is now. Passengers had to walk to the dedication site, which was about two blocks southeast on the corner of Arrow and Sierra Avenue.

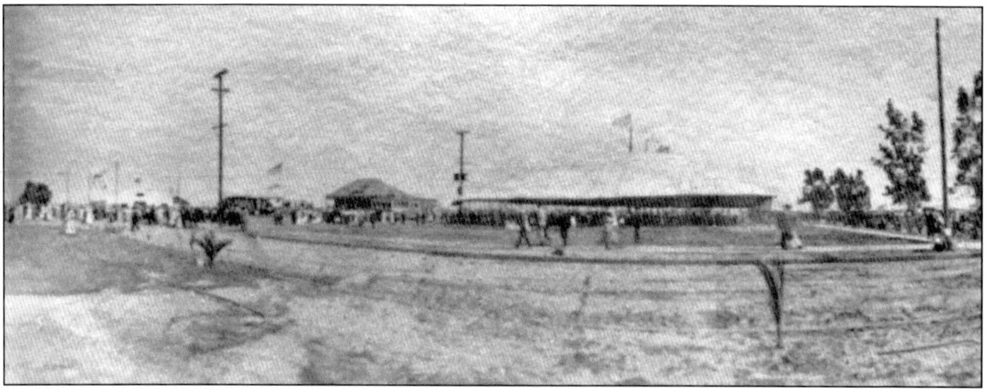

The huge Orange Show circus tent was the place to eat. Senor Garcia prepared the food; one of the most famous Spanish cooks in Southern California. If placed end to end, the tables at which the throngs were fed would reach an entire mile. More than 4,000 people were feasted. The menu included 1,500 pounds of beef, 500 pounds of mutton, 6 bulls' heads, 250 gallons of coffee, 110 gallons of red Spanish beans, 4 cases of sardines, 5,000 Spanish tortillas, 1,200 loaves of bread, 4 large cheeses, 50 gallons of olives, 25 gallons of pickles, 6 dozen bottles of catsup, 6 dozen bottles of chili, 6 dozen bottles of mustard, 200 pounds of sugar, 200 boxes of oranges and grapefruit, 1,000 pounds of ice, 15 barrels of "Fontana Smack," and between 5 and 6 cords of wood consumed during cooking.

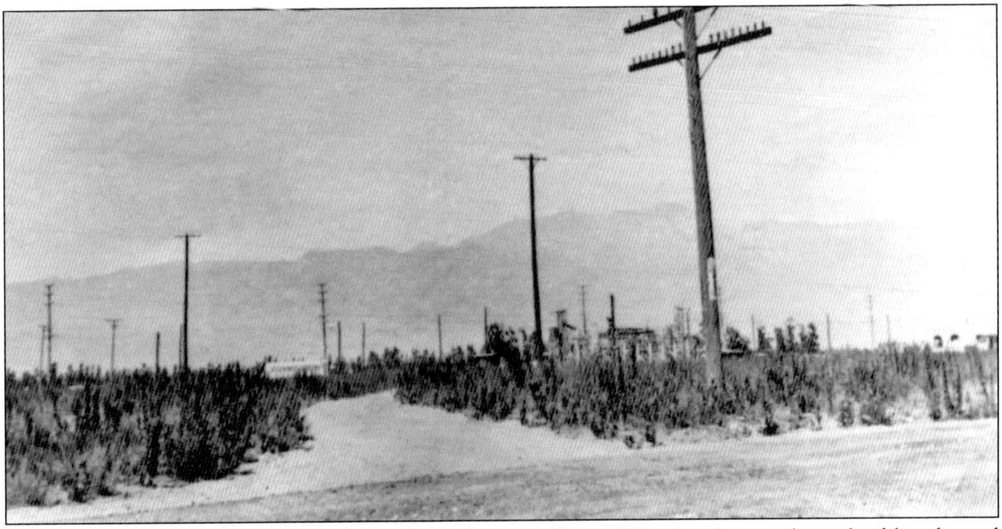

The town site was laid out with roads and power lines. The land was cleared of brush and rock. Some of these lots are still bare today, but are being in-filled. The town site was put up for public sale in 1927. Before that, the land was only built upon if A.B. Miller okayed the construction. He would usually donate the land or sell it at a lower price if he felt that his city needed the business. He sometimes even gave money to help build what was needed for the citizens of Fontana. There were 350 acres in the town site, and Magnolia Avenue ran north to south through the area. The County of San Bernardino Supervisors changed the name in June of 1927 to Sierra Avenue.

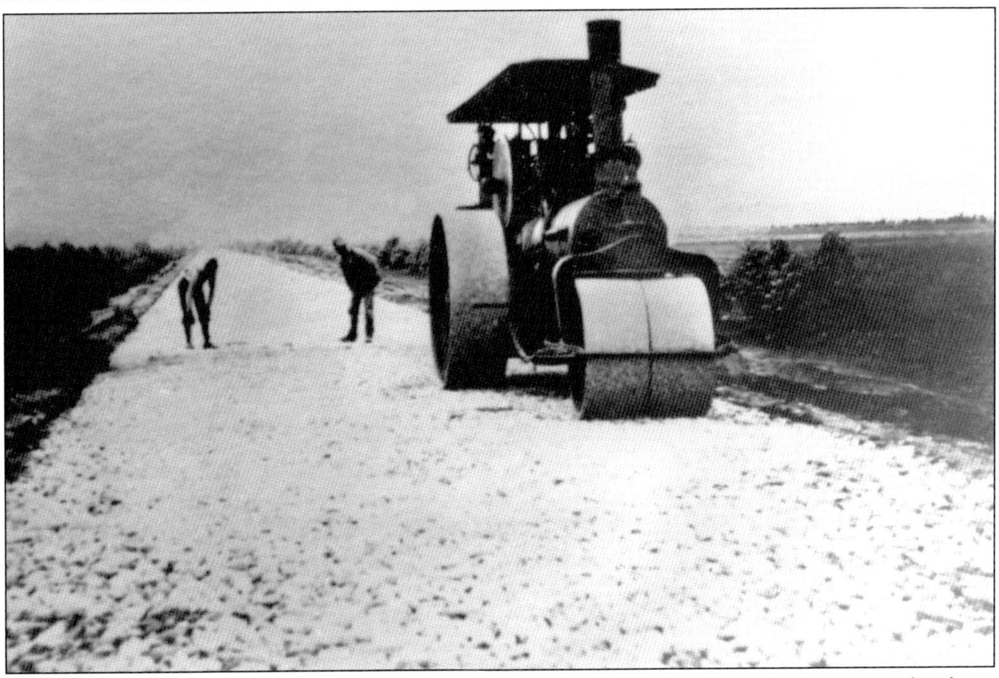

Creating the roads in the town site was a big job. The rocks from clearing the town site land was put into the streets to make a sound, deep bed to put the dirt or asphalt on. But in the future it was a mighty task to put water lines and other pipes in the streets, having to go through all that rock.

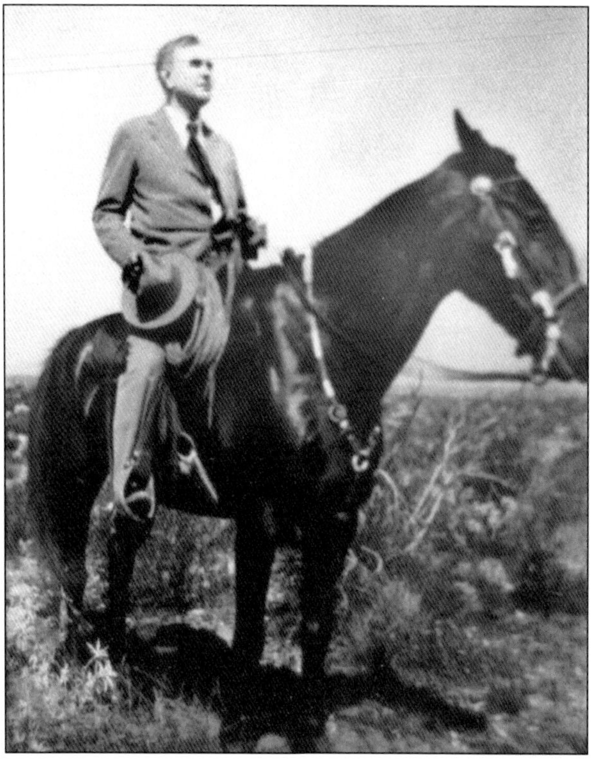

A.B. Miller, founder of Fontana, frequently needed a horse to visit otherwise inaccessible parts of the 1,300 acres managed for the Fontana Farms Company A proponent of agricultural experimentation and innovation, Miller supervised local planting of eucalyptus windbreaks and introduced many farming enterprises. These included the famous hog ranches, various types of fruit trees, flower bulbs, chickens, grain, and peanuts. An experimental rabbit station, established to find ways to provide more meat and protect against disease, was located here at one time. It now is a California landmark. Miller, seen here about 30 years old, gave Fontana its name in 1913. It had previously been known as "Rosena," a railroad stop.

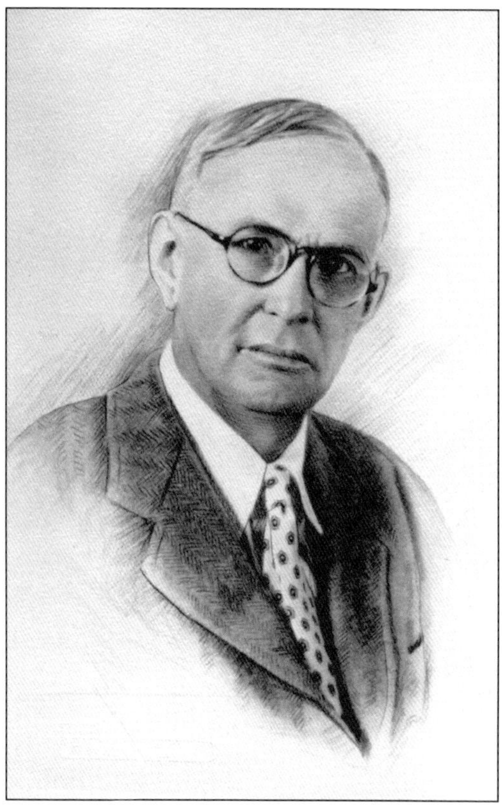

This is an image of A.B. Miller in his later years. Miller was an important person in California and around the world. He supervised the ranch in Fontana and several other locations in southern California. He had a cattle ranch with Swift of Chicago in Collinsville, California. An important figure for California agriculture, he was picked to be on the first agricultural board as well as president of the state fair in Sacramento. He also designed California's exhibit at the Chicago World's Fair in the 1930s. He died in 1941 at the age of 63. It was a great loss at the state level, to the point where they stopped the meetings in Sacramento when they heard of his death. He was highly thought of by many people.

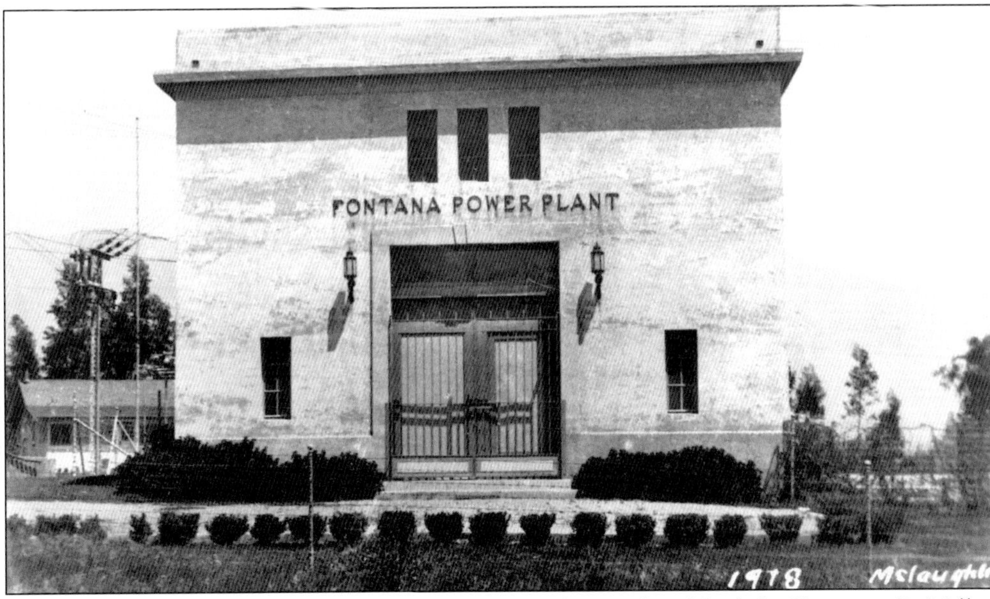

The Fontana Power Plant was built in 1916. It was designed and built by Kempster B. Miller, the older brother of A.B. Miller, a Cornell-grad electrical engineer. The plant developed over 2,000 horsepower and 18,000 kilowatts of power. Miller also assisted in the layout of the water system in Fontana, using the flow from Lytle Creek to generate 2,500 horsepower. The plant was leased to the Southern California Edison Company for 30 years, with half of the revenue belonging to the Fontana Union Water Company. In 1942, Edison purchased it outright. In June 1925, Fontana's "White Way" was installed, and a total of 40 lights along Magnolia, from Foothill to the Santa Fe tracks, as well as at the civic center, illuminated the night. There are three posts left, two of which are at the Woman's Club House and one at the Camp No. 1 Museum on Pepper Street.

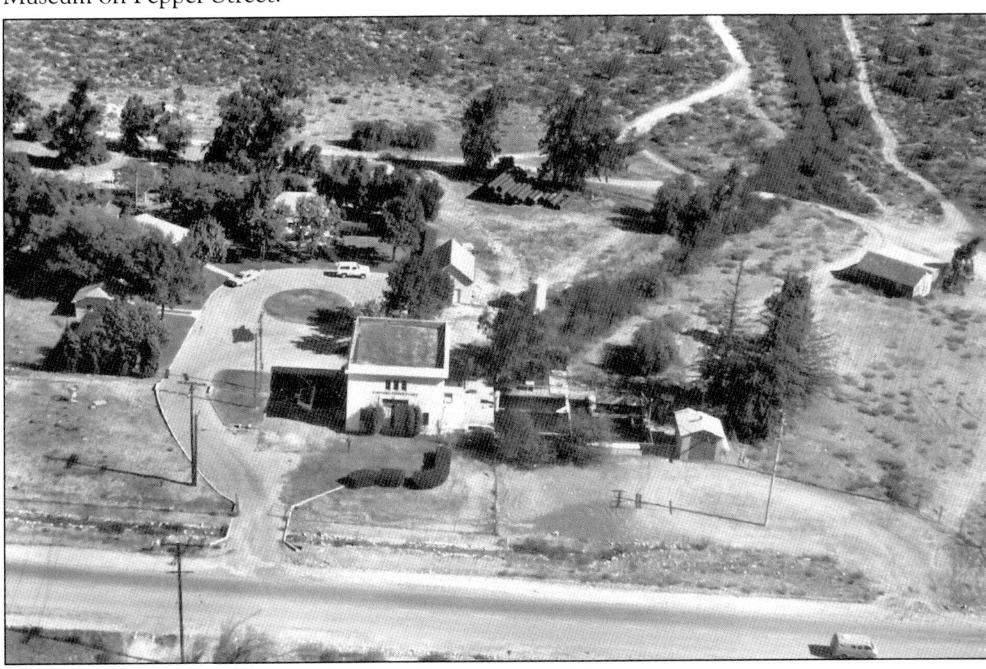

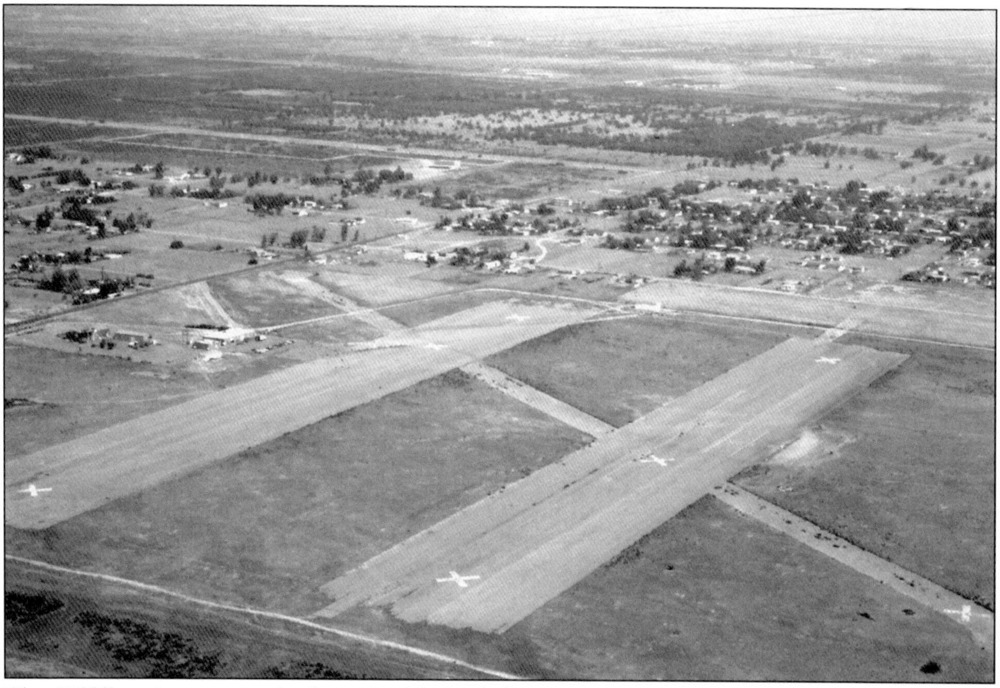

The Gilfillan Airport was built in the 1940s. A housing tract with a park and an airplane-style playground now occupies the land. Before Gilfillan, Fontana was home to Fontana Field, an emergency landing field that became outdated with the invention of radar. It was on 100 acres in North Fontana, above Highland Avenue, east of Sierra Avenge, fronting Sierra Avenue for a half-mile and extending east for a mile. It took three months for the Fontana Farms construction crew to clear the land of rock and brush. They constructed a diagonal runway that was 3,400 feet long, an airfield with a 70-foot tower, and a 24-inch beacon with two 18-inch green course lights of 27,000 candlepower. The field was part of a beacon system set up throughout the South during the early 1930s. Pilots would fly from beacon to beacon. The lights could be seen for 100 miles.

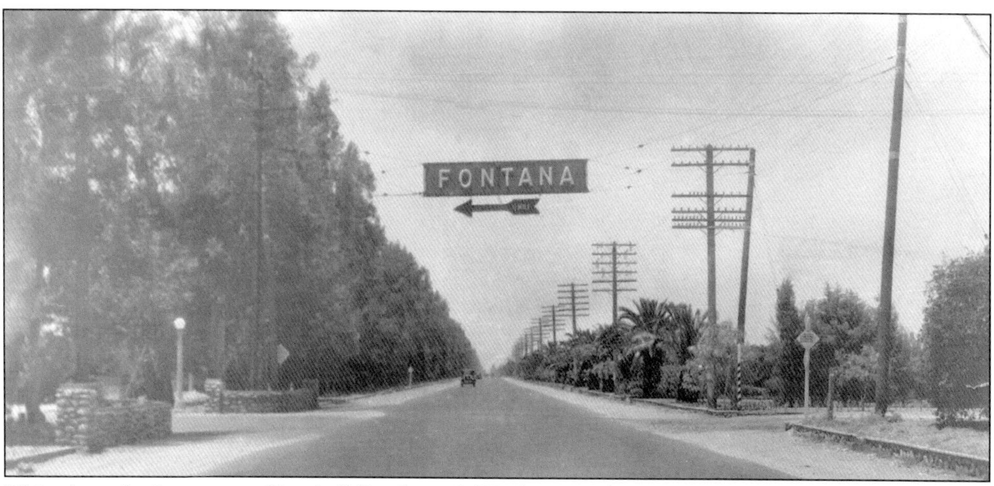

This photo looks west on Foothill Boulevard (Highway 66) in 1923. The Spring House has not been built yet on the corner to the right. The entrance to Magnolia (now Sierra) is on the left. You can see the Fontana sign with the arrow.

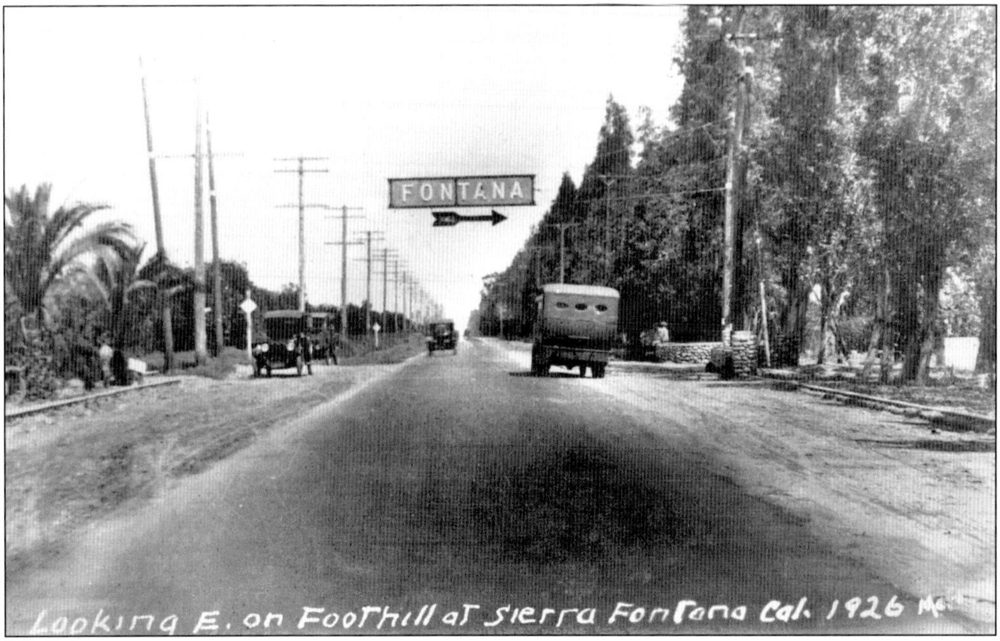

This image looks east on Foothill Boulevard (Highway 66) in 1926. The Spring House is at the left, as the landscaping and rockwork can be seen. Sierra Avenue is in on right.

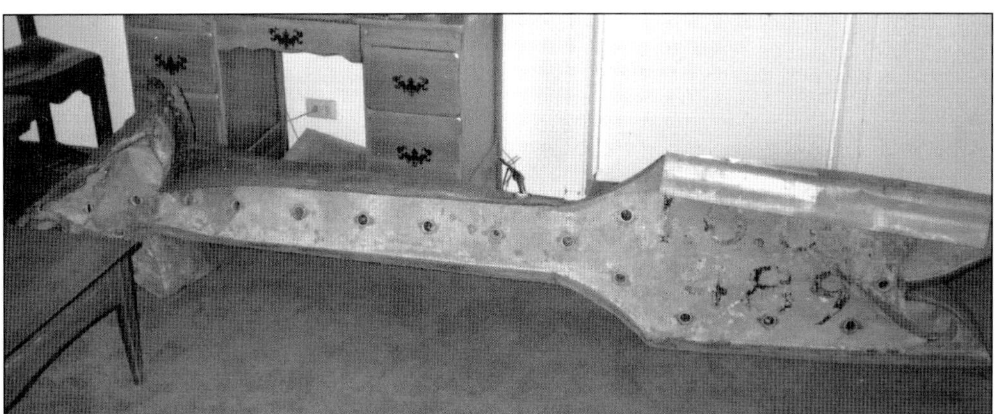
The arrow that hangs from the Fontana sign still exists, but is in Bloomington at the present time.

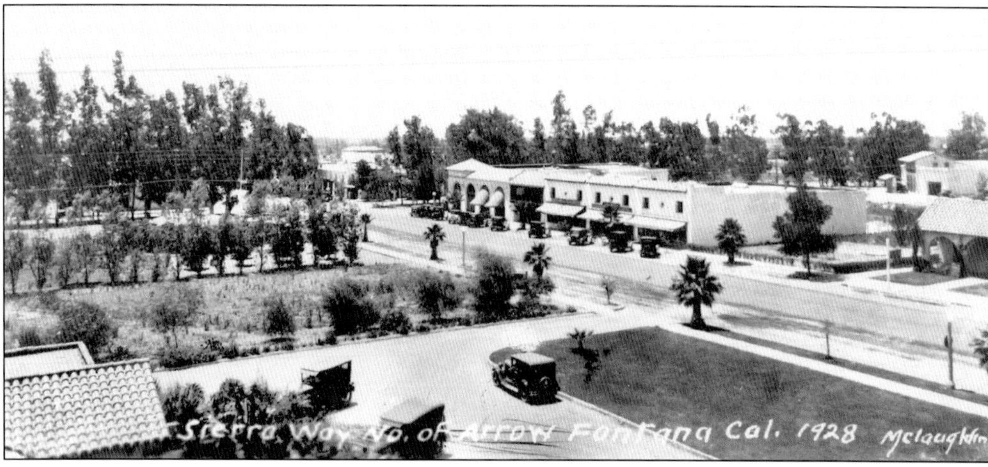

This is a 1928 view of Sierra Way, north of Arrow Highway, taken from the Fontana Farms administration building tower. The photo shows three stores on the Chomel block (built in 1926). These were the first business buildings of the new town site. The Bank of Fontana (later the Bank of America) is to the left of the three stores. It was constructed in 1924, and was the first building to have a second floor. All the buildings have disappeared and now a parking lot for the new Bank of America sits there.

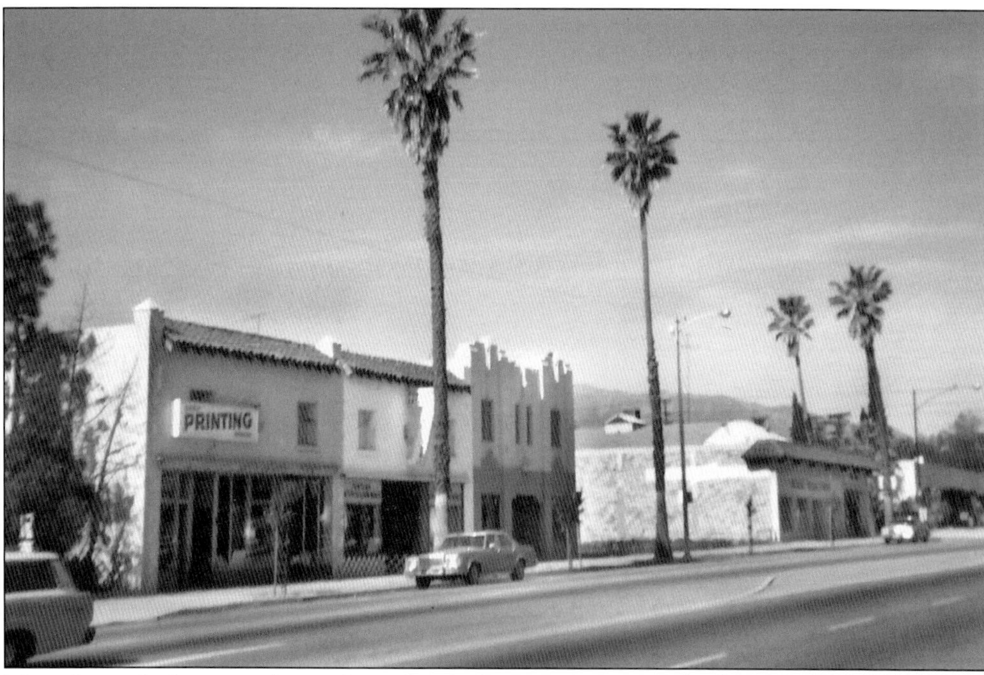

This photo, looking northwest from Sierra Avenue, contains the last two buildings on the Chomel block, the Kreis Building (constructed in 1937), and the Fontana Mercantile (built in 1921 and expanded in 1924). The Kreis Building is third from the left and was a two-story reinforced concrete structure. The Kreis Cafe and Store were on the first floor and the building also housed the 160 Club and the Parker Printing Company (now a law office).

The original sign of the Fontana Citrus Association is shown here. The name eventually changed to the Sunkist Packing Plant. The citrus packing house (for oranges and lemons) was built in 1914–1915 at a cost of $50,000. When grapefruit crops started to become available, an addition was built. In its day, this was the only concrete building in California's packing industry. In 1925, the Fontana Citrus Association bought the buildings. The rear section was built in 1936, and had air conditioning and storage areas for fruit. Fred Loeur was the manager when the addition was built, and held the position into the 1950s. The plant was sold to the Fontana Unified School District to create a warehouse and bus terminal.

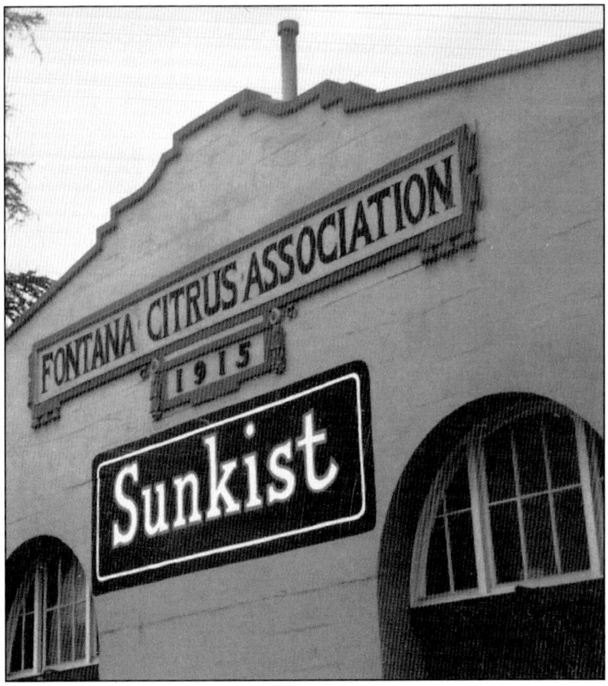

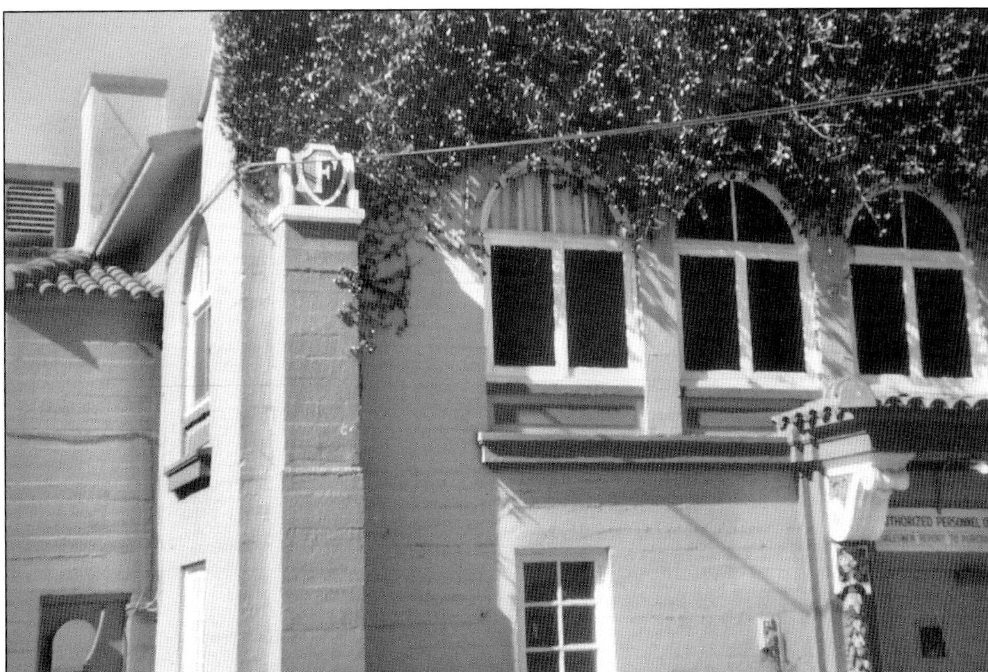

The Citrus Building had an "F" on all corners as a trim. The windows seen are where A.B. Miller had his first office, and the tiled section to the left is the vault area of that office. The vines used to cover the whole building and are remembered by the old-timers. The entrance at the lower right has details of fruit around the door opening.

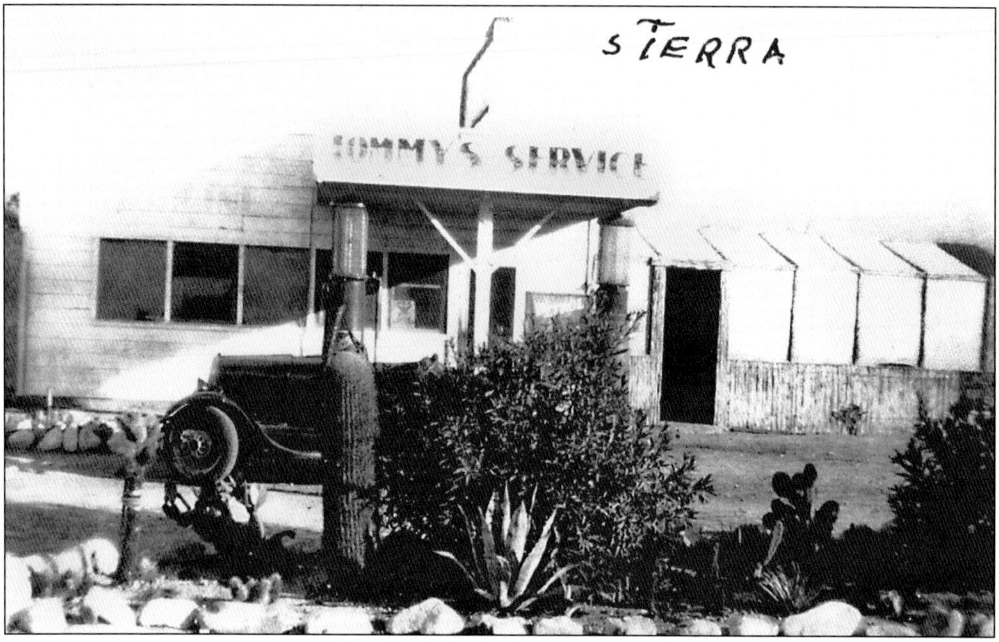

This is a summer view of Tommy's, the gas and service station formerly on the corner of Sierra Avenue and Highland Avenue.

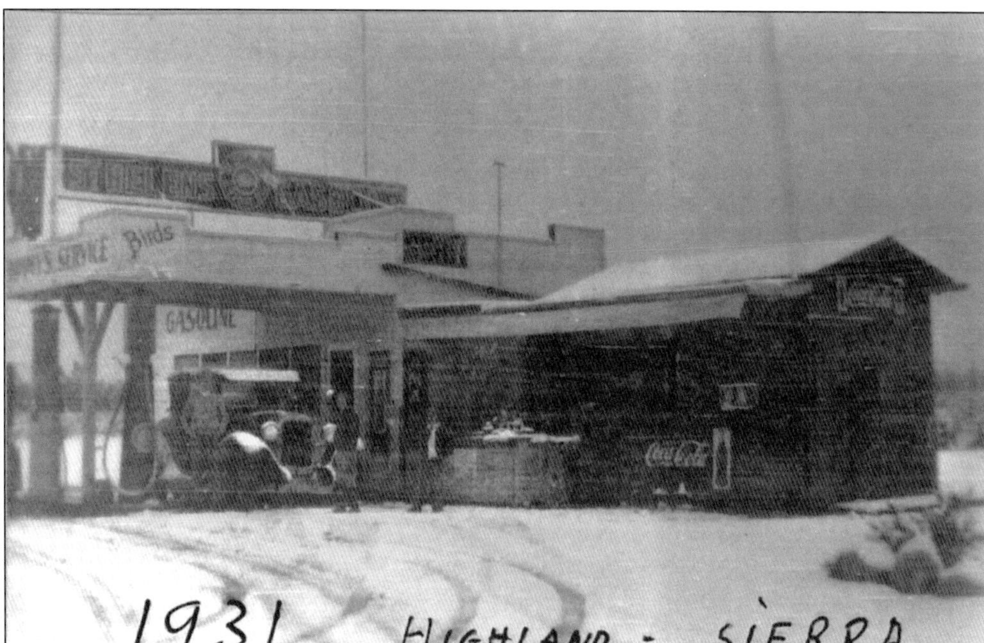

This is the same station, but during the winter of 1931. Ron Brower of Don's Trim-Rite barbers loaned both photos. He used to have a business in the downtown area on the northeast corner of Arrow Highway and Sierra Avenue.

Five

Growing Community

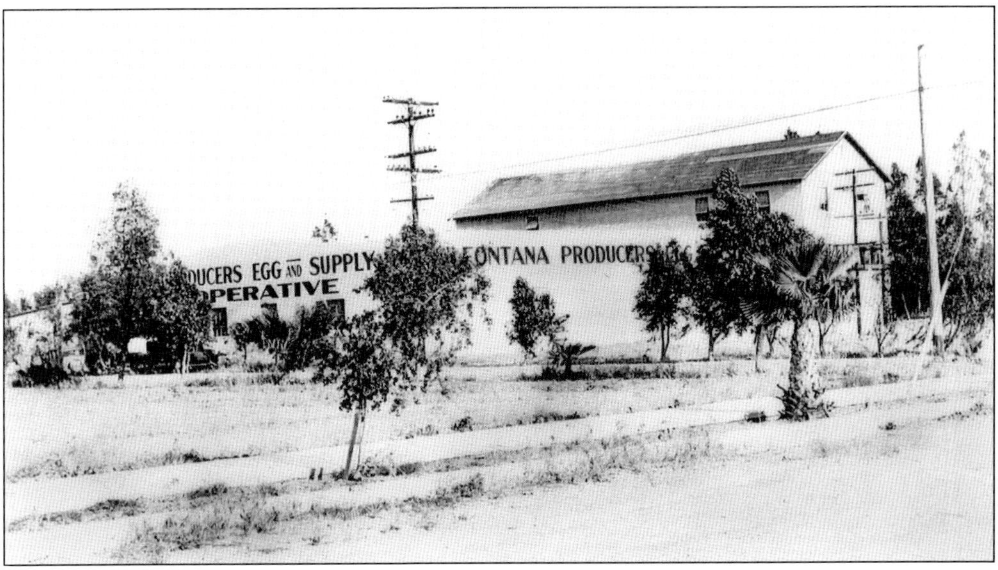

The new community of Fontana needed important buildings to support the growth brought by citizens from all over the United States and the world. Mr. Miller had an eight-millimeter film made on five reels that was shown to prospective buyers in Los Angeles at the sales office of the Fontana Farms Company It covered construction of the city and planting crops. Residents came from places like India and Europe, and they all blended together to make Fontana a success. Mr. Miller would sometimes donate land or money for a business or other buildings that the city needed to thrive. He never married, but he was married to his dream—the city of Fontana. The Fontana Producers Egg and Supply Cooperative was built in 1926, was added to in 1937, and it now sits on Orange Way and Sierra Avenue as a mattress factory. It was built so residents of Fontana had a place to buy cheap chicken feed, as well as sell their eggs and poultry. Miller felt this nonprofit business (buyers were stockholders) was needed to help his community to grow. The warehouse was made of concrete brick, was one-story tall, and had an elevated granary at the south end. The pits facilitated loading operations. The building included a 32-by-96-foot egg room, and the rest of the space was used for poultry feed and other sacked products.

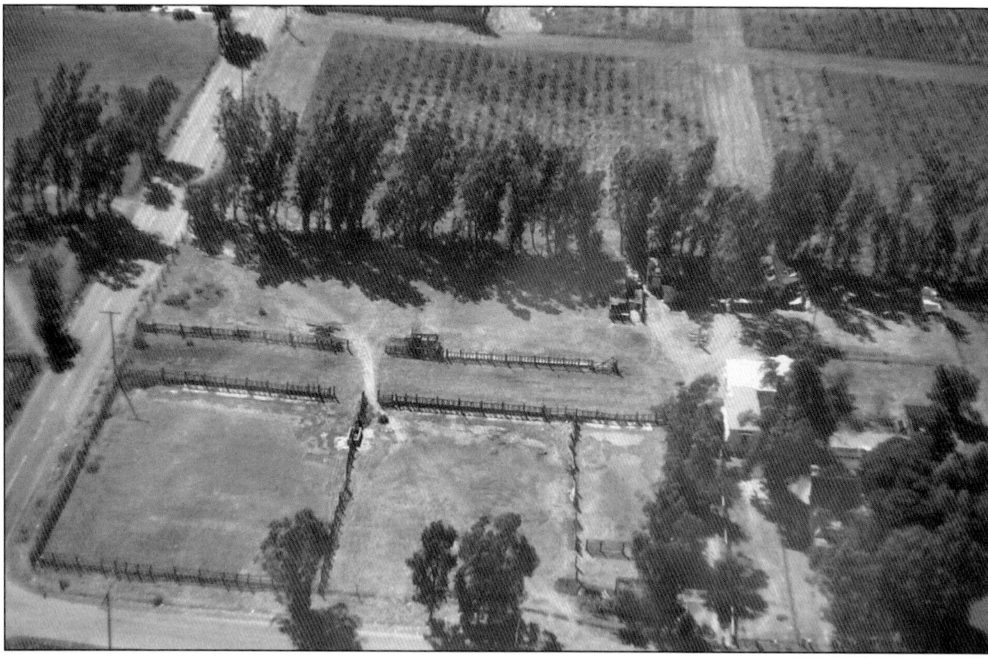

This is an image of the last original dairy farm on Beech Street in west Fontana. The old wooden fence is now chain link, there are two water troughs in the field, and the barn and other buildings are fixed up now.

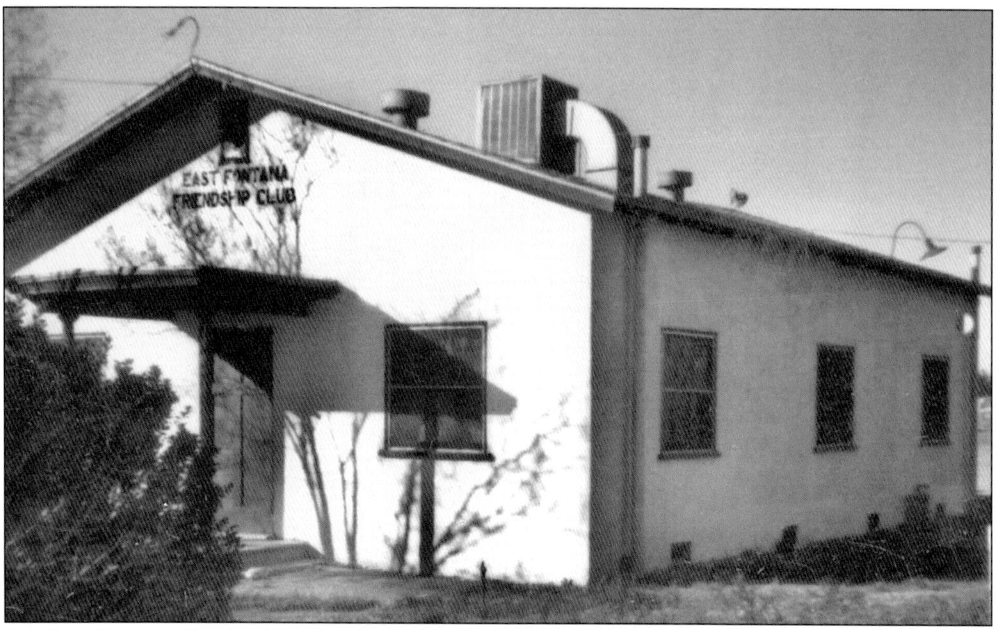

Displayed here is the East Fontana Friendship Club House on the southwest corner of Locust and Merrill Avenues. Residents had longed for such a building, and a big gala affair was launched for its dedication on June 16, 1933, attended by many dignitaries of the community. There was also a West Arrow Tract Friendship Club House built in February 1928, near the corner of Arrow and Almond Avenues. Both clubs, still around today, were built so residents could use them for meetings on agriculture and animal care. Parties and socials were also very popular.

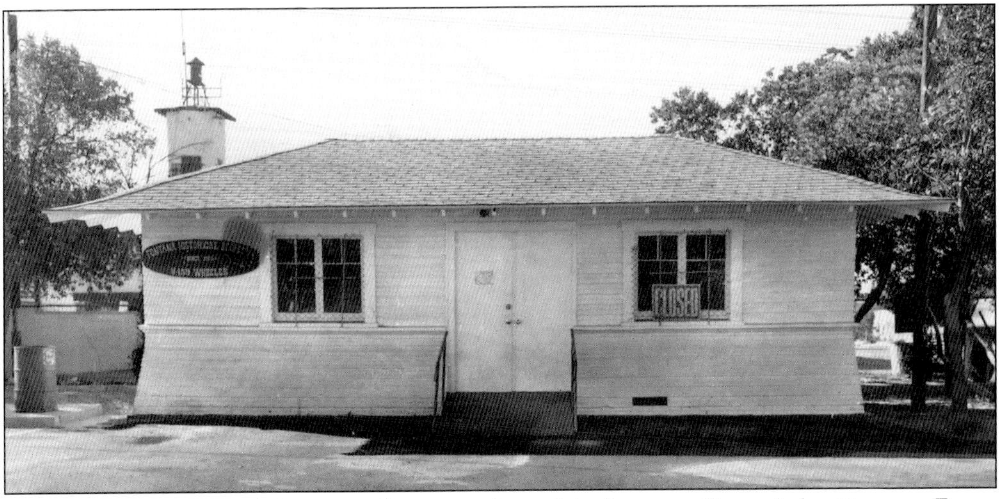

The Fontana Historical Society office was the original tract office of the Fontana Farms Company in Rialto (built c. 1911) and was brought to Fontana in 1912. It was placed on the northeast corner of Arrow and Sierra from 1912 until the 1950s. During that time it was a branch office of the library system from January 1926 until 1947. It was moved to the northwest corner of Arrow and Wheeler Avenues in 1947 where it became home to the Red Cross and then the chamber of commerce. In the 1950s it was moved east of the fire station in the park when it became the parks and recreation office of the newly incorporated city of Fontana. It was then transported to the north side of the fire station to store park equipment before it found its final resting spot west of Sierra Avenue in the Hazel Putnam Plaza next to the Pacific Electric Trail. Hazel Putnam and members of the society restored the building in 1977 (when the author joined the society), and the City currently leases it to them.

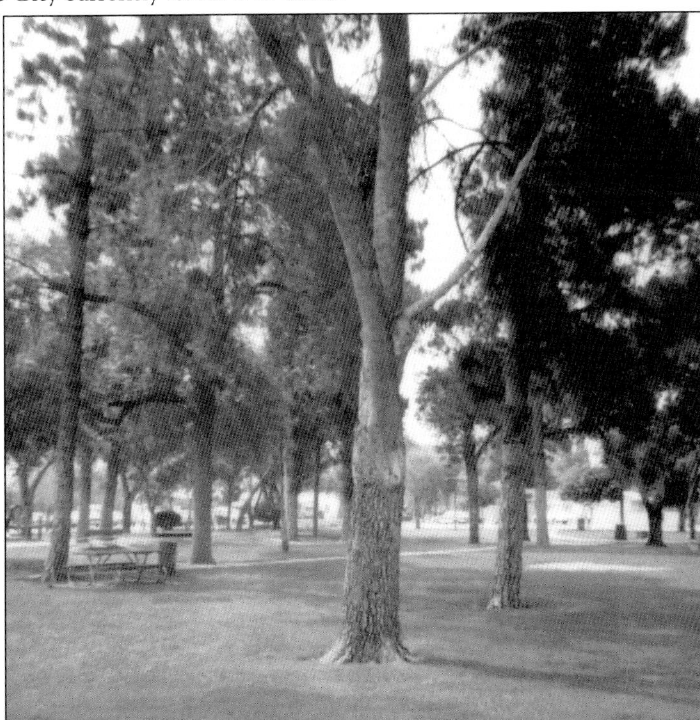

Citizens of Fontana donated the trees in A.B. Miller Park, and E.F. Bradbury did the landscaping. Most of the trees are still there, but some have been lost to Santa Ana winds.

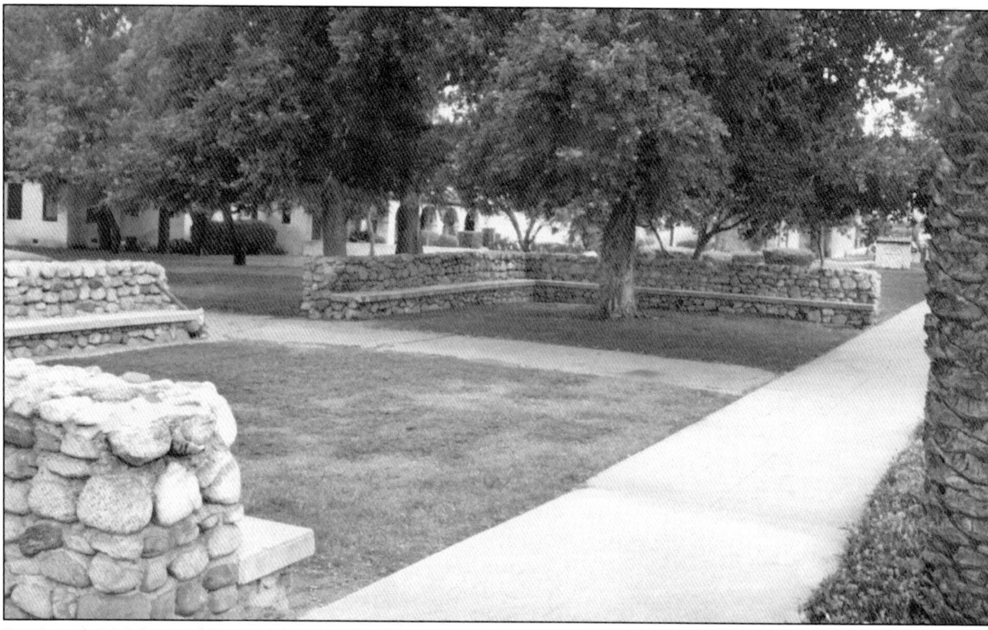

In April 1925, work started on Fontana's new park, landscaped by E.F. Bradbury. Construction took four weeks, and seats were molded into a semicircular wall of stone masonry with walkways leading in two directions into the interior of the park and a fountain in the center. It was called Eliza Miller Park in honor of Mr. Miller's mother. Troop 501 from the community church keeps it clean as the area, with its landscaping, was donated to the church.

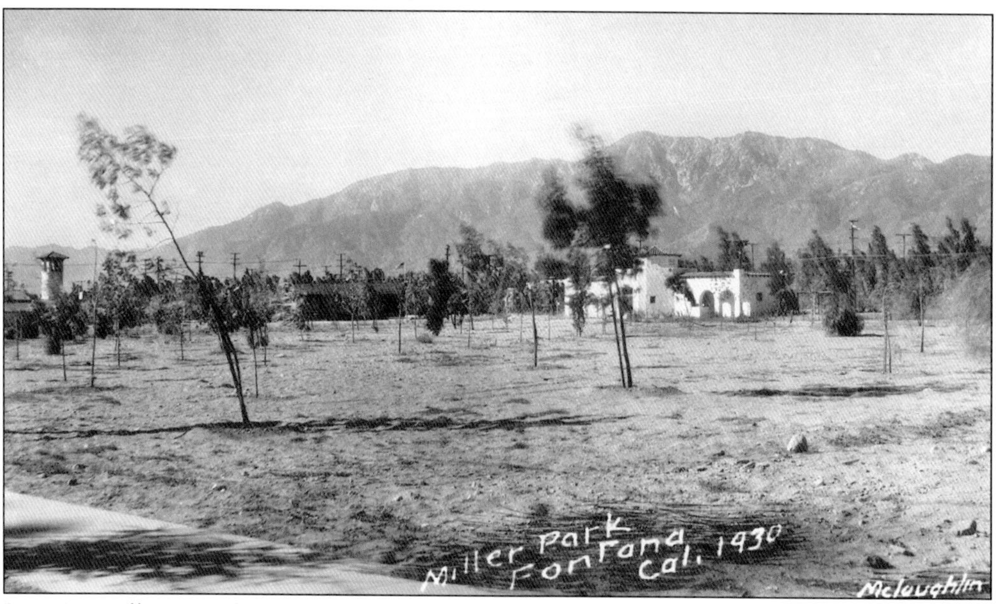

In 1928, Miller gave the citizens of Fontana a great gift—a second city park. Known as Miller Park, its official title is A.B. Miller Park. Once again, E.F. Bradbury did the landscaping. Citizens could buy a tree in the park with their family name on it. The committee authorized placing a tag on every tree. In the first week, 60 trees were donated at $1.75 each. By the end of the second week, 100 trees had a tag, and 50 more each week after. It was decided that 200 more trees were needed.

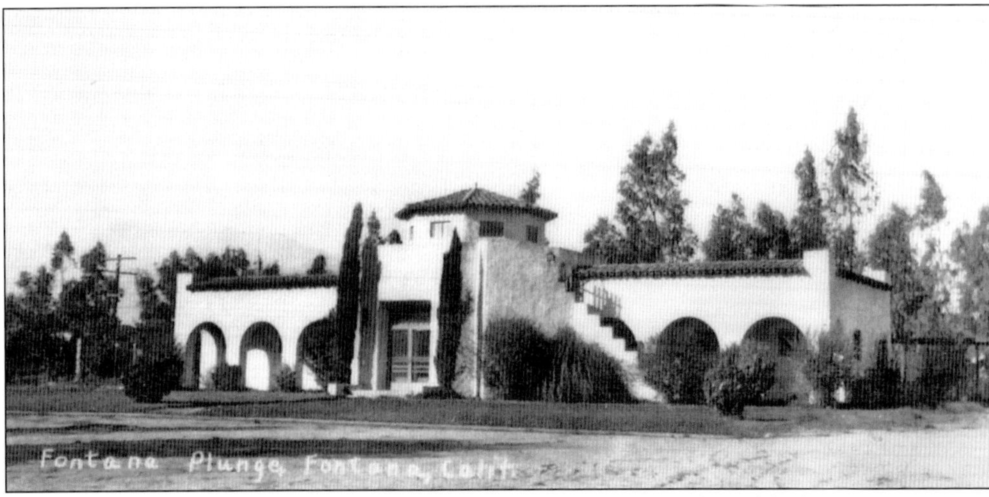

The Fontana Community Park Plunge was designed by Hugh Kirk and built in 1929 at a cost of $7,400, with the money raised by a grand ball. H.J. Ross was awarded the contract and completed construction in 60 days. A.B. Miller, who of course donated the property, requested Spanish architecture. An eight-sided tower in the center was the location of the office, equipment room, and 150 lockers. Stairs led to the top for a view of the town site. The wings to the east and west provided dressing rooms and arches on the north side, facing the Pacific Electric Line, were the main entrance. The pool also was completed, with trees and landscaping finishing off the grounds. Some of the original tiles were saved by the society, taken down by John Anicic Sr. to be put on display at a later date. William Chantry built the swimming pool, designed to complement the plunge building, at a construction and maintenance cost of about $4,600. The Fontana Farms Company provided the excavations and water, E.L. Bash and R.B. Doney donated the sidewalks, and residents donated money and labor. The pool opened with a "bathing girl" contest. The queen of Fontana, Kitty Powell, christened the pool with a bottle of pure Fontana grape juice. At 60 by 120 feet, the pool had a walled area for children with a shallower depth that was 20 feet wide. After many years, it succumbed to the rigors of wear and tear, and a new pool was built on south side as the old area became a racquetball court.

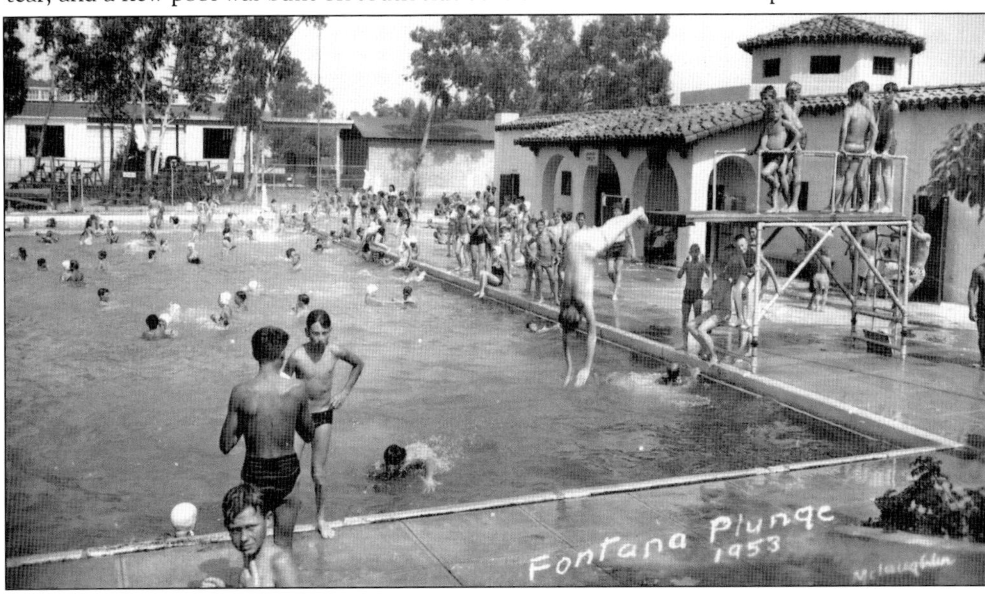

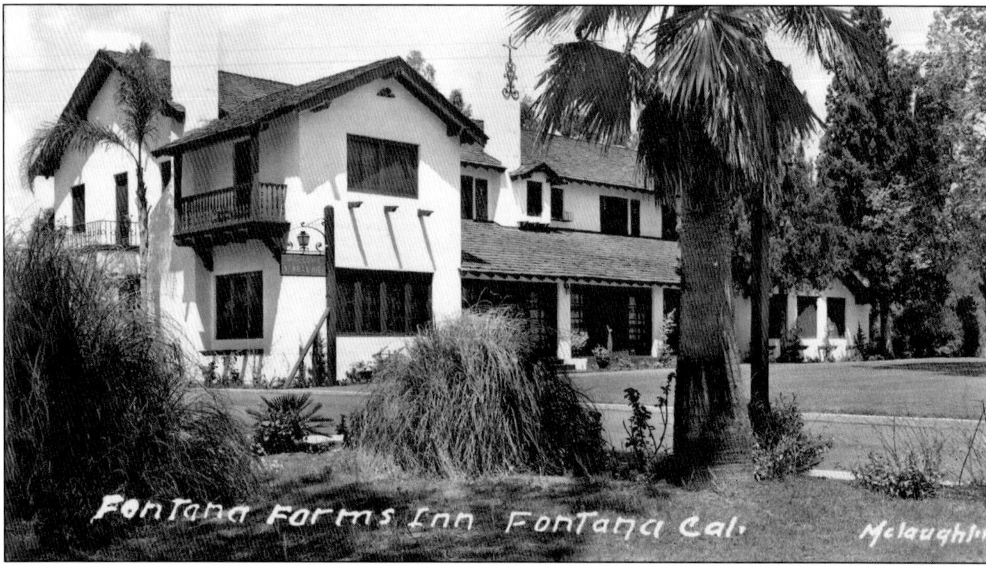

The Fontana Inn was built in 1924 as a hotel and restaurant for businesspeople and house hunters. It had a pool, bungalows to rent, tennis courts, and was the center of social doings in the new community. In 1931 and 1932, local groups were planning to help with the 10th Olympics in Los Angeles and met at the inn for months to decide how to help the metropolis. The committee in Los Angeles received word from Count de Baillet-Latour of Switzerland that there were 2,000 sons and daughters from 35 countries that would attend in 135 distinct programs of competition from 15 branches of sports. The West Enders helped the 1932 Summer Olympics from these meetings. The inn closed when it was bought by the San Diego Archdiocese to be used as a boys' school.

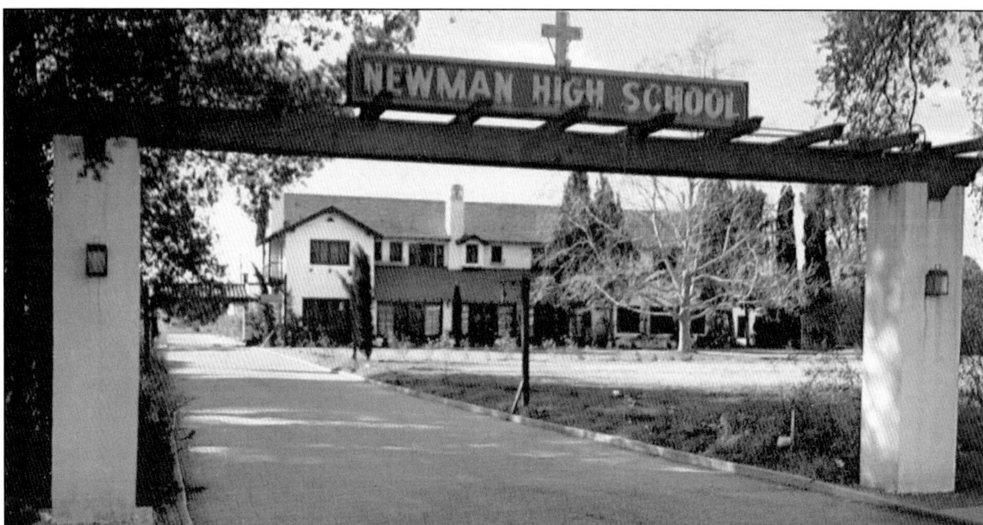

The Fontana Inn became Newman High School, a private boys' school. The bungalows were used as classrooms, and the inn became housing for out-of-town students. Many key enrollees were successful after they graduated, becoming lawyers and judges. The school developed a good reputation. When it closed in the 1960s, the buildings were left vacant and were later torn down to make room for a shopping center and post office. One of the classroom units was moved to Resurrection Parish. It is the only surviving building of the Fontana Inn.

On the northeast corner of Miller and Mango is a large, two-story structure known as Camp No. 4. Fontana Farms Company had camps all over the area, so the men always lived near their work. This house was home to foreman Frank Williams and his family. Mr. Williams later became supervisor of agriculture. The palm trees along the driveway and in the planter are still there, as well as the garage in the back.

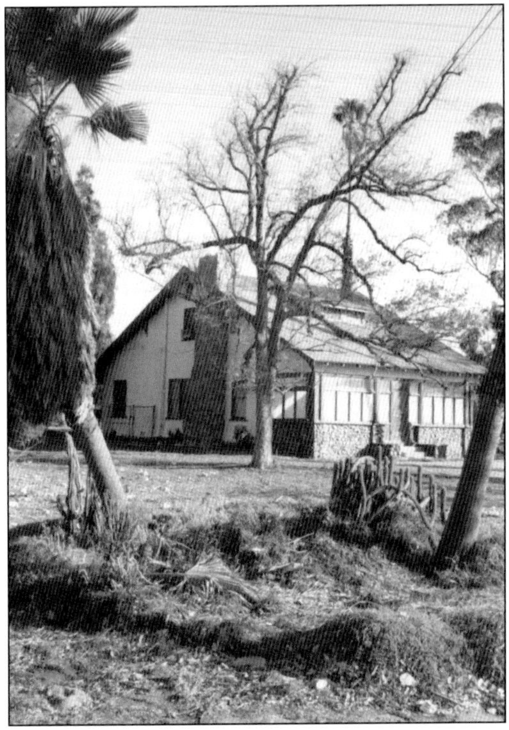

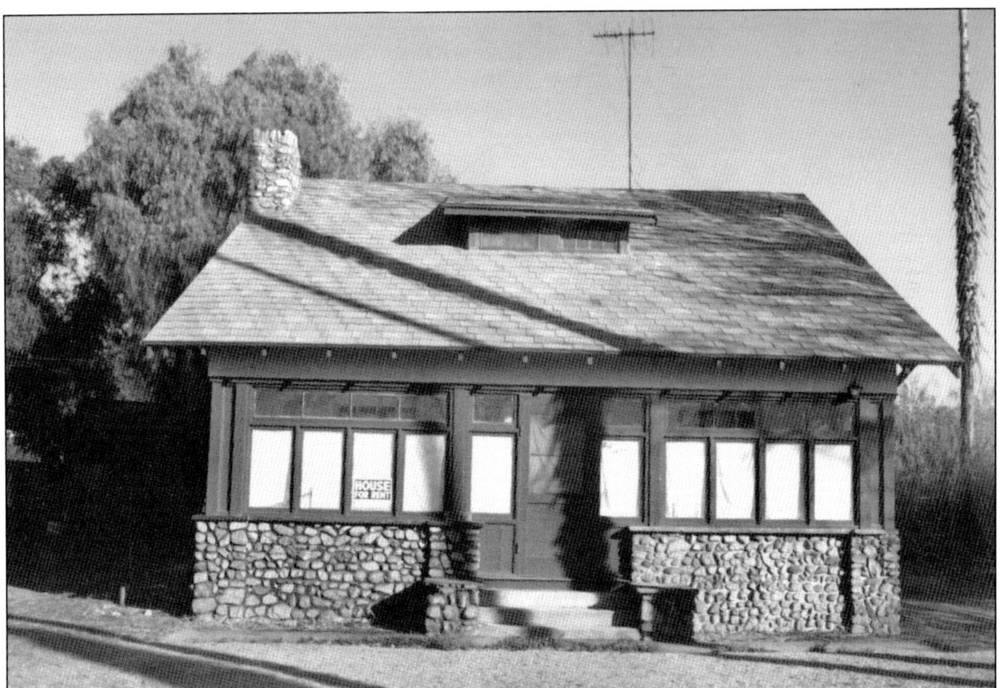

This is a view of the front of the house, which had a large, knotty pine kitchen and summer porch. The lower floor had a dining room that joined the living room (also the master bedroom) and fireplace. On the second floor there were two bedrooms and storage space used by Williams's daughters, Kay and Emmy Lou.

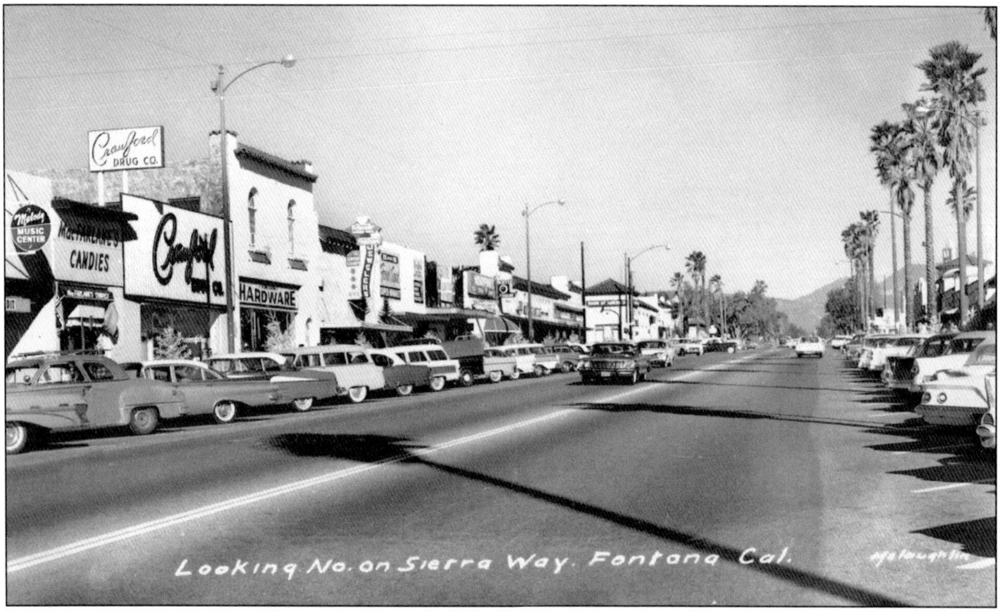

This view looks north on Sierra Avenue from Valencia, showing the Crawford Drug Co. and the Tudor two-story hardware store (on the left). The buildings on this west side were built between 1925 through 1929: the Henry Building, in 1925; the Nichols Building, in 1926; the Sinclair block, in 1926; the Cohen Building, in 1926; the Crawford Building, in 1928; and the Tudor two-story building, in 1929. All of these buildings still remain today, but have been altered.

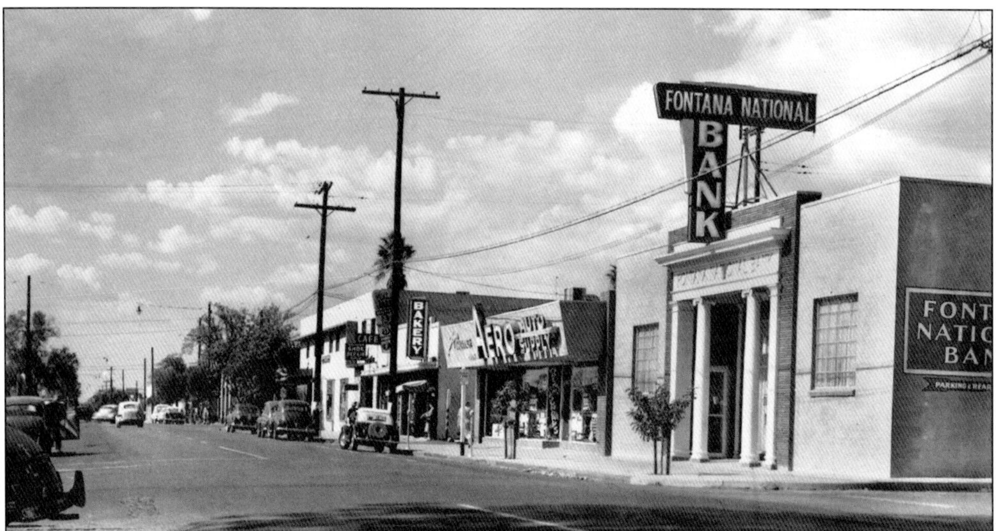

This is a view of the buildings on Arrow, looking west toward Sierra Avenue. The far corner building is gone now. The stores on that block were Don Brower's barbershop, the Aero Auto Store (later the Knights of Columbus Hall), and the Fontana National Bank (on the northwest corner of Wheeler and Arrow). City councilman Don Day helped the society one evening take down the gold-leafed sign over the door. The columns, with its top and bottom caps, the doors, paneling, and plumbing items were all used for the restoration of Camp No. 1. The corner is now the chamber of commerce and housing department.

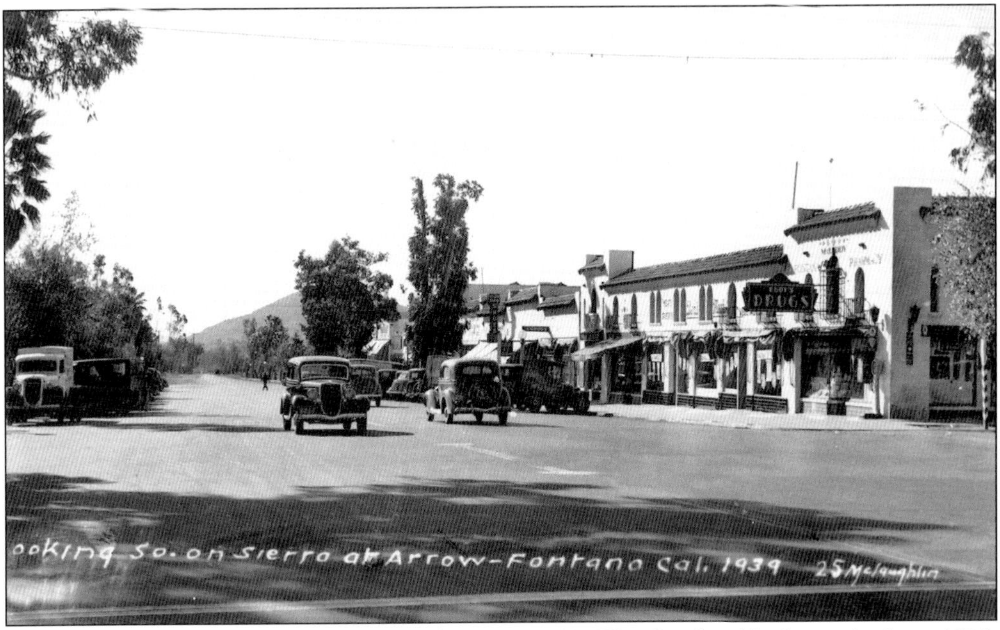

This image looks south from Arrow Highway in 1939. The Sinclair block was built in 1926. Finley's Rexall Drug Store, opened in July 1926 by A.M. Bell, was in the building for many years. The sign was up from 1926 to 1939 before it was covered. In May 1928, J.H. Burris bought the business, which is now a pawnshop. The Sinclair block is a California point of historical interest. The day it was listed, they took off all the coverings to expose all the old details and signage.

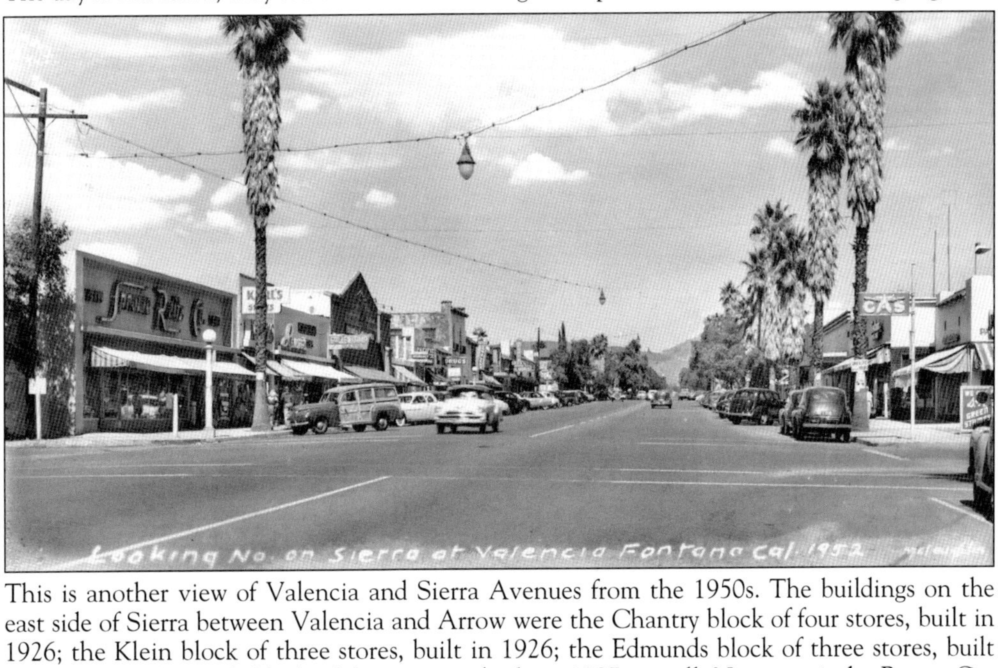

This is another view of Valencia and Sierra Avenues from the 1950s. The buildings on the east side of Sierra between Valencia and Arrow were the Chantry block of four stores, built in 1926; the Klein block of three stores, built in 1926; the Edmunds block of three stores, built in 1937; and the Fitch block of three stores, built in 1937 as well. Not seen is the Rocco Gas Station, to the right. Some of the businesses on this side of the street were Eva's Beauty Shop, Arrow Travel, Miss Juliet Bornefeld's Gift and Gown Shop, and L.I. Jecker and O.G. Daab's barbershop. The Prato Store was also on this side of Sierra, next to the Hunter block.

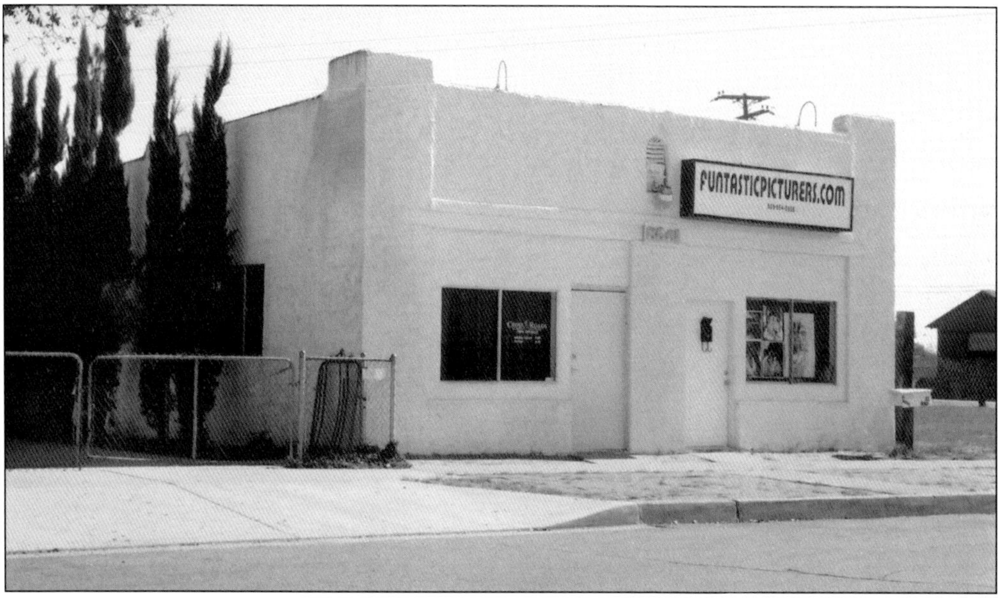

This building, on the corner of wheeler and Orange Way, shows up in very early photographs and is believed to be one of the oldest structures in the area, dating back to the 1910s. It still is a business today and has been kept in very good condition.

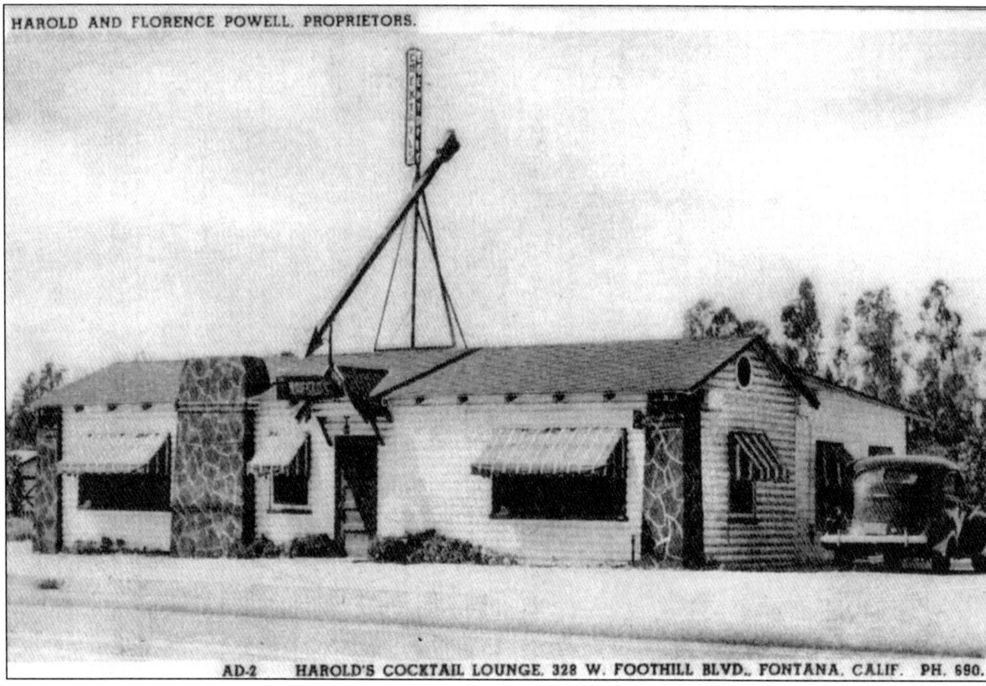

This is a shot of Harold's Cocktail Lounge, owned by Harold and Florence Powell, on Foothill Boulevard (Route 66). The couple lived in a home behind the business. The lounge was a stop for many Hollywood stars and important people on their way to Palm Springs and the mountains who ate and drank as they wished. The lounge burned by a fire in the kitchen and was never rebuilt. The lot remained empty until a few years ago when a new building was constructed on the lot.

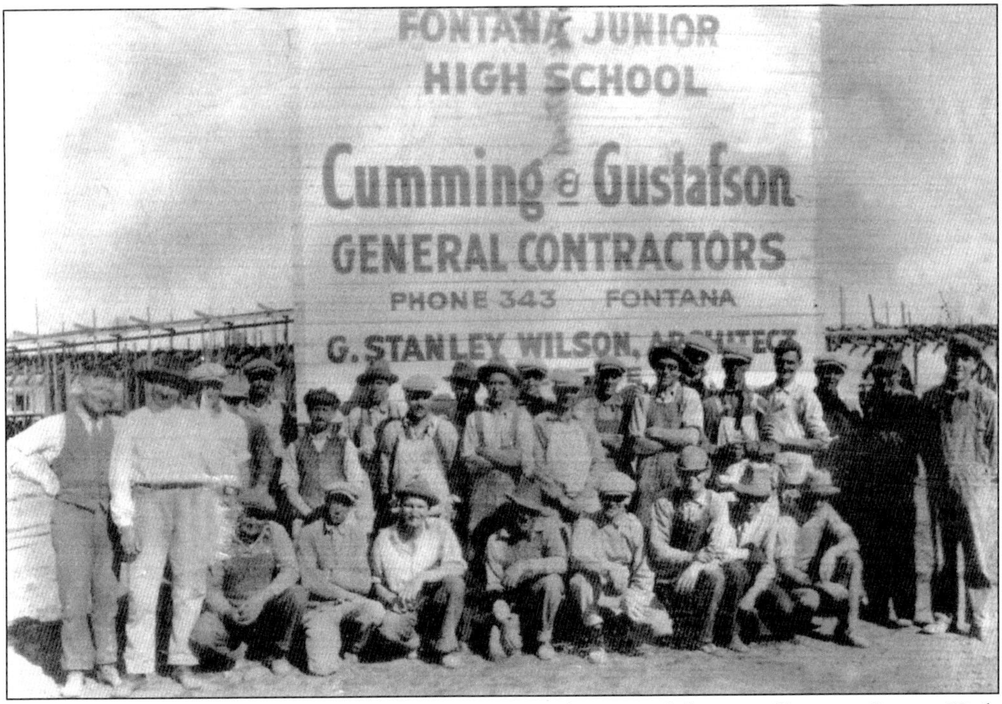

This photo shows a construction crew in 1927 at the site of the new Fontana Junior High School, located at the corner of Arrow Route and Mango Avenue. William Cumming, at the far left, and Axel Gustafson, second from the left, were the general contractors for the building. William (Bill) Cumming also constructed the first church in Fontana—Fontana Community Church. He and his wife, Ivy Cumming, and their four children arrived in Fontana from Canada in 1925. Eva Cumming Hall is the only remaining family member, residing in Redlands, California. (Courtesy of Pat Alexander Murray.)

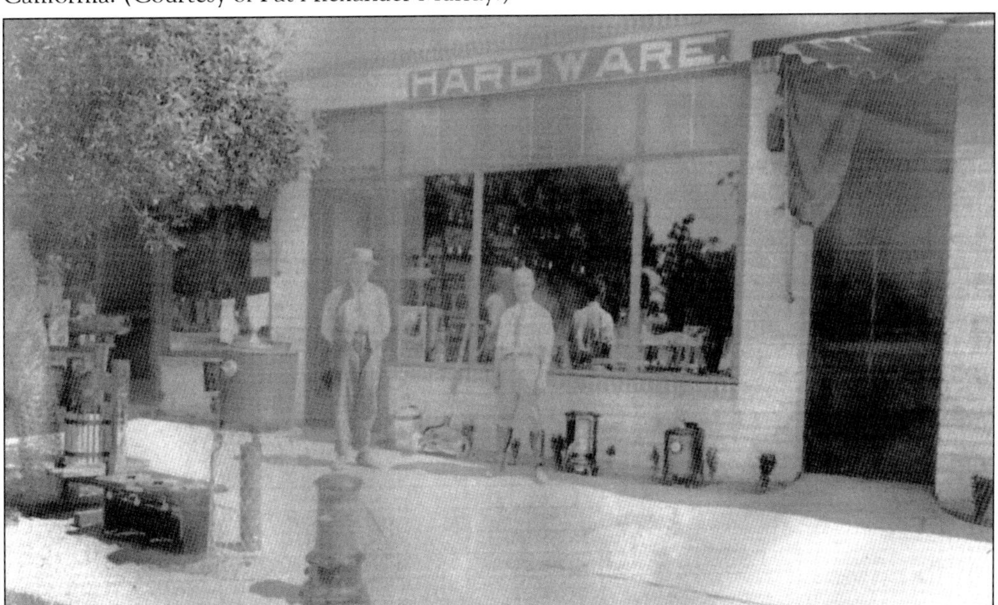

One of the hardware stores in the downtown area is depicted in this image.

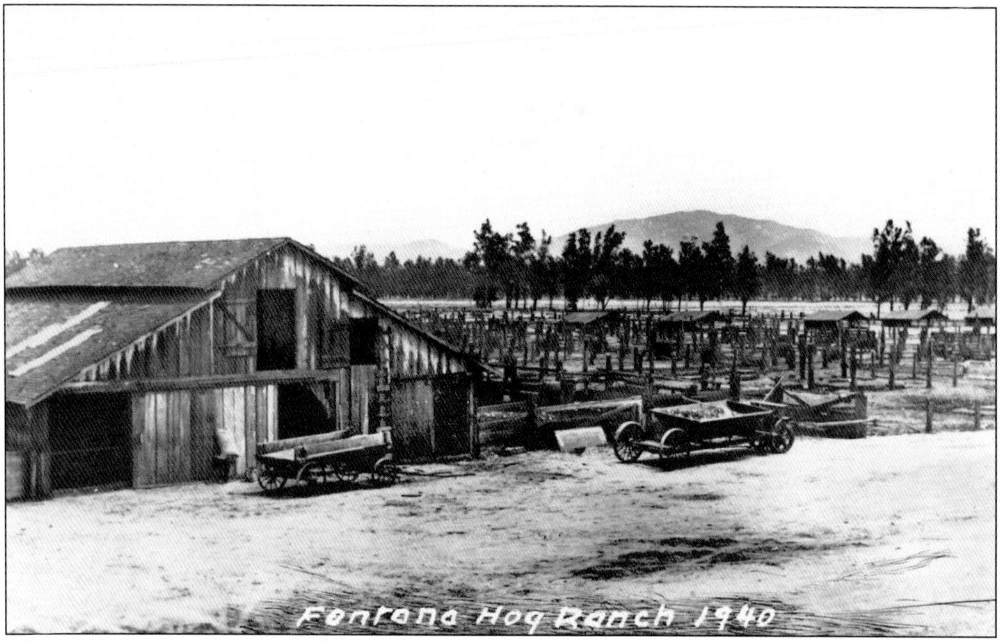

The Fontana Farms Company had a camp called Wade, used for breeding pigs, which was also a stop on the Santa Fe Railroad. The sows and piglets were kept here in pens until they could be taken to Declez and were fed with garbage from Los Angeles. This photo was taken in 1940.

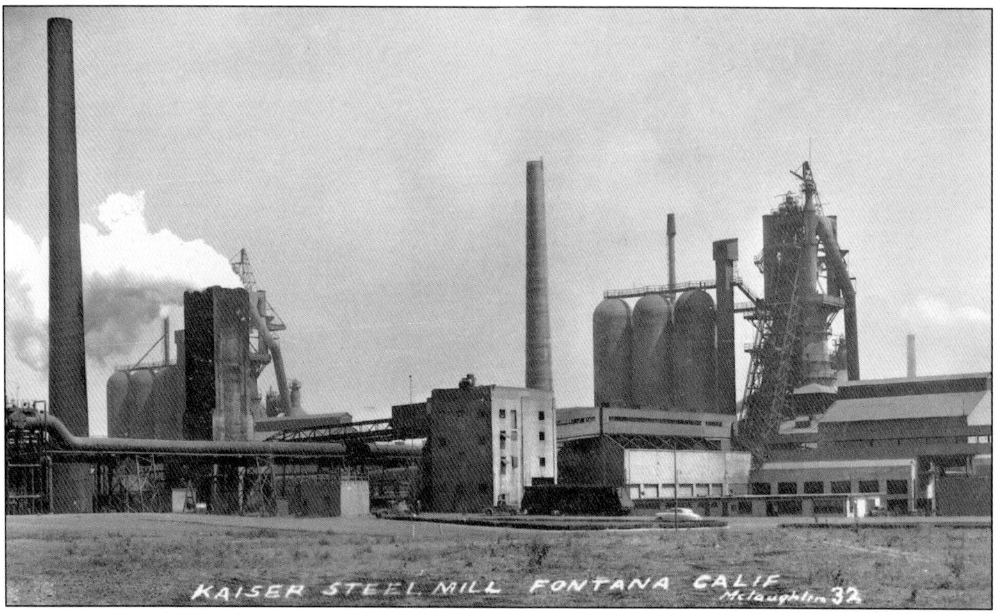

This is a photo of the Kaiser Steel Plant in Fontana on the old breeding camp of Wade. The land was sold to Henry J. Kaiser to build his first steel plant west of the Mississippi River in 1942. Henry and his wife lived in Fontana during construction of the plant, on Miller Avenue east of Mango Avenue. Kaiser even had owned a trailer park for employees to live in until homes could be built. California Steel bought the plant after Kiser Steel closed and the blast furnaces were taken down and shipped to China. The area of the blast furnaces is now the Fontana California Speedway Automobile Race track.

Six

IMPORTANT PEOPLE AND BUILDINGS

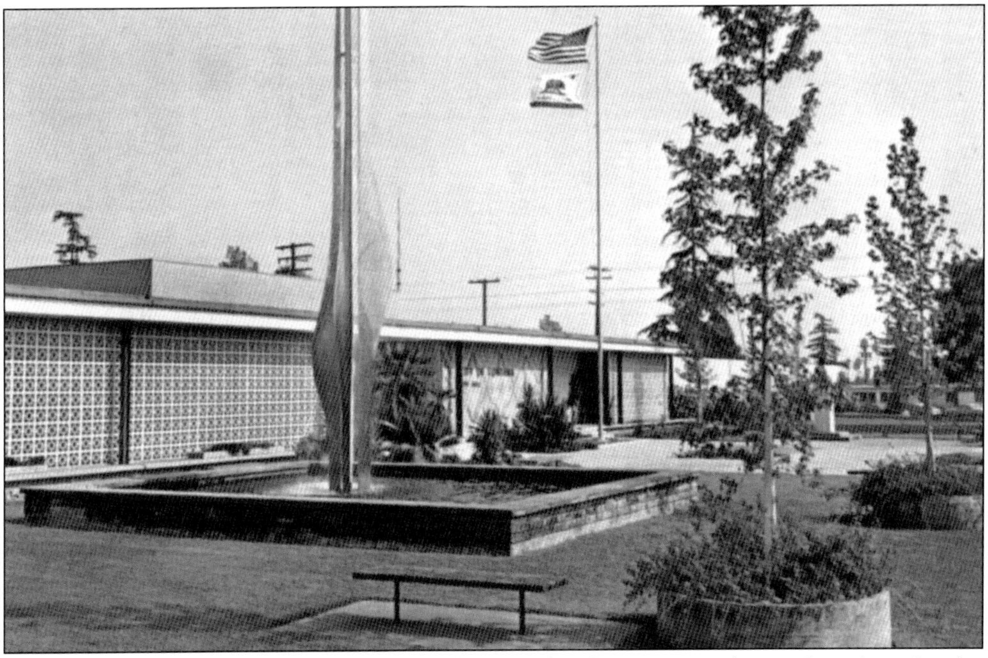

Fontana continues to grow today, with new housing developments on the north and south sides of the city. But the most important place is the historic core of downtown. The Downtown Revitalization Committee has done a great job with the help of city staff to carry the downtown area into the future. Pictured above, the Civic Center City Hall, on Sierra Avenue between Upland and Seville Avenues, was built in 1961 and dedicated on June 25. It was constructed on the grounds of the Sierra-Seville School after it was torn down and rests across from the Fontana Community Church and the Fontana Woman's Club House. The building served the community until 1983 when a new wing and council chambers were built. The first city hall was on the west side of Sierra Avenue and Spring Street, placed in a set of offices in 1952 that are still standing today. The second city hall was stationed at the Sierra-Seville School in 1953, and the third was placed at the Fontana Farms Company administration building in 1961. It was also a county building until 1962. Nat Simon was mayor when they moved to the new city hall in 1961. The soaring steel fountain that graces its front was donated by Kaiser Steel and arrived in 1962. It was commissioned by Kaiser to international sculptor Francois Stahlyl, who designed the fountain at the Seattle World's Fair.

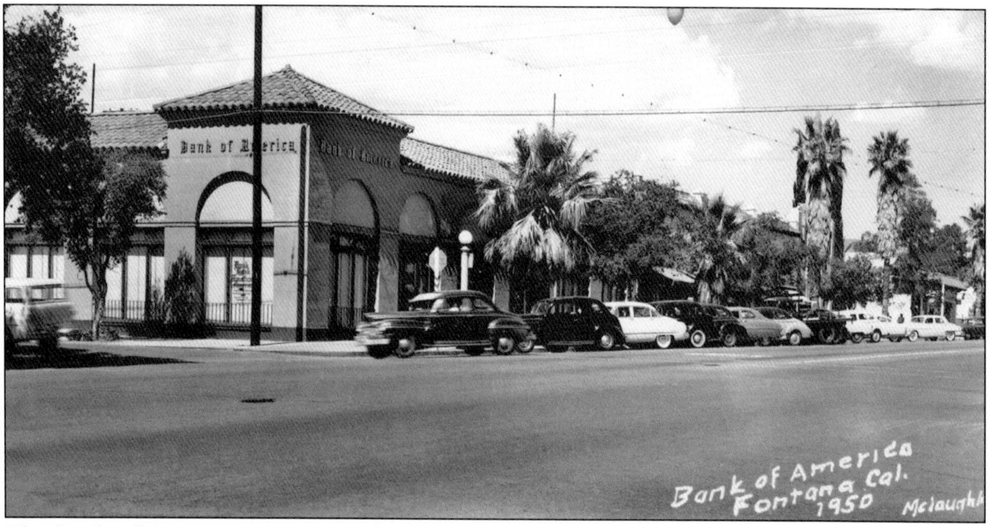

The Bank of America was originally the Fontana National Bank when it was constructed in 1924. It was a two-story modern structure with rooms for meetings and offices. This photo was taken in 1950. It opened as the First National Bank on August 21, 1926. Depositors on the first day were given a gift of $250 each. It issued its own currency in 1930, allowed by the law at the time. The Bank of America purchased the property in June 1937 and they still are on the old site, but in a new building on corner of Arrow and Nuevo Avenues. The old building was torn down to create a parking lot. The Chomel block of three buildings was also torn down to make the parking lot larger.

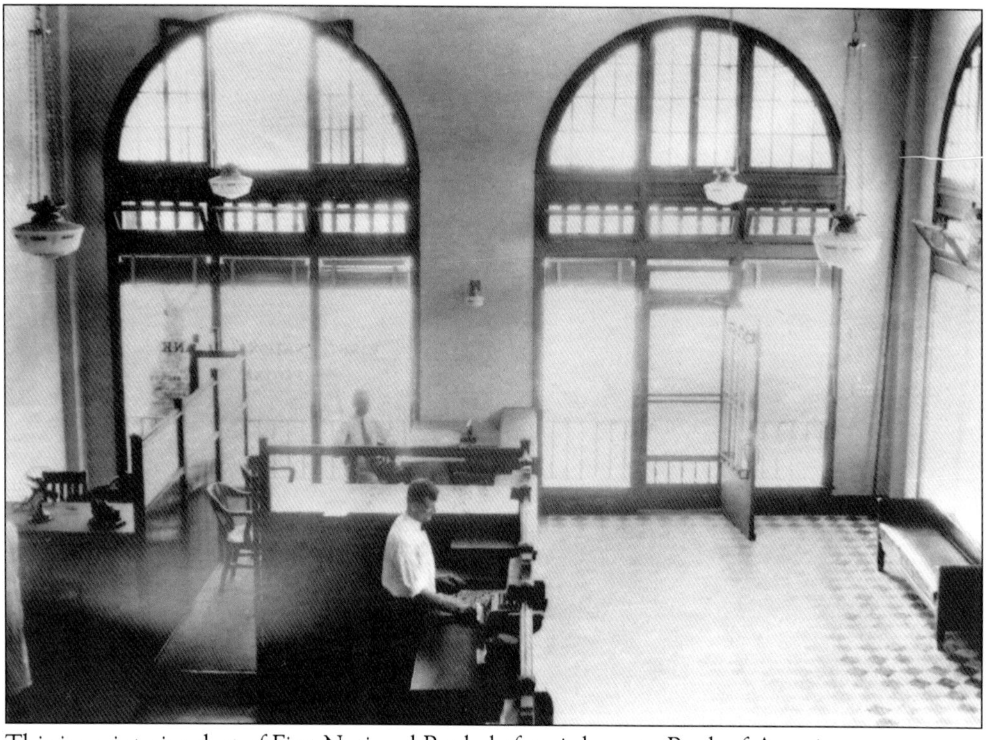

This is an interior shot of First National Bank, before it became Bank of America.

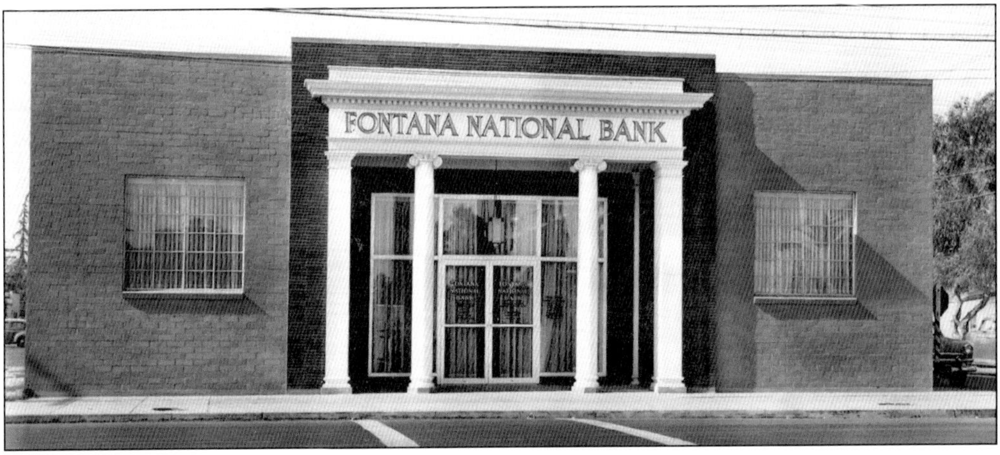

The Fontana National Bank, built by residents, became the second bank of Fontana 14 years after the Bank of America arrived in 1937, opening on June 1, 1952. Its first manager was Walter Wachtel and Rudy Gazvoda was the first director. Contractor Charles Henningsen constructed it, using 5,800 square feet at a cost of $12,500. Three years after opening, Riverside's Citizens National purchased the bank. The original principals had achieved a 100 percent return. Those who held their stock when it split reaped another 50 percent profit when Citizen's merged with Security First National, later to become Security Pacific. Security Pacific bought the whole northeast corner of Sierra and Arrow to build a larger bank building in December 1978, which opened on October 22,1979. The old building became vacant, and they needed parking and access to the new bank, so it had to be torn down. The only items saved were the sign and columns. Many other items were donated to the Fontana Historical Society.

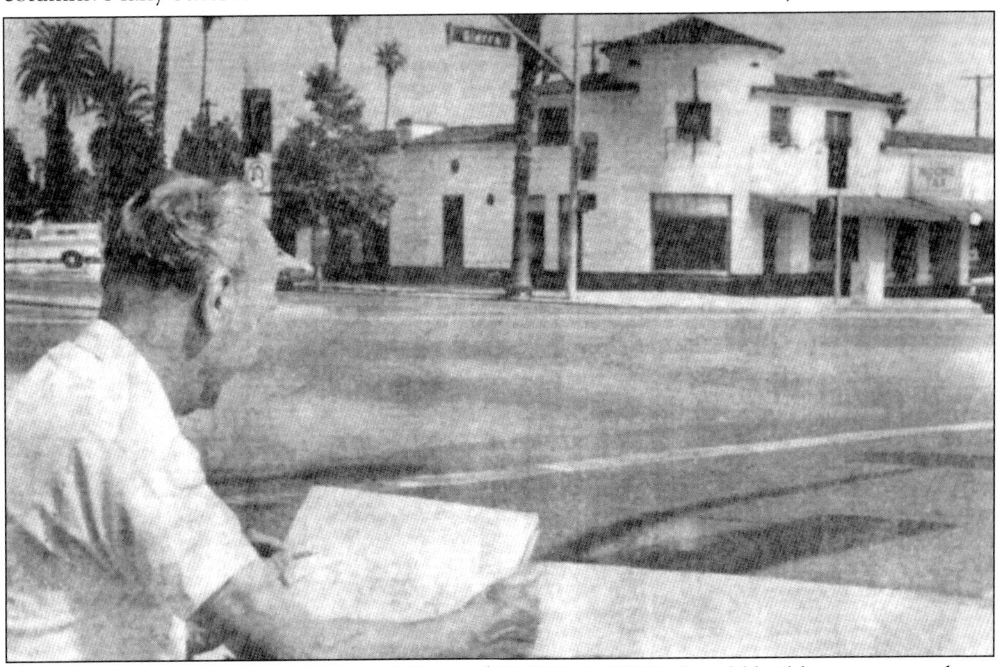

The M.C. Hunter block was built in 1924 for $20,000. In 1926, the old building was torn down and the new one constructed. Here, Ray Rosenkild sketches the new building, which was also torn down and replaced by the Redlands National Bank. Citibank is now on the southeast corner of Arrow and Sierra.

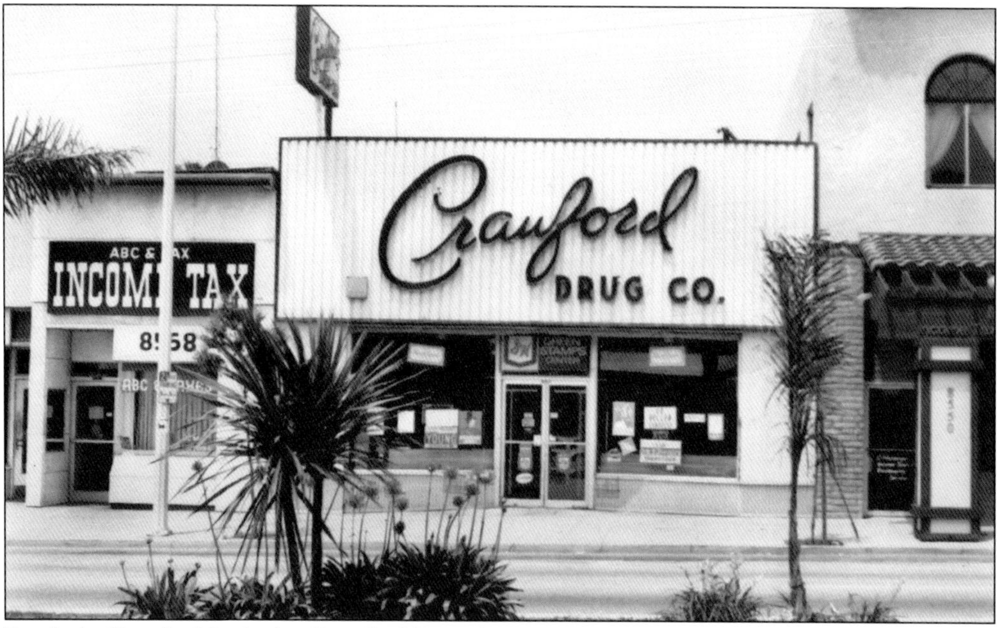

Frank A. Crawford built the Crawford Drug Co. in 1928. His son Harold worked there during the summer while attending Oregon State, and later in the 1930s he took over the business. Bud, as everyone knew him, is remembered also as a member and president of the rotary club and school board. He died in October 1959. His eldest son, Harold Jr., took over the store and was rotary club president as well. Harold Jr. ran the store until he retired, and later sold the business, but it still serves the community as it has for 87 years.

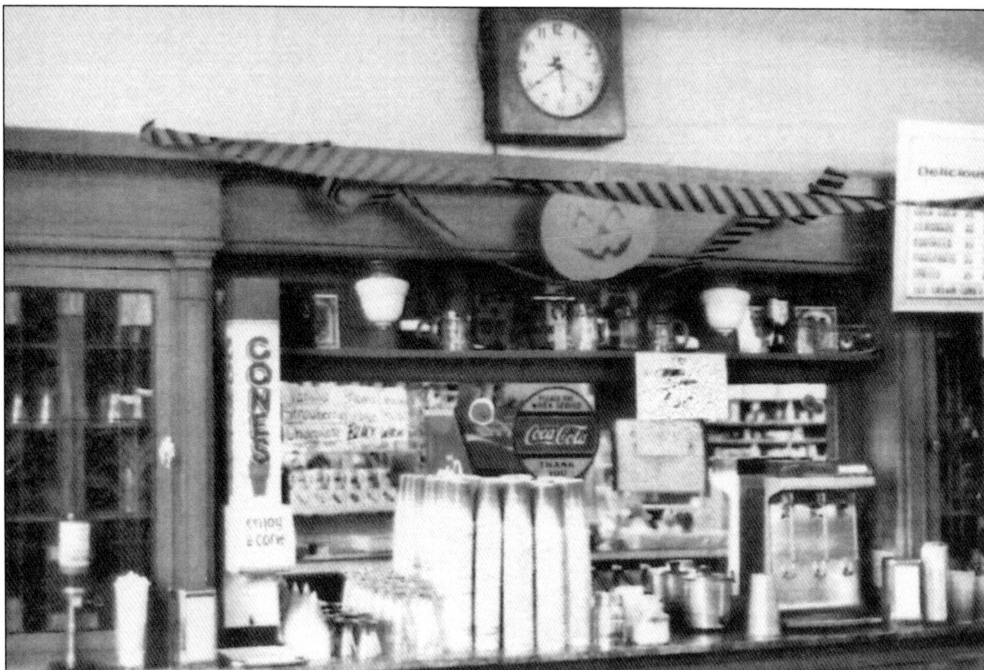

The soda fountain and the wood cabinets seen here are still part of the drugstore. They are all original and very few soda fountains are left in the West.

This fine lady was the matron of her family, was a grand lady who loved her community, and her name was Mildred Hilton Crawford. She was born in Redlands, California, and was brought to Fontana as a young girl. Her parents were Roy Thurston and Victoria Hilton. They arrived in Fontana on a "cold, north-windy day." Their first night was at the Evergreen Rooming House on Wheeler Street, then called the Lodge. The winds were so strong, they blew smoke back into the Lodge Room. She attended school at the Fontana Grammar School, later known as the Sierra-Seville, where city hall is now. Mildred was very active in the community until she died. She even wrote letters to the *Fontana Herald-News* about things she knew and saw about Fontana's history. She loved her family, community, and her Fontana Community Church. She lived on Mango Avenue with her husband and family before moving to a home near city hall.

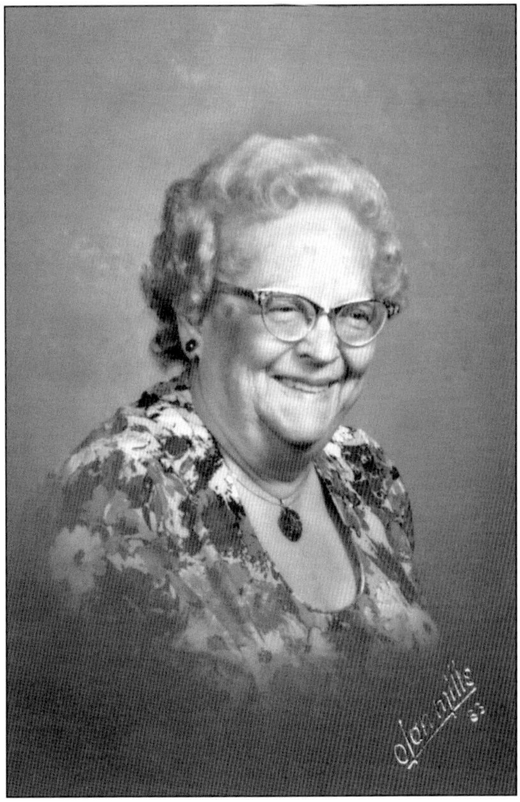

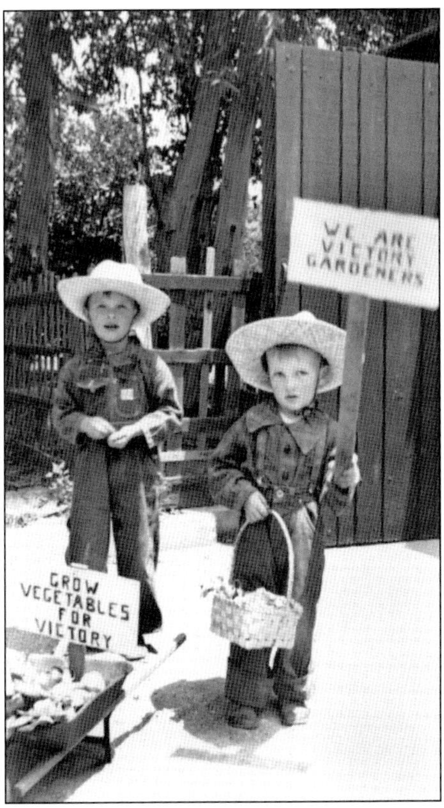

Seen here are the Crawford boys with Victory Garden items to sell during the war. Harold was seven years old (on the left) and Charlie was five. The photo was taken on North Juniper.

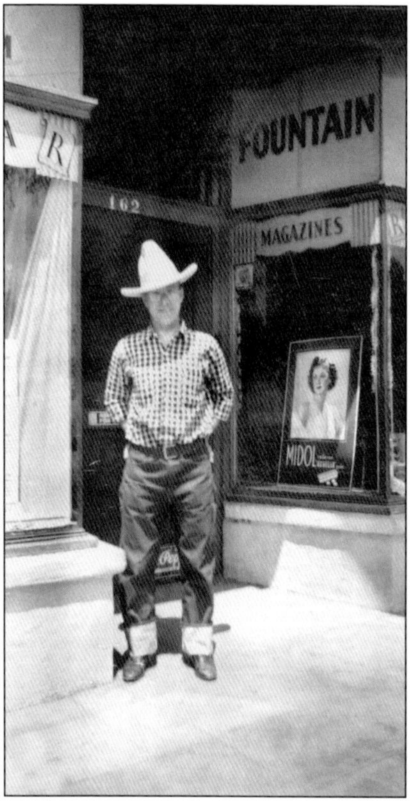

Harold Crawford (Bud) is the focus of this photo in front of the drugstore in 1939.

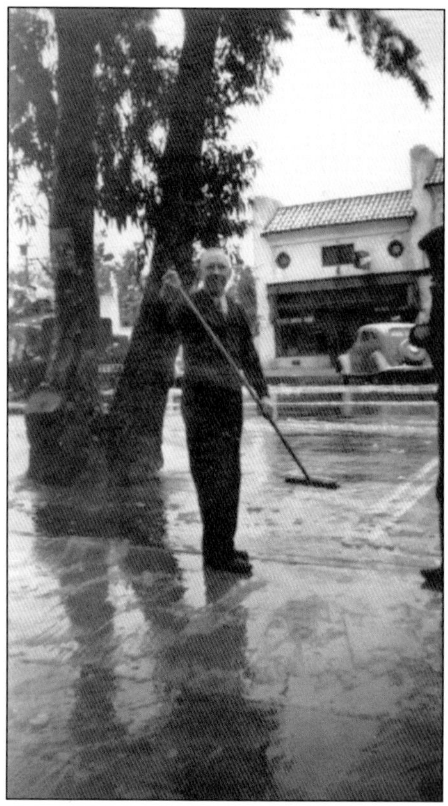

Frank A. Crawford is seen here shoveling snow off the sidewalk in front of the drugstore in 1939.

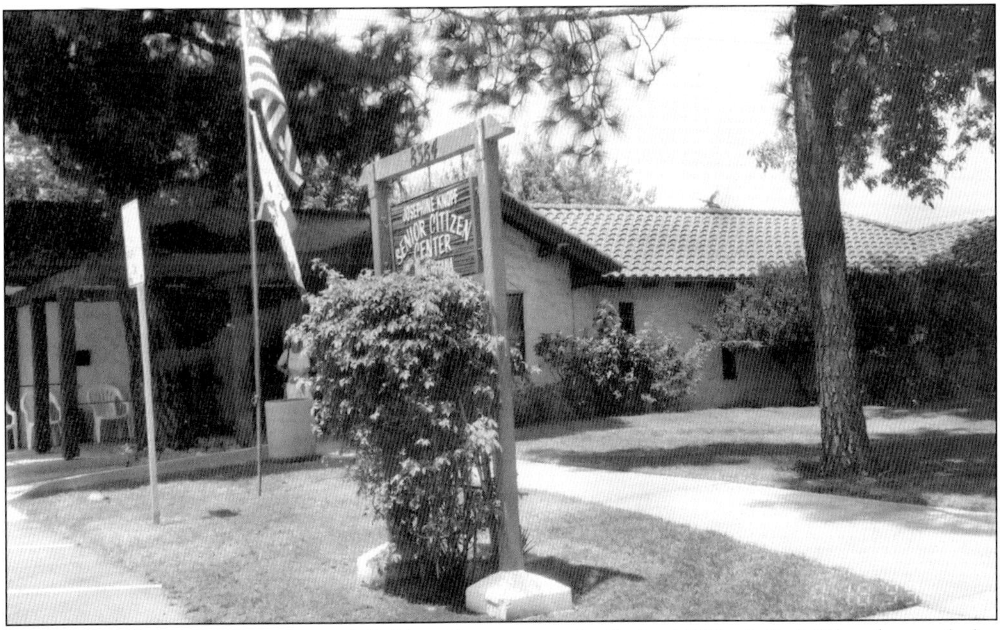

The United States Experimental Rabbit Station was built in 1928. A.B. Miller donated the land so it could be built in Fontana. The large, Spanish-style administration building had a spacious lobby, offices, and laboratories. The lobby was 20 by 40 feet with a fireplace at one end. There are two oil paintings by William A. Bixler called "A bit of California Coast" and "The San Gabriel Mountain." The fireplace and lobby remain about the same today. There is a feed barn with mixing and sterilizing rooms, a garage, a carpenter shop, and several types of breeding houses and additional buildings with a capacity for 5,000 animals that are all equipped with modern pens and nest boxes. A six-foot wire guard fence encloses the five acres and the walks are graveled between buildings with a beautiful fountain amid orange trees and velvety lawns. The entire site and all the buildings were designed and built by H.L. Larsen, local contractor picked by A.B. Miller. There were eight varieties of rabbits there: White and Red New Zealand, Blue and White American Flemish, Chinchilla, French Silver, Havana, American Sable, and Polish. In 1965, it became the Josephine Knopf Center, a senior center. It is California Landmark No. 950.

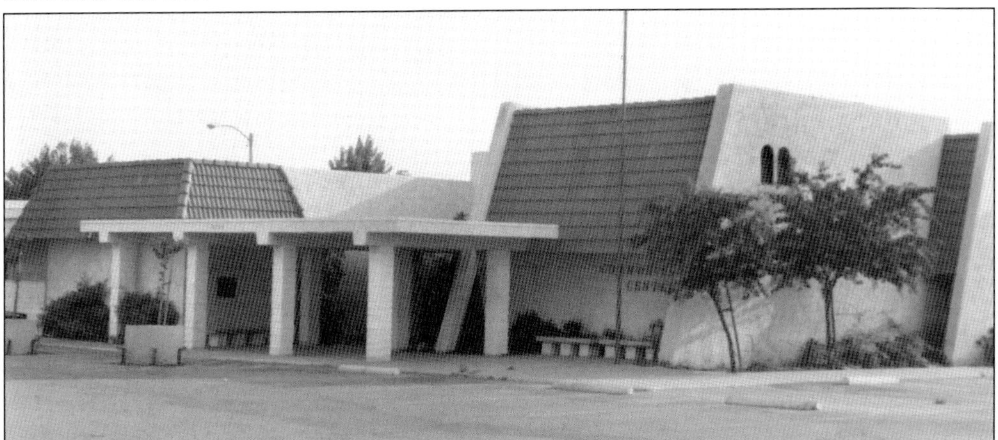

This is a shot of the Cypress Community Center, which is next to the old Rabbit Station (now the senior center). The author's father sat on the design committee for the AARP building.

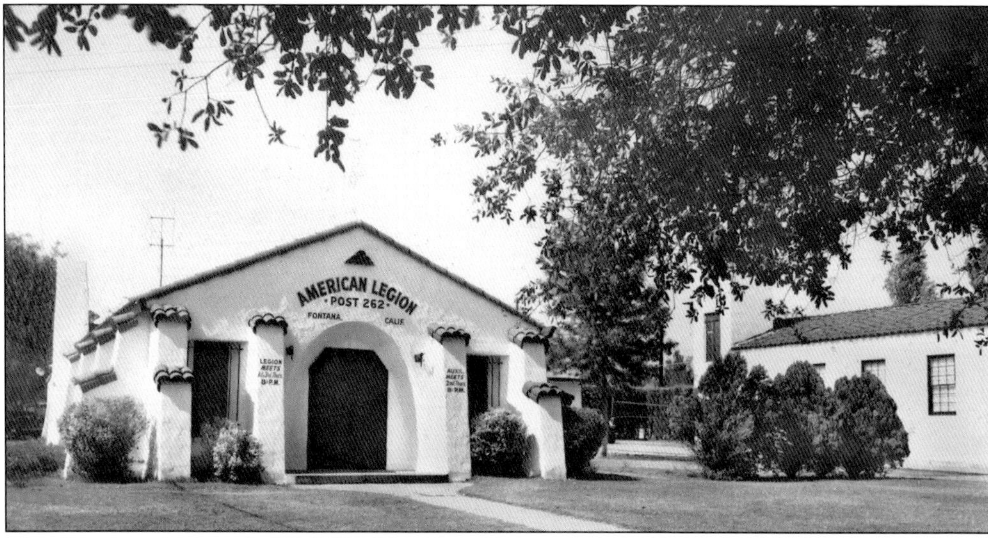

The American Legion Post 262 building was constructed in one day in 1926, but not for them. It was built for the Fontana Boy Scouts as a lodge to meet in. The property was donated by A.B. Miller through the Fontana Farms Company. Citizens donated materials and labor to build the lodge. It was also the headquarters of the Chaffey Scout District. It was a log cabin with windows and had a huge fireplace with a side patio.

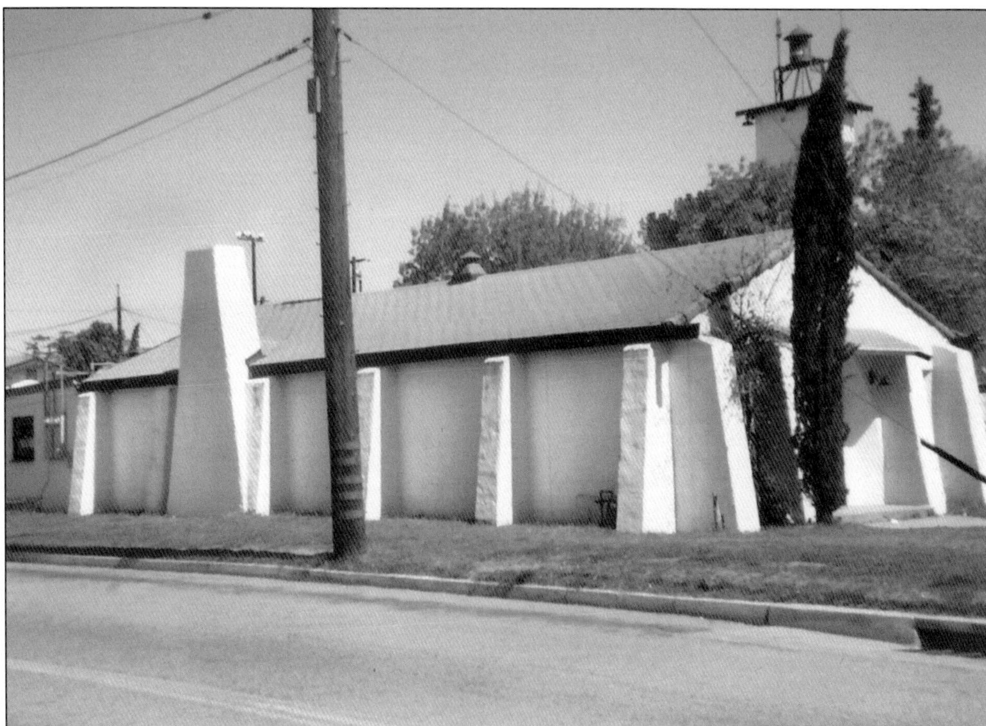

This view shows the walls where the windows used to be located. The outlines can be seen with close examination. Stucco now covers the logs. A year after the lodge was built it was turned over to the American Legion Post 262. Their first meeting was February 21, 1927. It has been the American Legion Meeting place ever since.

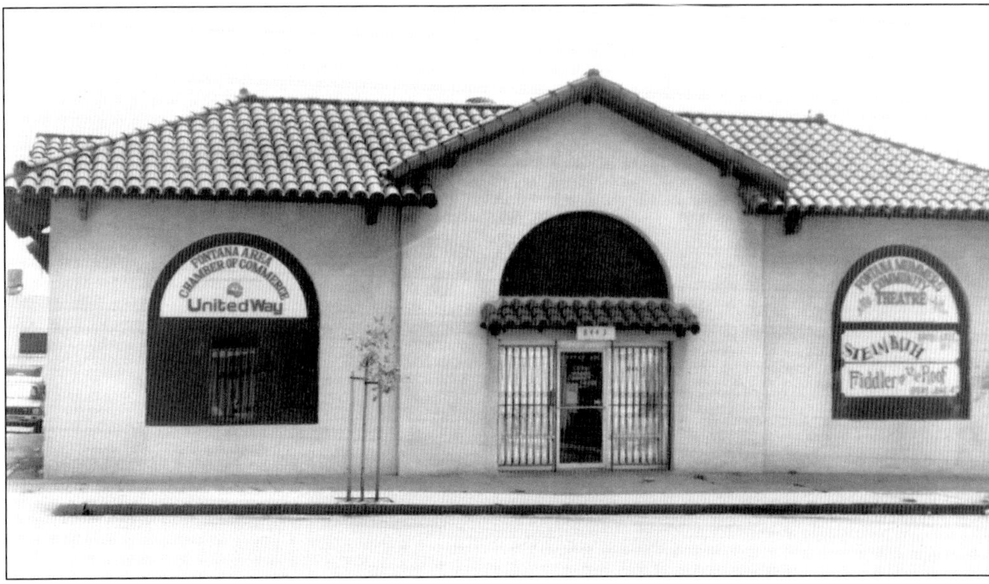

The second Fontana garage was built in 1926 after the boom of automobiles demanded more space than the first garage offered, so a new site was located across from the Pacific Electric Depot on the southeast corner of Nuevo and Spring Streets. It cost approximately $18,000 and was designed by Fontana Farms own architect, Hugh Kirk. The ornate structure of modified Spanish architecture had two entrances on Eureka, now Spring Street, and was built by the Fontana Farms Company and the Johnson Construction Company Included in the building was a double display room, mechanical and repair departments, battery, oiling, and grease departments, washing and cleaning equipment, accessories and gasoline, oil service departments, an office, and a Buick agency. It was the most up-to-date garage in the San Bernardino Valley. The garage remained in operation until 1952 when Walker's Market took it over until 1961. Other businesses included the Sierra Trading Post; Service Systems in 1973, a vending company; Mummers Theatre rented the building; a church; and eventually Mummers took it over and is still there.

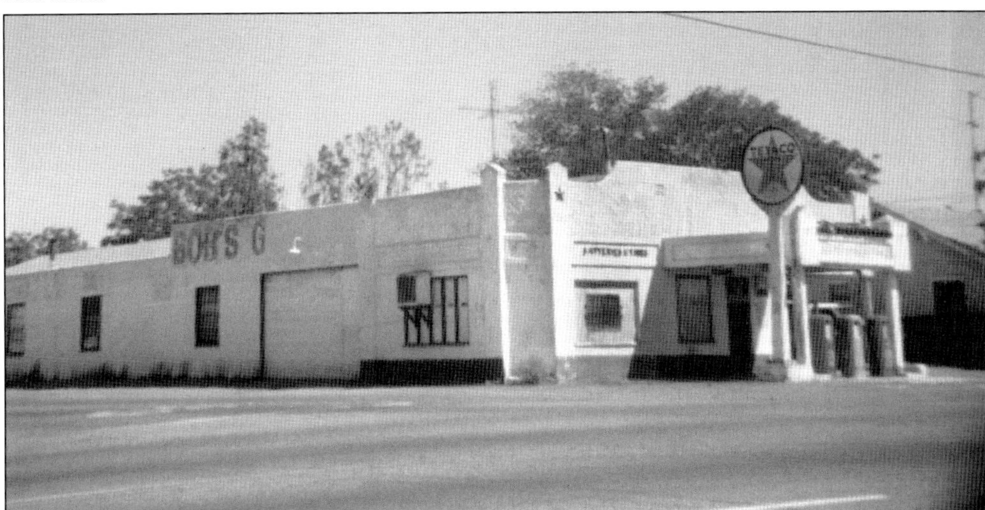

This is a shot of Bob's Garage on the northeast corner of Cypress and Arrow Highway. It is no longer there, and the home next to it burned down in 2004.

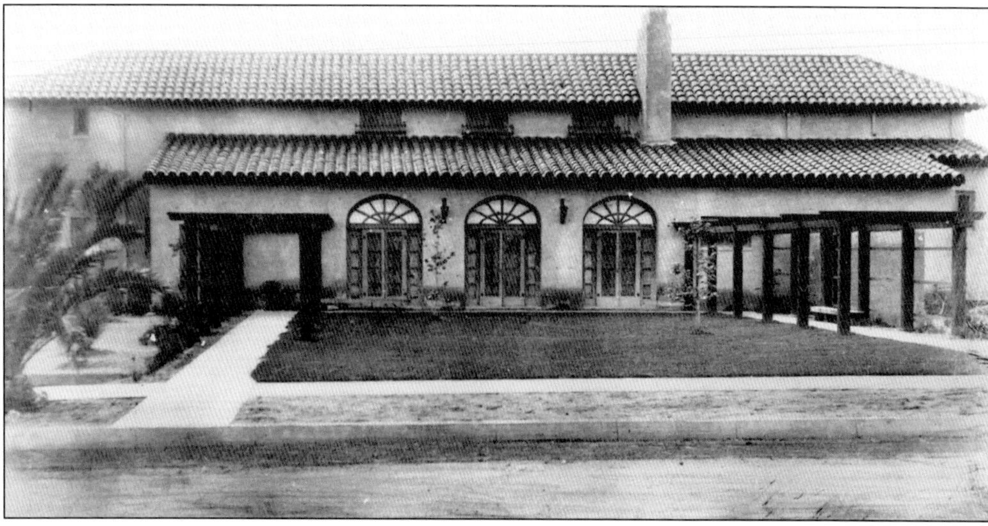

The Fontana Woman's Club House was built in 1923–1924, the first commercial building in Fontana. It was designed by Hugh Kirk and constructed with an auditorium and stage, a small clubroom, a library, a kitchen, and two dressing rooms. Above the foyer, a motion picture booth was constructed. The structure was Spanish Mission style, with a red tile roof and plastered walls. The interior of the auditorium was tinted a soft sage green, and the foyer was finished in Tiffany with a tiled floor. Spanish lanterns greeted visitors on each side of the entrance. Balconies of wrought iron, exterior doors of the arched Mission type, and a patio on the east front brought the total cost to $16,000. The first meeting was held April 17, 1924.

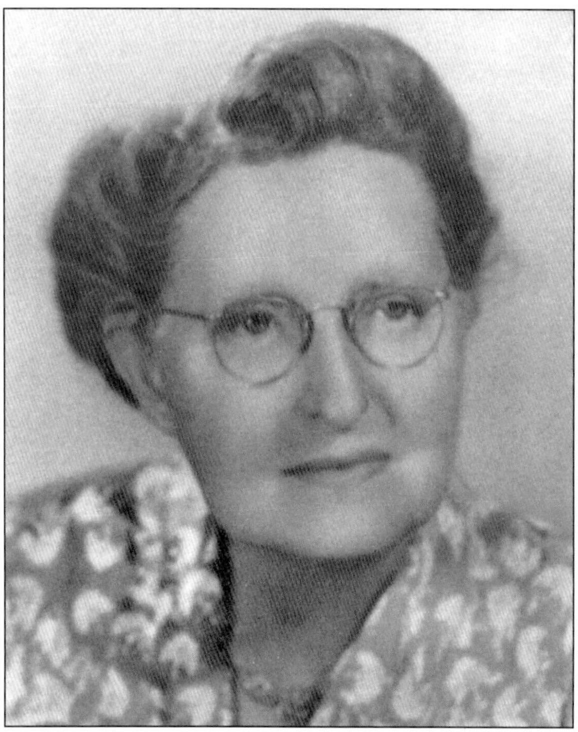

Early in the spring of 1912, a group of women gathered at the home of Mrs. Kelshaw (pictured) for tea and needleworking. There were 13 ladies in attendance—the only women in Fontana at that time. They agreed to meet every two weeks on Thursdays, and they called the gathering the "Helping Hand." In 1914, the name was changed to the "Fontana Thursday Club," and in 1923 to the "Fontana Woman's Club." The group is still going strong today.

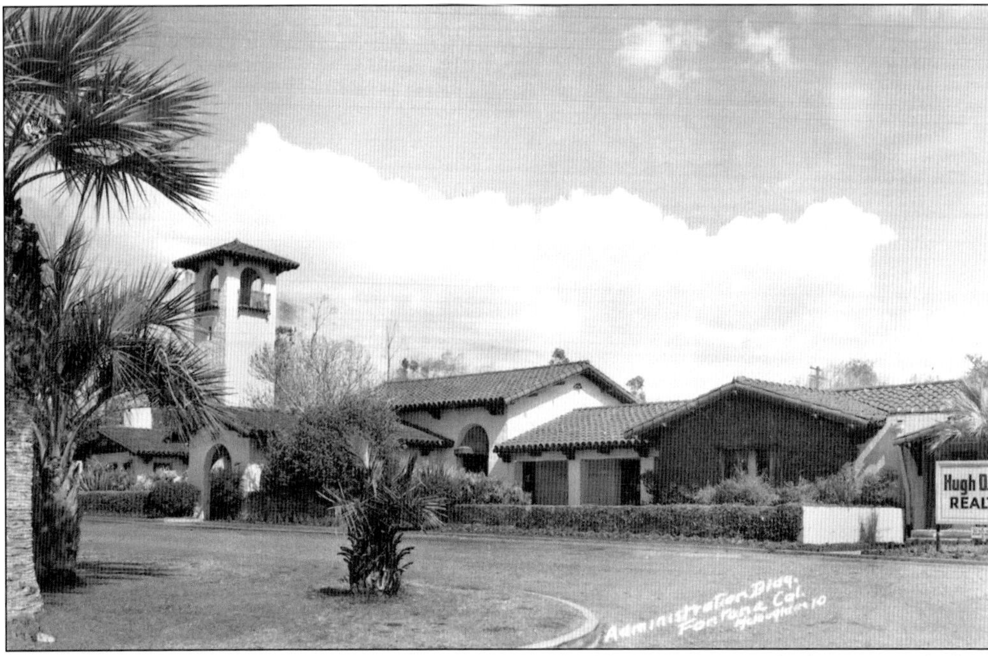

This is the Fontana Farms Company administration building, constructed of stucco and tile at a cost between $18,000 and $20,000. It was completed in 150 days instead of the 90 they had planned. It sat on the southeast corner of Seville and Magnolia (Sierra) Avenues, just south of the Pacific Electric Tracks, facing Sierra with 142 feet of frontage. The observation tower of 42 feet was the center feature of the building designed by Hugh Kirk, Fontana's own architect. The building was the home for city hall in 1952 before it became the county building. Dynamite had to be used to level the building that was 45 years old when it was torn down.

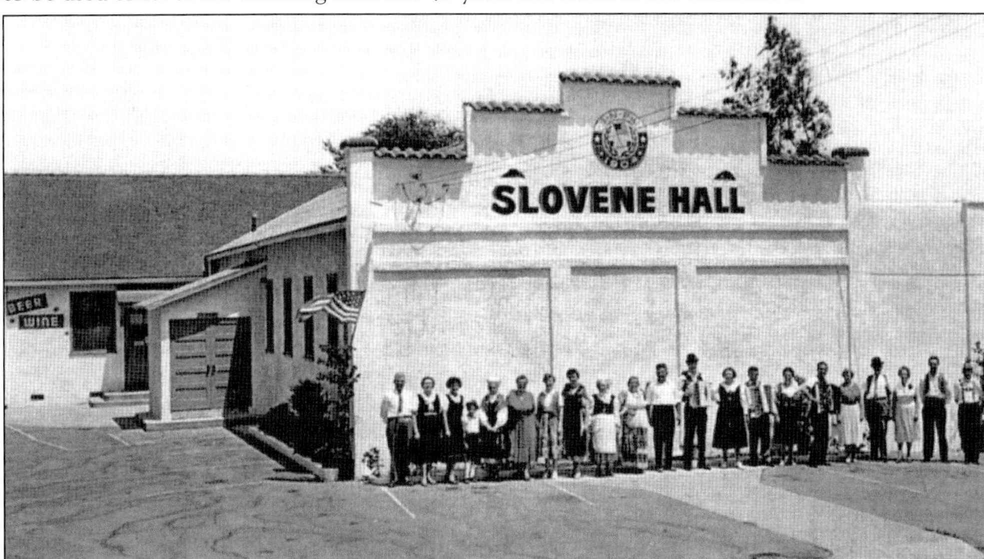

The Slovene Hall was built in 1939 on Cypress Avenue. The community had a large Slavic population that used the building heavily. It has a stage, dance floor, kitchen, and a bar with dining areas both inside and outside. There is a fenced and covered play and game area with outside seating.

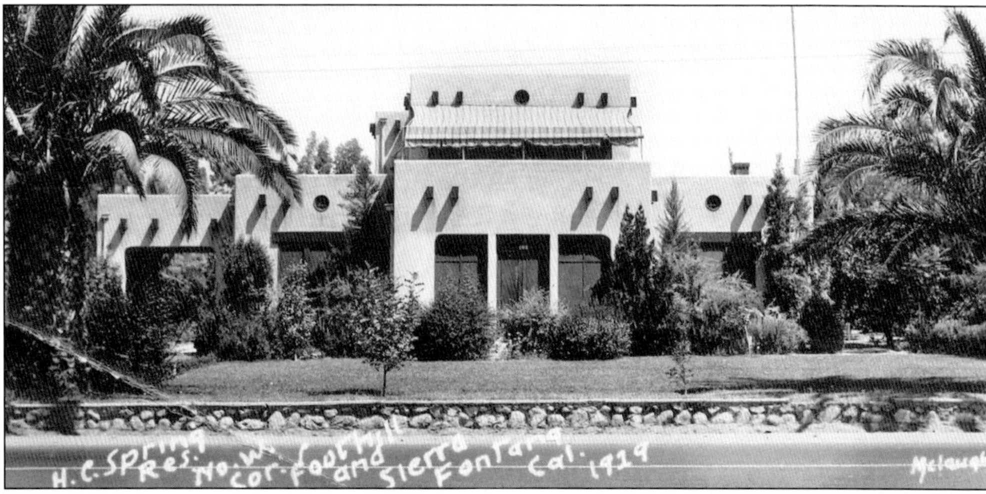

This is a photo of the H.C. Spring home in 1929. It was built in 1925 on the northwest corner of Foothill (Route 66) and Sierra Avenue. Mr. Spring organized the chamber of commerce and was its president. The structure was moved from the 40-acre estate to between the Sierra Liquor and the Firestone Store. It was the largest home in Fontana at the time with dimensions of 60 feet wide by 60 feet deep, and was a two-story adobe style in cream stucco with brown trim surrounded by 150 square feet of gardens and lawn. At a cost of $14,000, the building was designed by architect Shelby R. Coon of Los Angeles, and the contractor was Charles D. Platt of San Bernardino. It had a sun terrace, and the original dining room corner wood cabinets and doors are still there, though house was destroyed for development a few years back.

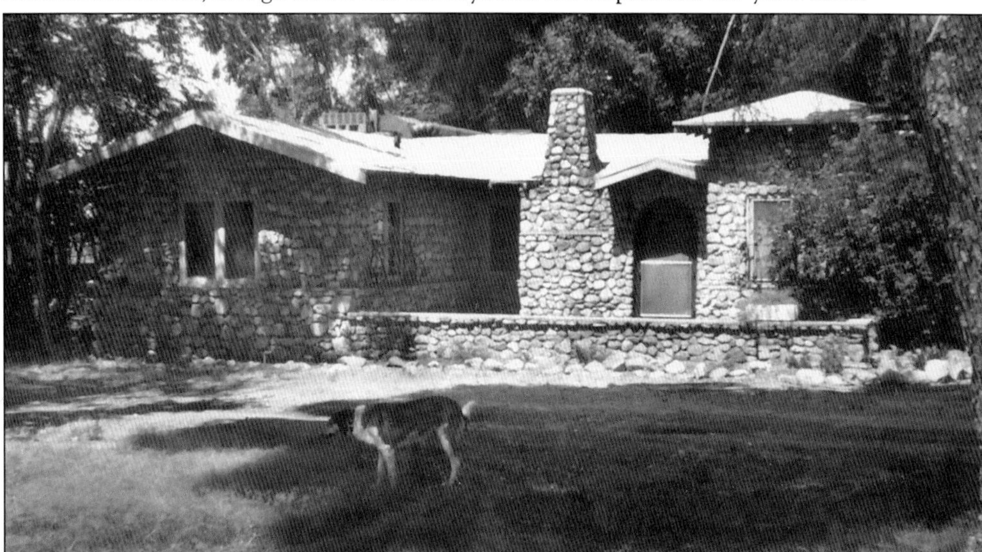

The E.P. Bradbury residence is a unique home built with Lytle Creek rock. It has an inside garden room, a living room, bedrooms and bath, a kitchen of odd size, a large fireplace, and a large outdoor front patio. It has a rock pillar entrance to driveway and there is a guest building. The property was the Fontana Nursery for the family business. They raised tropical flowers and orchids, as well as cacti of all types. The family landscaped most of the older homes in Fontana and shipped their fauna all over the world. Many royal palaces had cacti from Fontana. When he retired, he moved to Bradbury, near Pasadena.

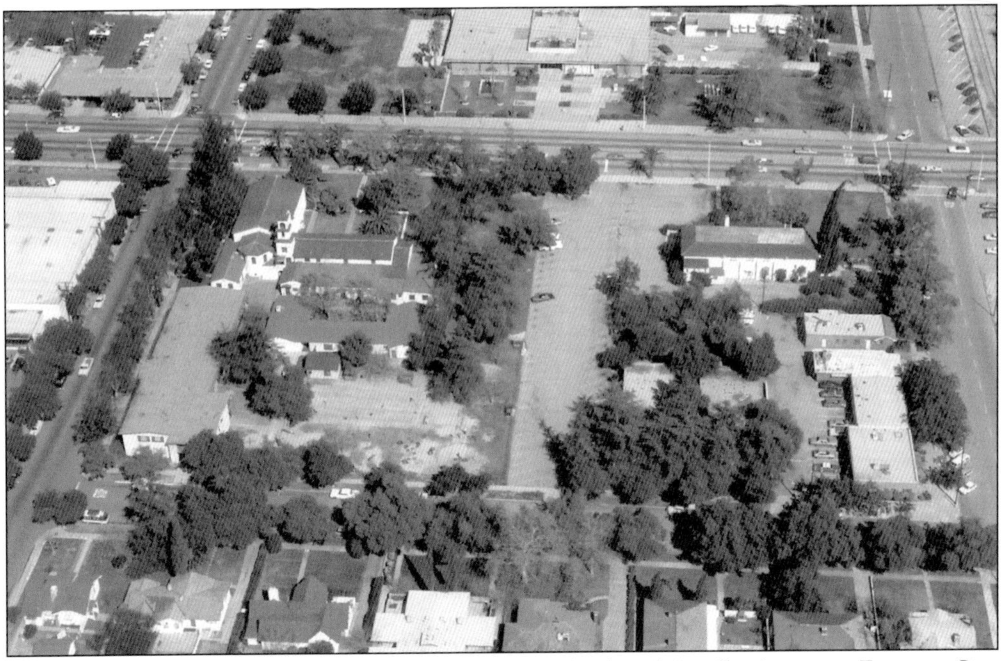

This is an aerial view of Sierra Avenue between Upland and Seville Avenues. Fontana City Hall is at the top, built in 1962. The Fontana Community Church is at the left, with a school and parking lot. The Fontana Woman's Club House is to the right, next to offices and Senior Housing. The street at the bottom of photo is where many of the pioneer settlers lived and could walk to work.

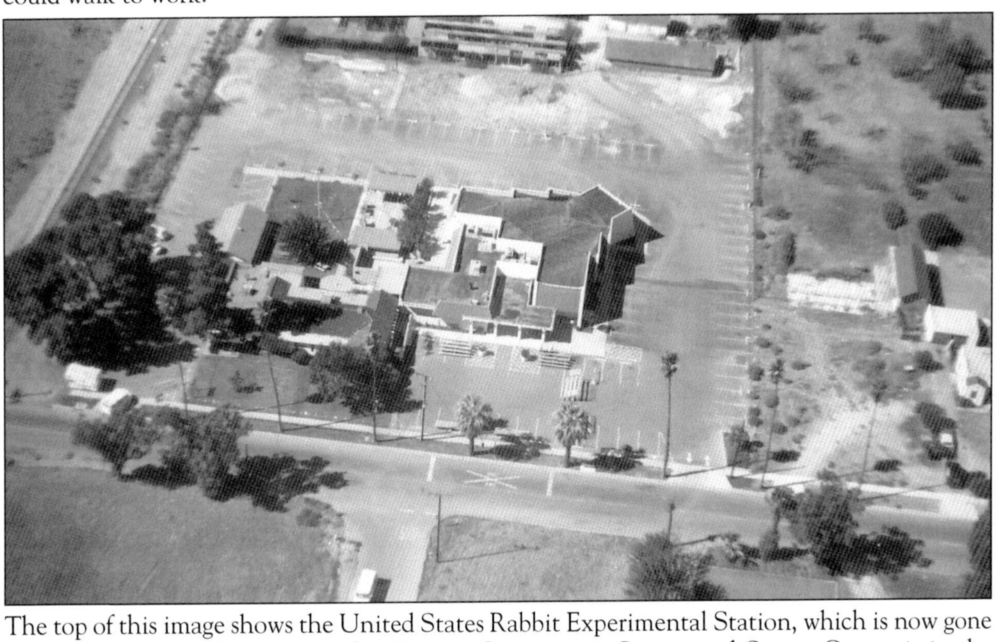

The top of this image shows the United States Rabbit Experimental Station, which is now gone except for the slaughterhouse. The Cypress Community Center and Senior Center is in the middle of the photo. The supervisor lived in the house on the right in this photograph. The Josephine Knopp Center is the main center, with gardens, a city nursery, and a horseshoe pit area. The Pacific Electric tracks (now the Pacific Electric Trail) are at the left.

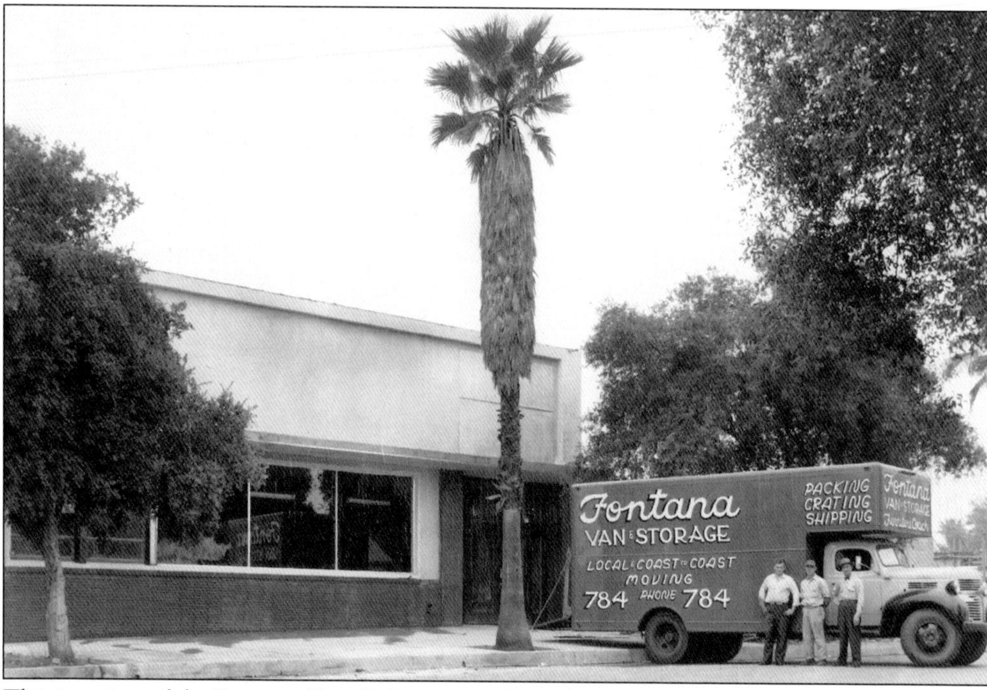

This is a view of the Fontana Van & Storage truck at the post office that used to be on Wheeler below Valencia Avenue. The persons in the photo are the Hickey brothers, Pete and Walt.

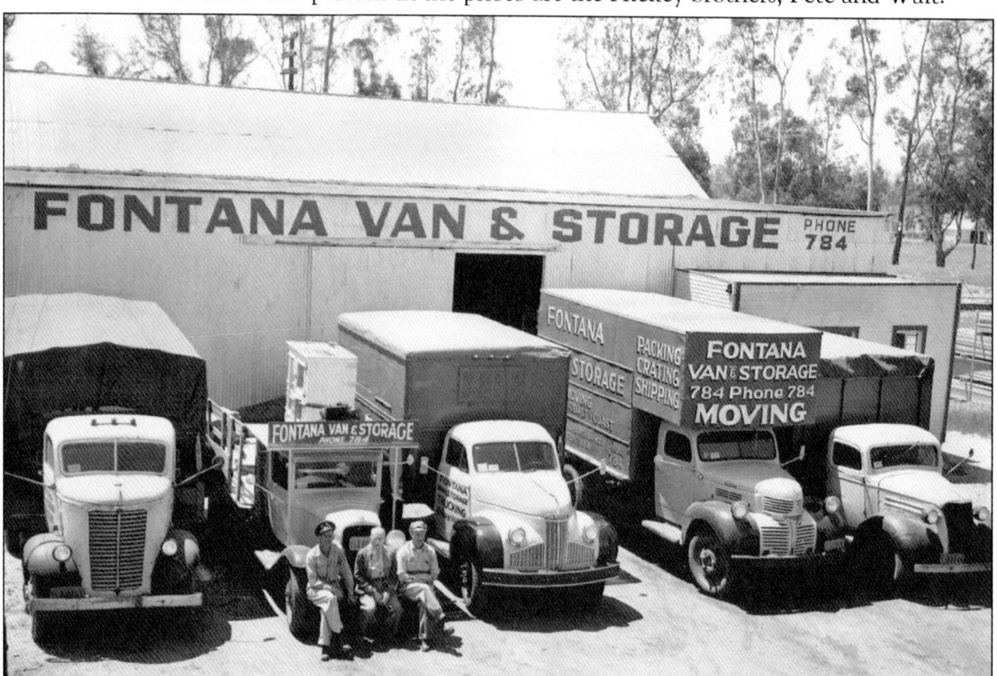

This is an image of the Fontana Van & Storage Building and trucks on Orange Way near Mango Avenue. The business is now owned by Chuck Hickey, the son of Walt Hickey. Seen here, from left to right, are Walt Hickey, Bill Neine, and Pete Hickey. (Courtesy of Chuck and Sue Hickey.)

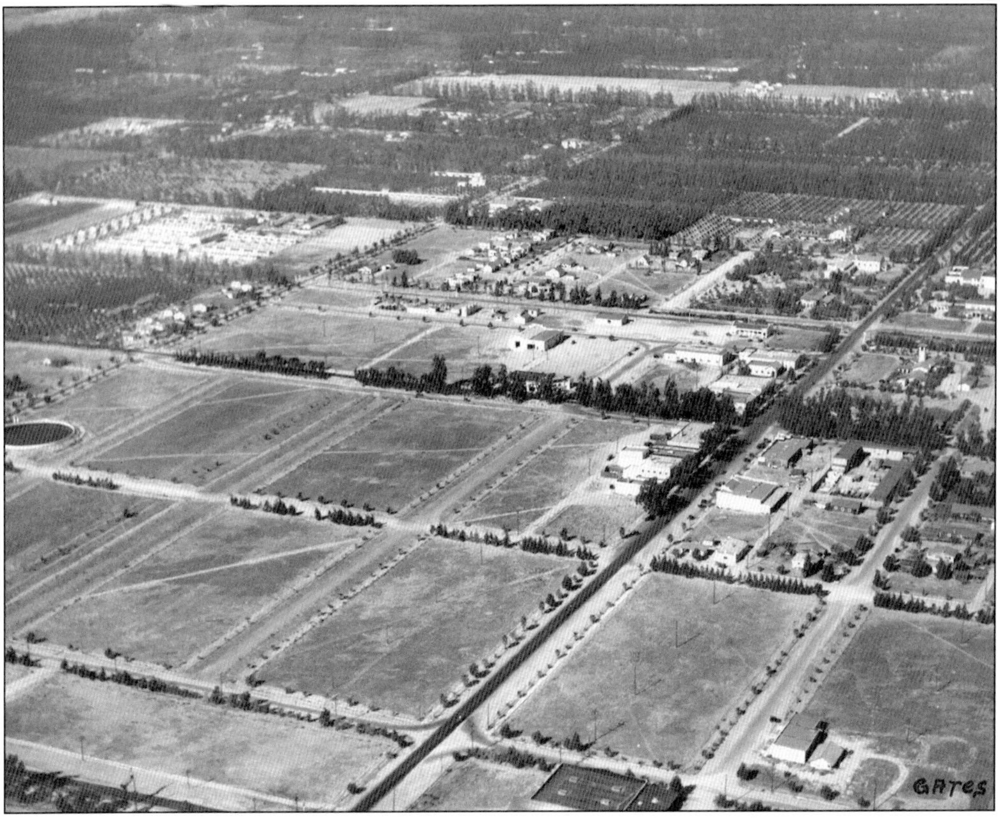

This 1929 photo of Fontana shows the town site in detail, looking northwest. Sierra Avenue is the dark diagonal street at the lower right, and the reservoir at left is on Juniper and Valencia Avenues. Notice that there are no buildings between Juniper and Sierra Avenues and Valencia and Orange Way. At the upper left is the Fontana Poultry Plant. The Fontana Producers Egg and Supply Cooperative is at the bottom center. Arrow Highway runs across the center.

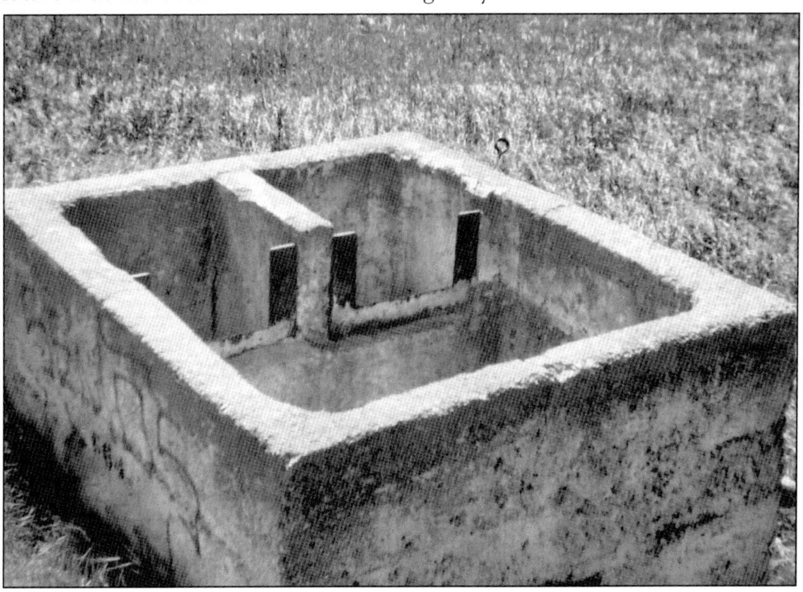

Weirs like this one brought water to properties in Fontana. They were along all the streets in the city, and many still remain.

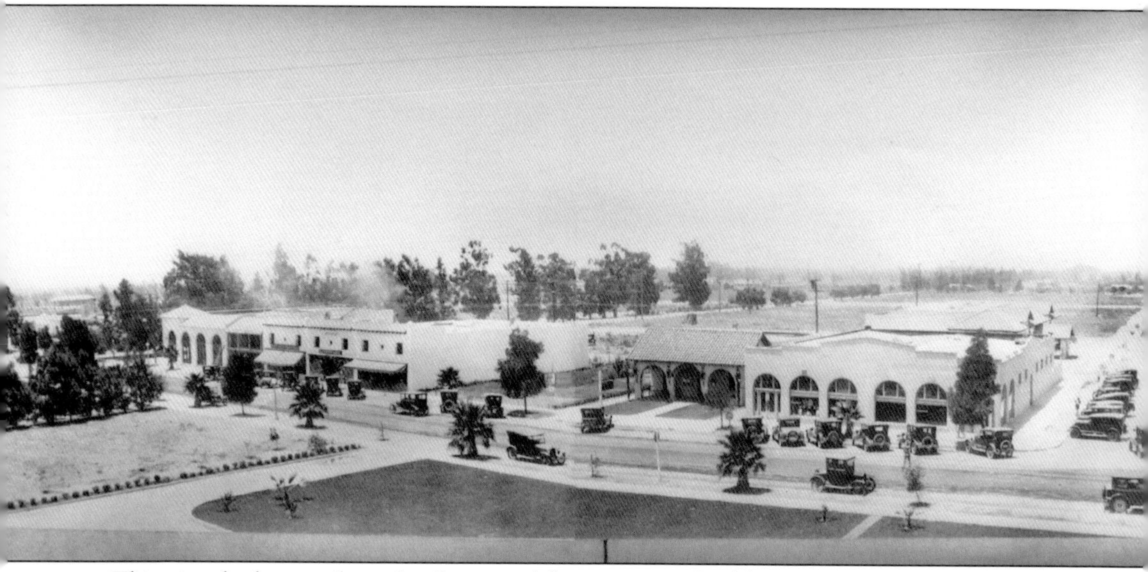

This view looks west from the Fontana Administration Building tower. Fontana First National Bank is on left, then the Chomel block consists of the next three stores before an empty lot, the 1924 C.L. Montgomery and C.H. Shaw Jr. Realty Office (built for $10,000), and the Fontana Mercantile building (later the Thorpe Building) take up the space. Sierra Avenue runs across the bottom, and Spring Street is to the right.

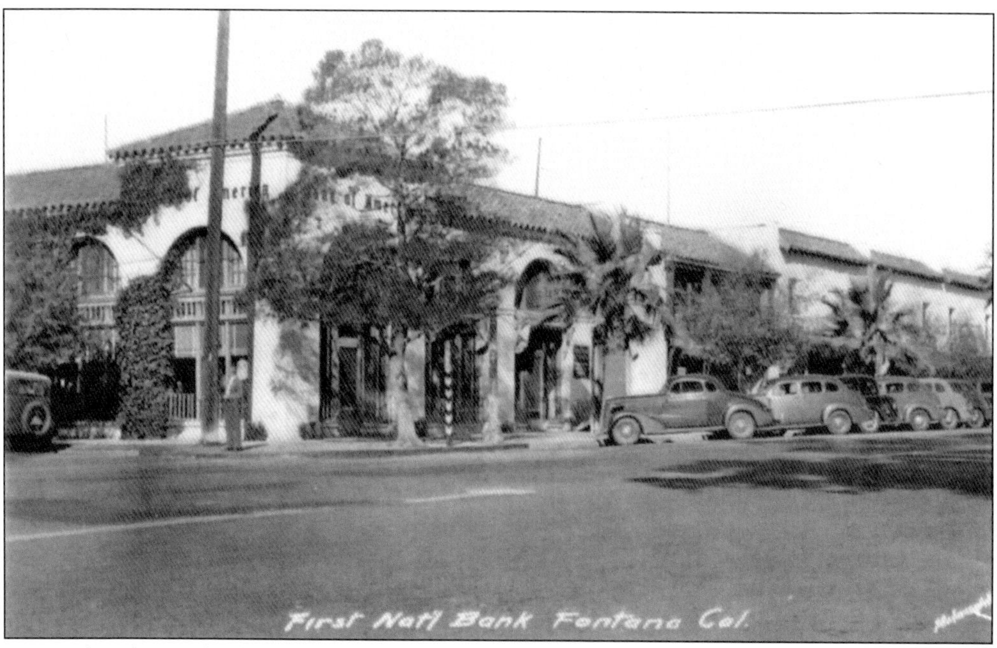

Pictured is the Bank of America, which had previously been First National Bank and Fontana National Bank.

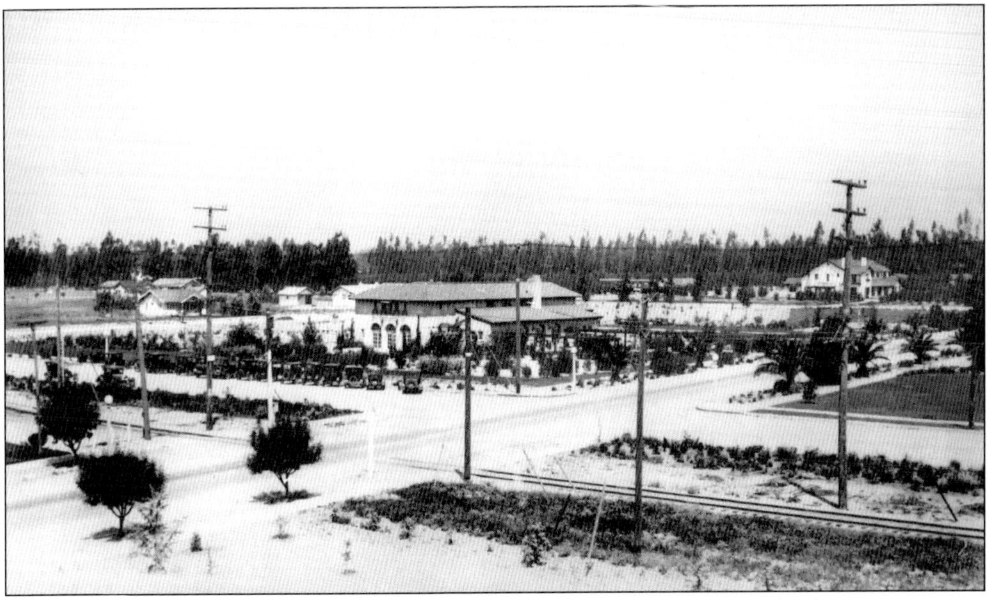

This town site image, c. 1925, shows the Fontana Woman's Club House, built in 1923–1924; the Fontana Inn, built in 1924; and some homes in the background. The Pacific Electric track runs diagonally across the photo.

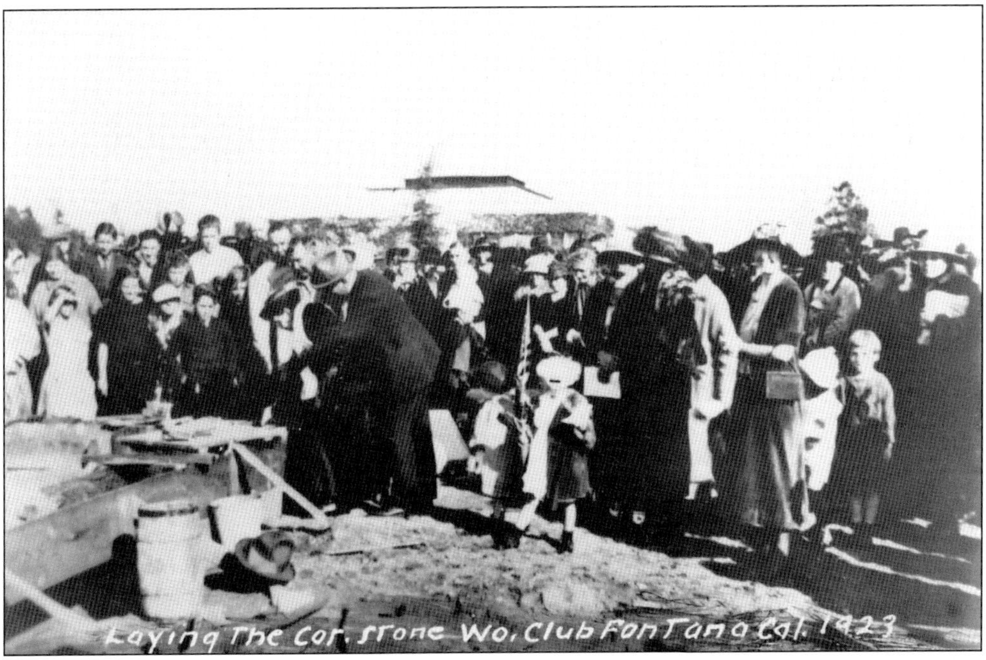

The laying of the corner stone for the Fontana Woman's Club House is shown here, October 30, 1923. Eliza Miller, the "Mother of Fontana," is receiving help from her son, A.B. Miller, as she puts mortar on the corner stone.

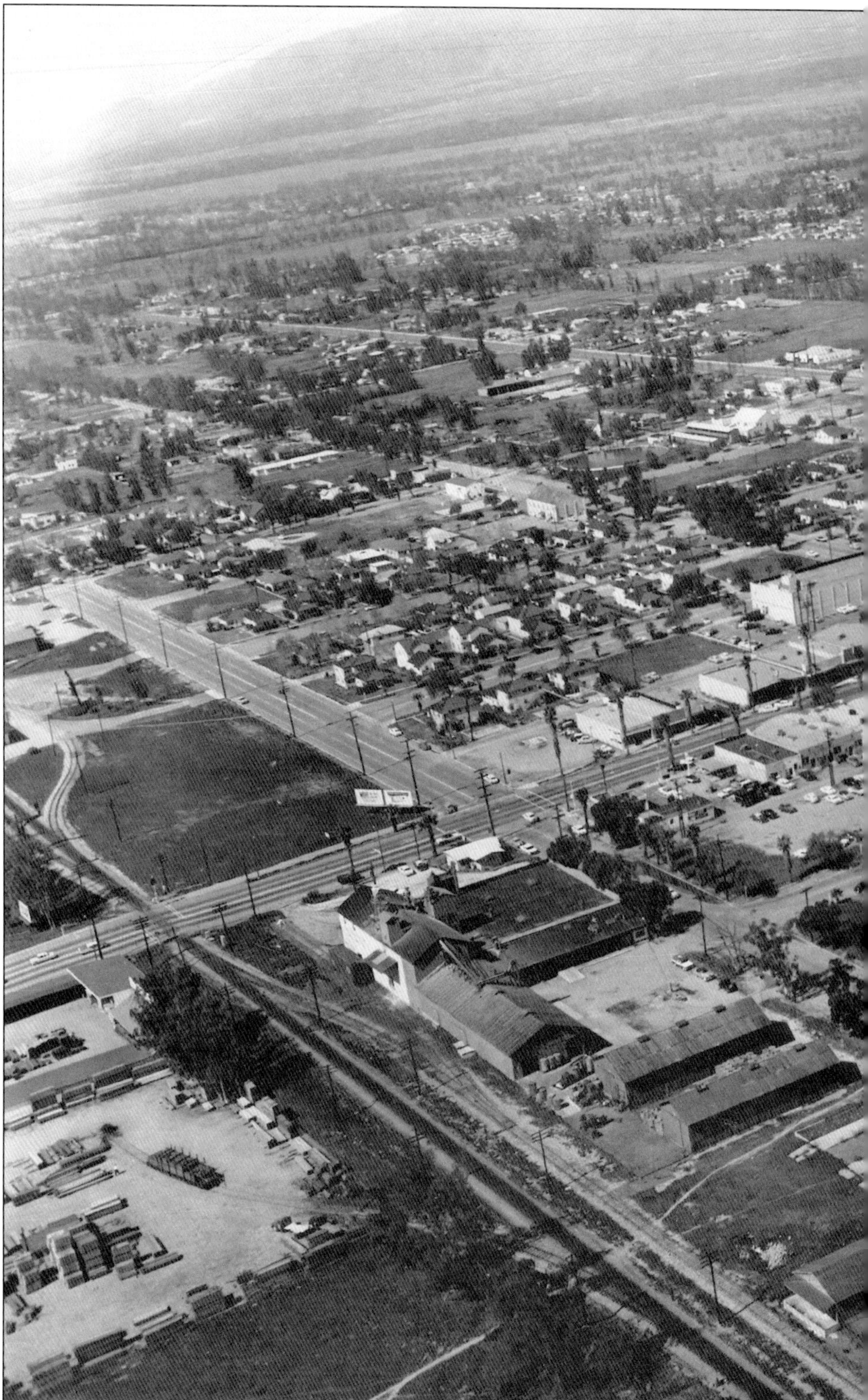

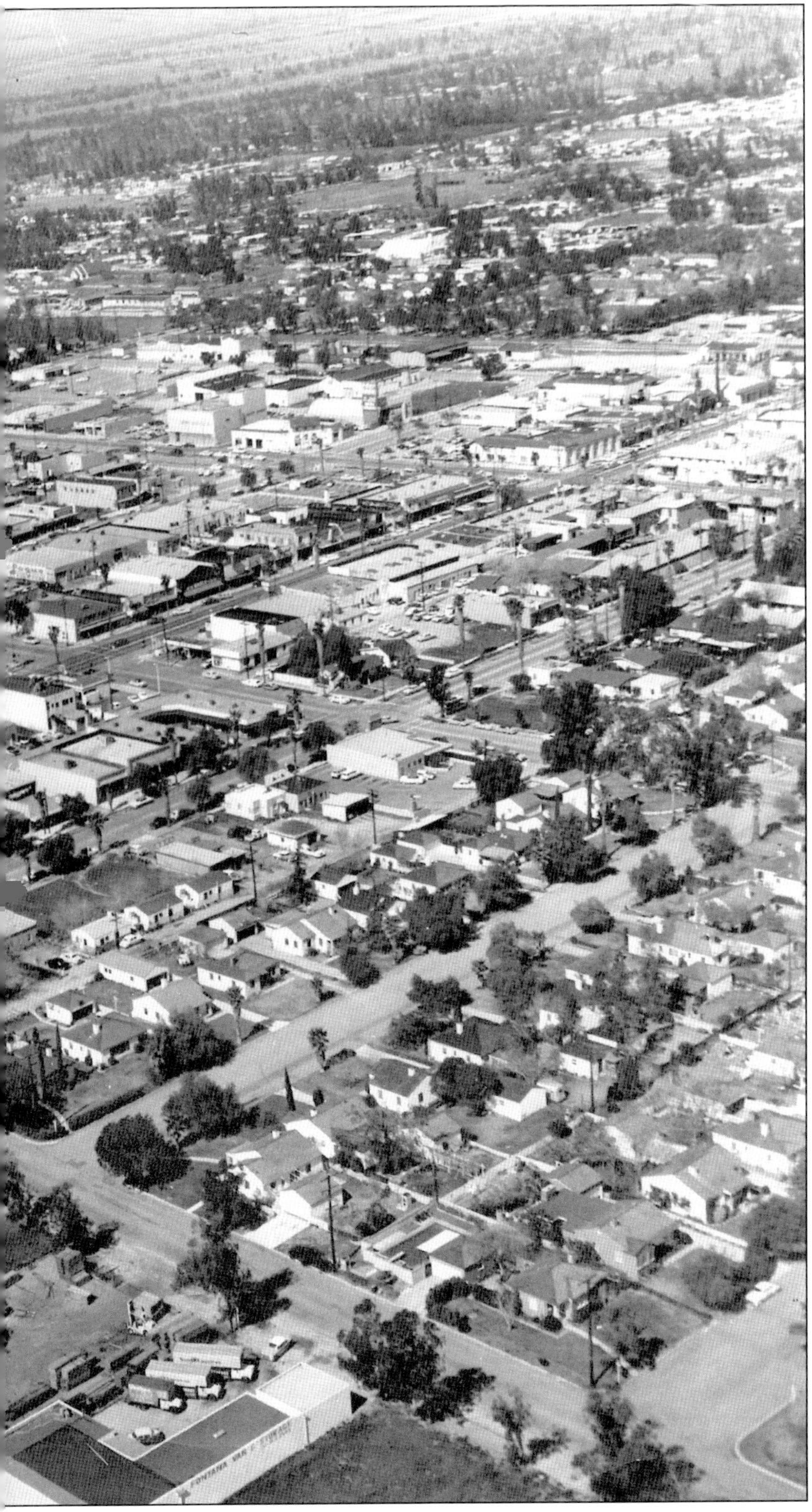

This aerial view shows Fontana in the 1950s, looking northwest. (Courtesy of Chuck and Sue Hickey.)

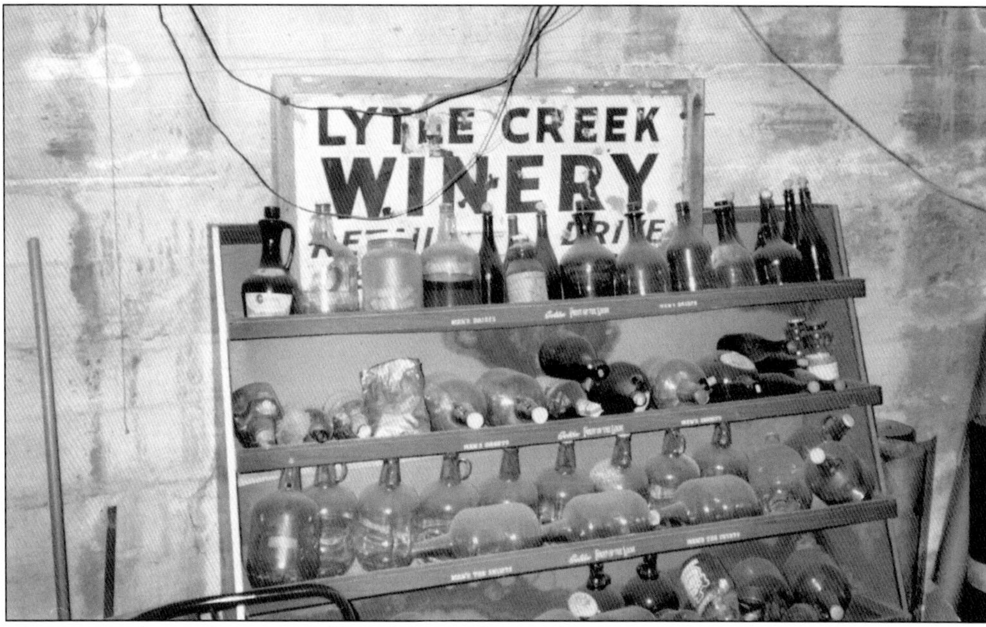

This image shows the wine cellar of the Lytle Creek Winery in a rock concrete, metal, and wood building on the Taylor property in what was Grapeland. The site is on the southeast corner of Duncan Canyon and Lytle Creek Road. The site goes back to the 1880s.

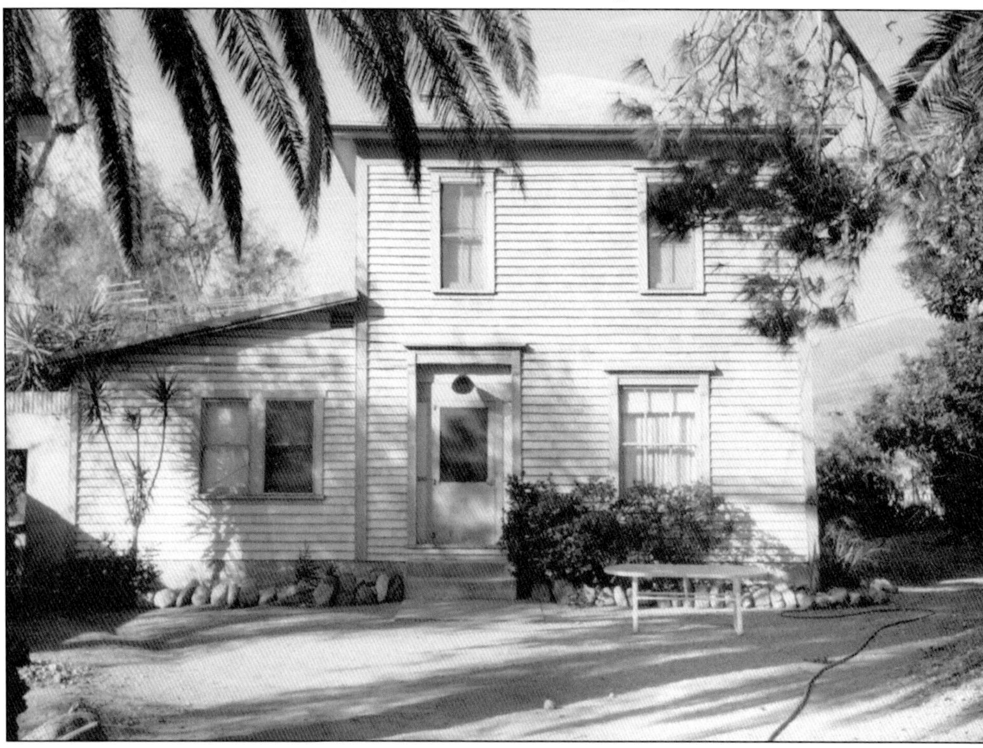

The Taylor residence in Grapeland, across the street from the Perdew schoolhouse site, is shown in this photo. The property contains the winery, house, barns and sheds, farm equipment, and a water reservoir to the east.

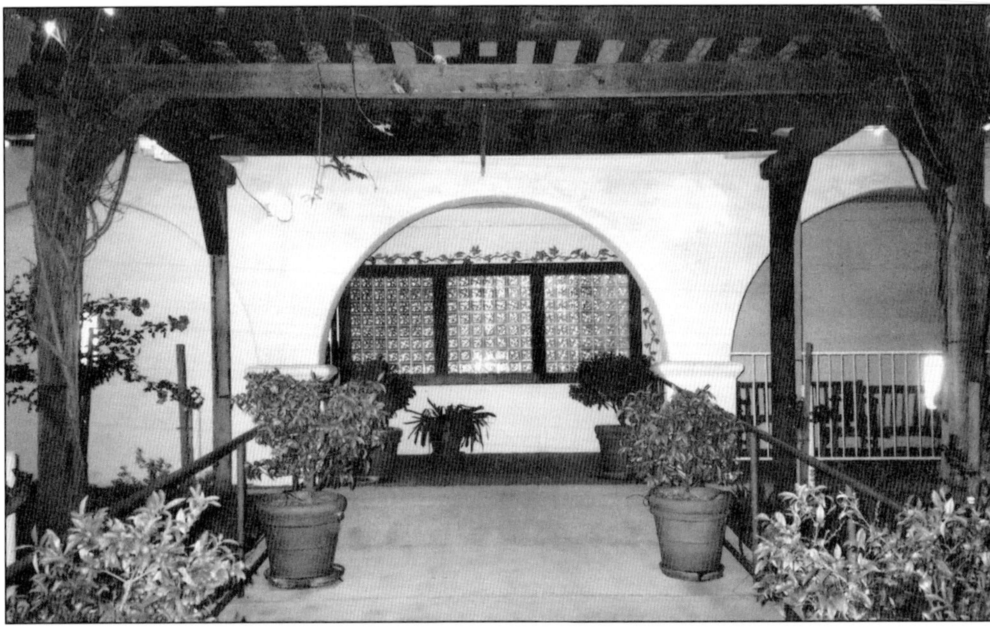

This is the new Filippi Winery in Rancho Cucamonga on Baseline, west of Etiwanda Avenue. The original Filippi Winery was in South Fontana on Etiwanda Avenue. They have a wine-tasting counter, a gift shop, an art gallery, and historic display cabinets of the valley's vineyard and grape history. This valley had the largest vineyard area, and A.B. Miller had the largest watered vineyard in Fontana along Foothill Boulevard. There are newly planted vineyards around the winery with picnic grounds. The building is the original Regina Winery, the first restaurant winery in California.

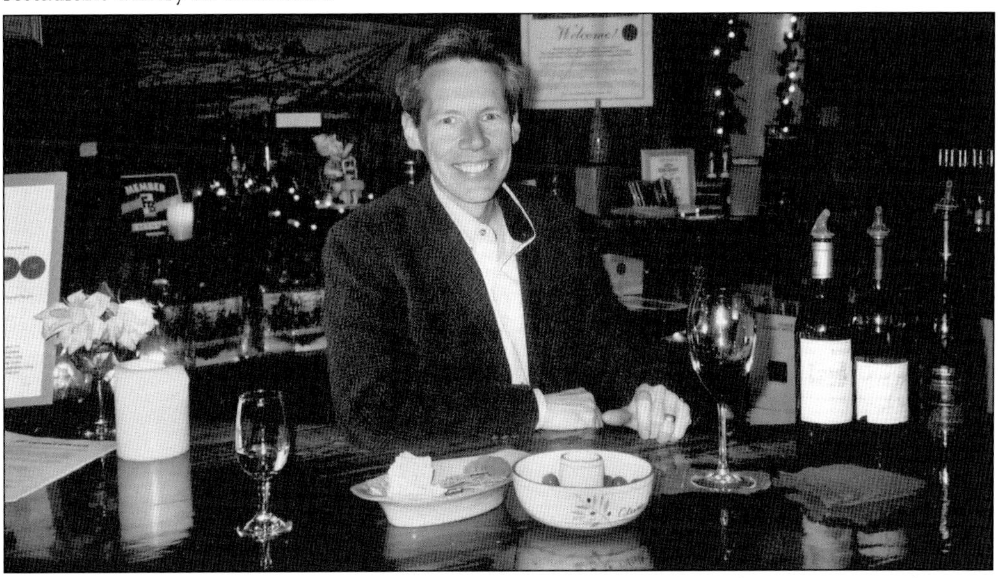

This is a shot of a happy Gino Filippi, a fourth-generation Filippi from Fontana, who runs two winery outlets in the area. This location and one at the Guasti Winery site are next to Ontario International Airport. The original winery was on Etiwanda in Fontana, below the I-10 Freeway, south of Slover Avenue where the new industrial park currently rests. Gino is working with vintners from France to join the wines of both valleys.

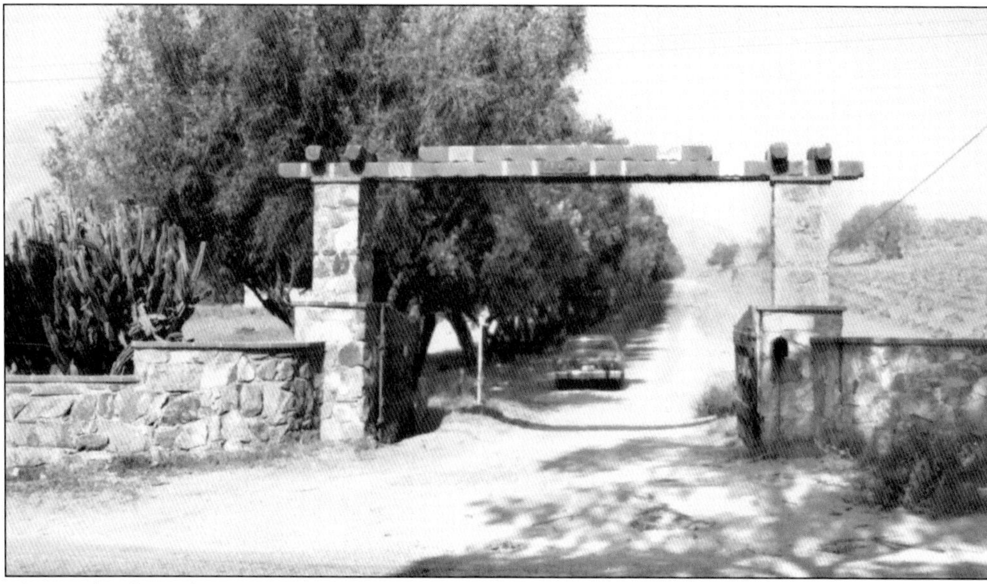

This is the formal entrance to the Santa Fe Winery Ranch in South Fontana, below Jurupa Avenue in a valley of its own, with a line of Olive trees marking the boundary of the ranch. The vineyards covered this small valley. The ranch and vineyards are gone now, making way for a housing tract. The ranch was also a Butterfield stage stop in the late 1880s. The route was from Southern Arizona to Los Angeles through the riverside area and this ranch. The entrance is gone now also.

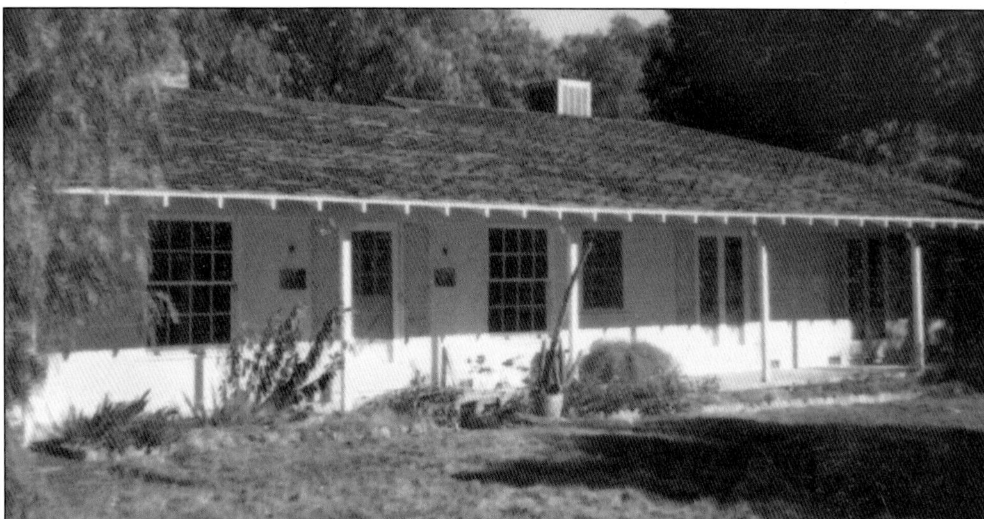

This is a photo of the Santa Fe ranch house. A rock wall surrounded it and the interior of the yard area was landscaped with 100-year-old trees and shrubs. The house had a covered porch with access from each room, a large kitchen and summer porch, a large living room with carved beams in the ceiling, bathrooms, bedrooms, and a cellar. The patio had a waterfall in the rock wall and a large barbeque also covered one end. There was a caretaker's house, plus an outside restroom. The winery barn had a covered sorting building, with benches and tables for the ladies to sort the grapes. Many items were saved from the ranch before the whole site was destroyed.

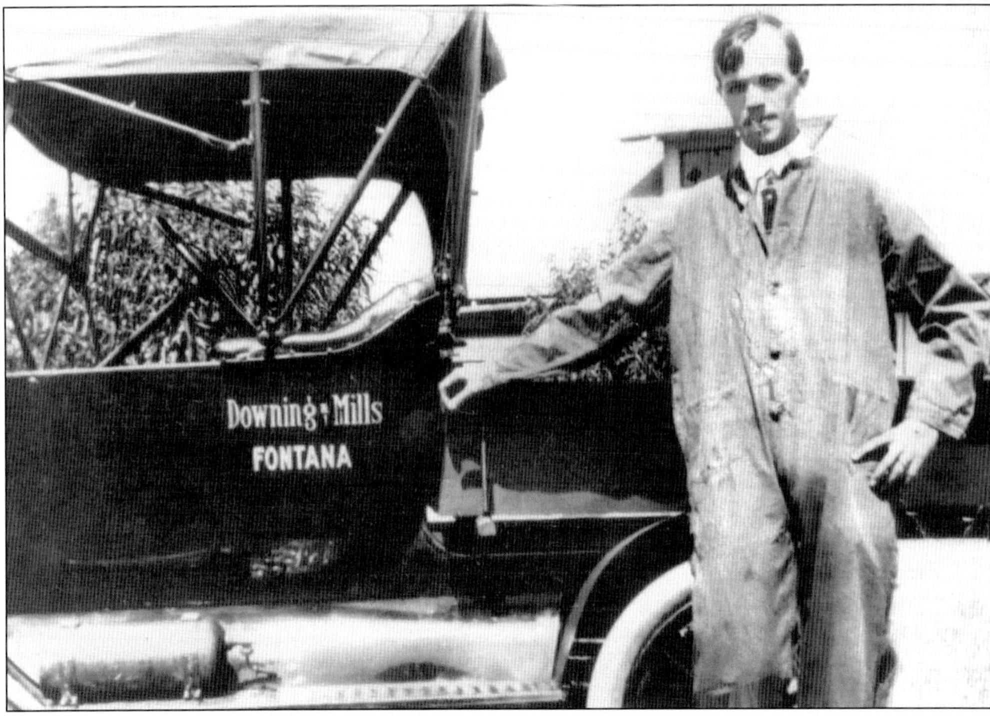

This is an image of the Downing & Mills delivery truck that used to deliver for the Mercantile Store in Fontana. They would go as far as Declez and the hog ranch or up Lytle Creek to the Glenn Ranch to make deliveries. Business became so brisk that they started their own business. Earl Downing and Lloyd Mills were the deliverymen in Fontana.

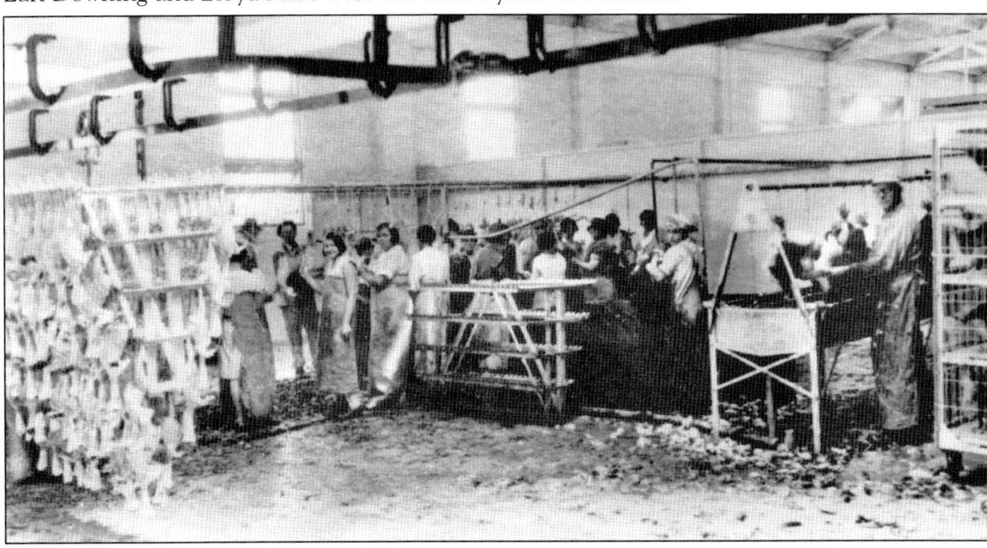

Pictured here is the Poultry Packing Warehouse that was owned by L.F. Swift of Chicago. It was on the south side of the Santa Fe tracks at Juniper and Ceres Avenues, on the northwest corner. The first poultry plant was built in 1913, and the poultry plant and hatchery was constructed in 1919. In 1926, the egg cooperative was formed at the time Swift signed his first contract. In 1928, there were 7,939 ducks, 1,122 turkeys, 2,240 pigeons, 50 geese, 425,000 chickens (306,573 hens, 59,359 pullets, and 47,028 baby chicks), and 45,000 rabbit does roaming Fontana plants.

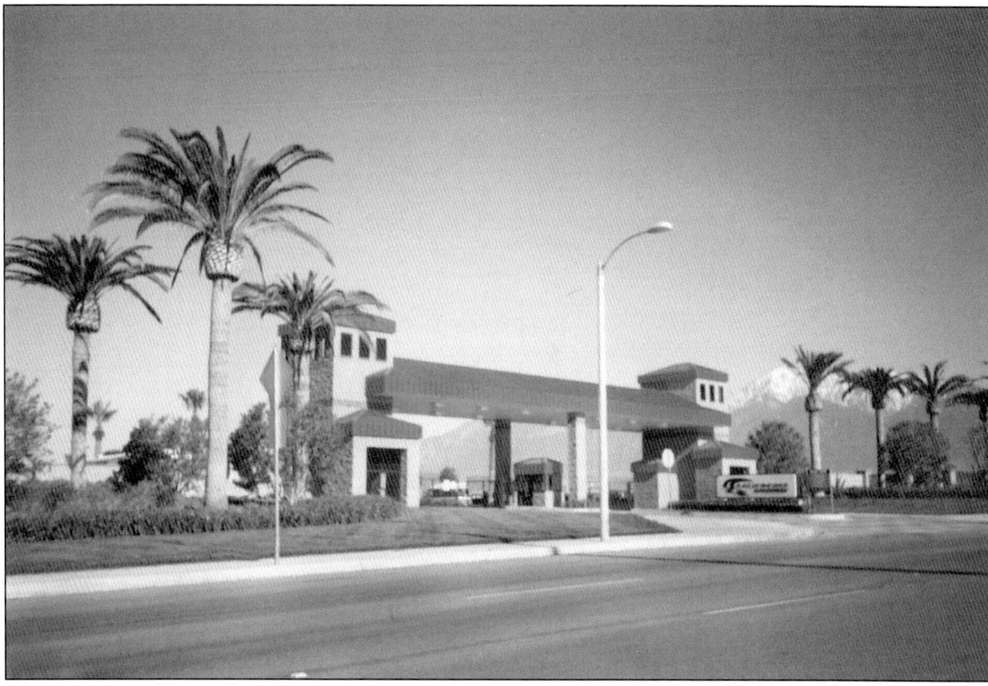

The main entrance to the Fontana California Speedway on Cherry Avenue sits on the land once occupied by Kaiser Steel's blast furnaces.

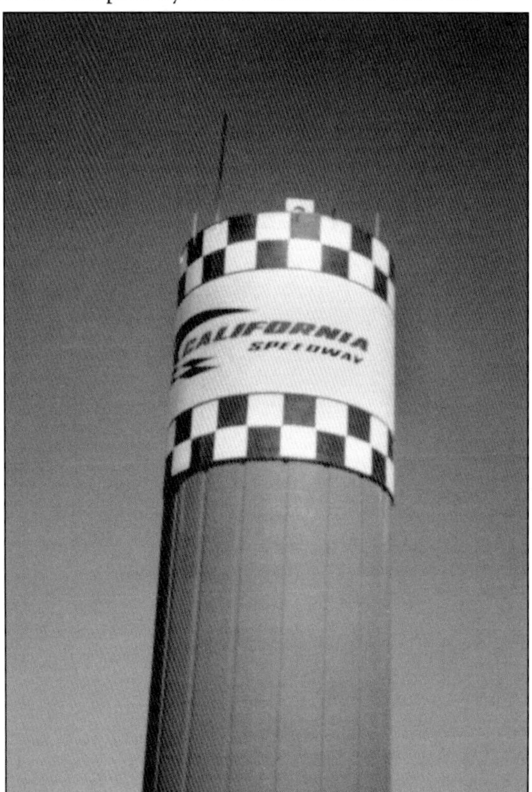

The old Kaiser water tower was saved for use at the Speedway. It sits across from the grandstands by the racecar buildings.

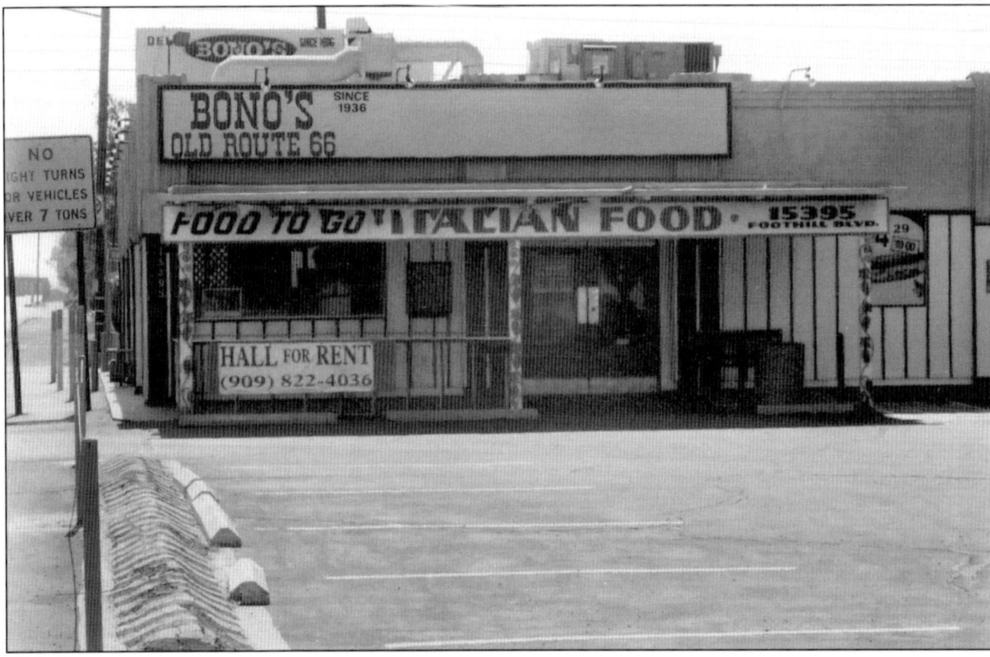

Shown here is Bono's, a family-run Italian market and deli that has been on Foothill Boulevard (Route 66) since 1936.

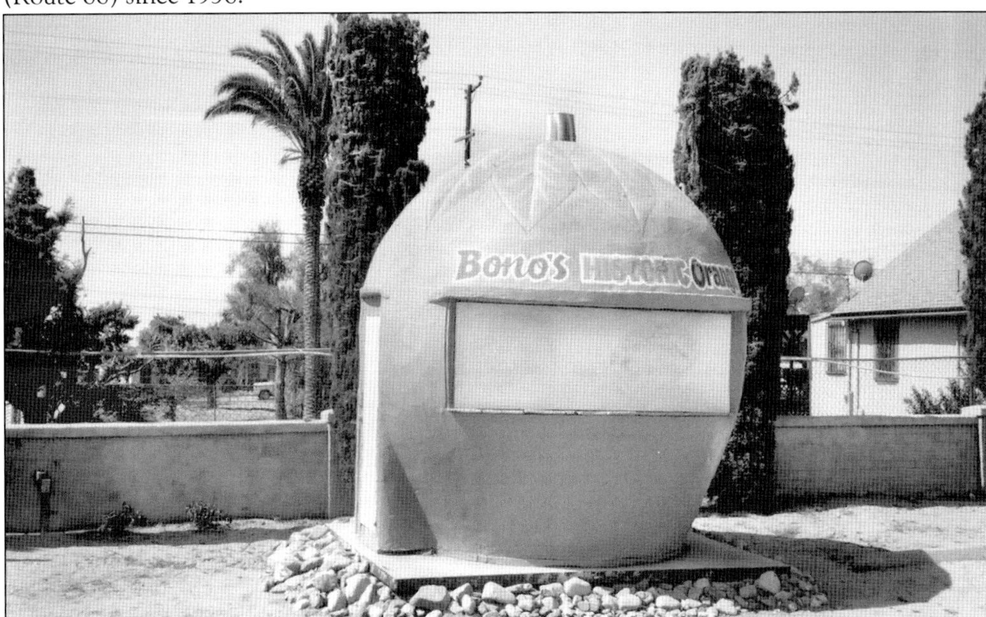

The last original orange stand in the valley is now at Bono's and belongs to the Fontana Historical Society. Loomis P. DeVries built the orange stand in 1936 from wood and stucco. He sold oranges (10¢), large black olives and stuffed pimento green olives (98¢ per gallon), honey from Colton, and dates from Indio. Originally on Foothill Boulevard near Laurel Avenue, it was in Wal-Mart's parking lot for a few years, but Mr. Bono moved it to this location on Route 66.

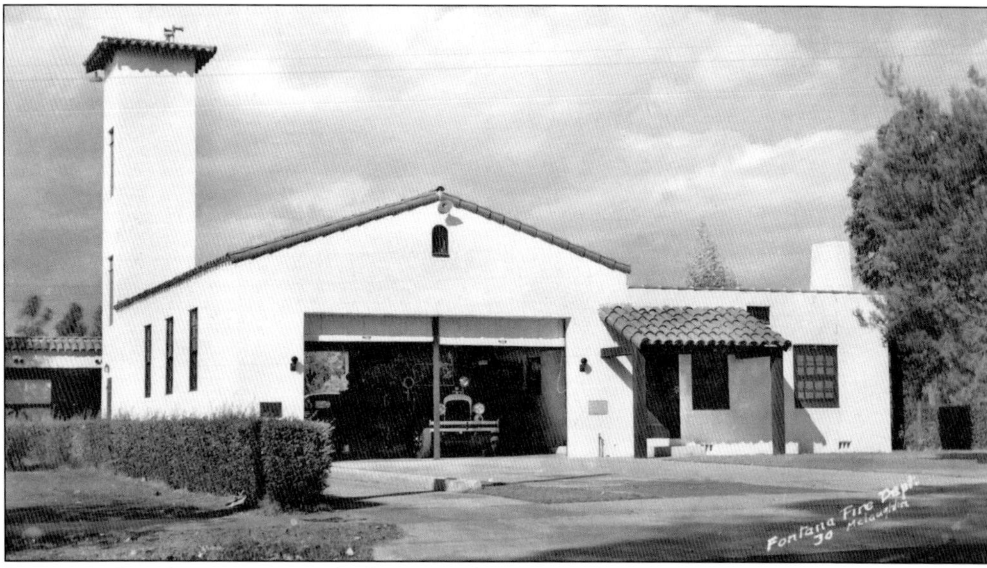

Fontana's first fire station was built in April or May of 1929, and had a room for apparatus storage and another for use by firemen on duty. The contractor of the Spanish-style building was H.J. Ross, who also installed the siren. An addition was made in 1939 for an office area. There is a later building at the rear, put in for repairs and storage of the first engine that has been restored by the firemen, led by Robert Green.

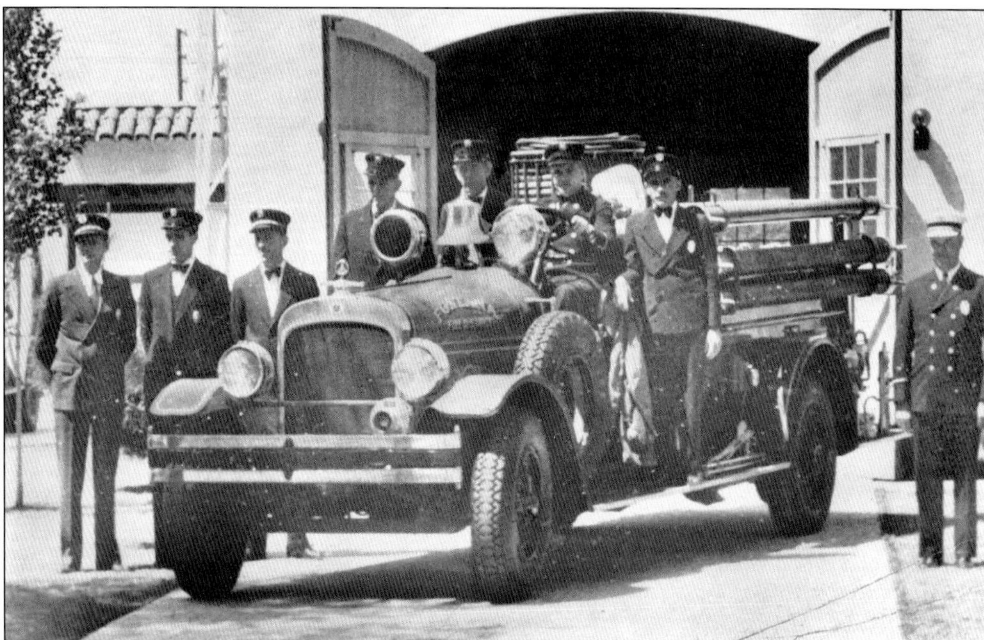

The first engine of the Fontana Fire Station was delivered on Thursday, November 22, 1928. The truck was built and shipped from Columbus, Ohio, to Los Angeles, and then brought immediately to Fontana. It was a 600-gallon Seagraves Pumper, which was best suited for the Fontana area. This equipment cost $9,000. Hoses, ladders, extinguishers, and other necessary equipment were delivered on November 1. The pumping apparatus worked directly from the motor of the truck and afforded the necessary pressure to throw a strong stream of water.

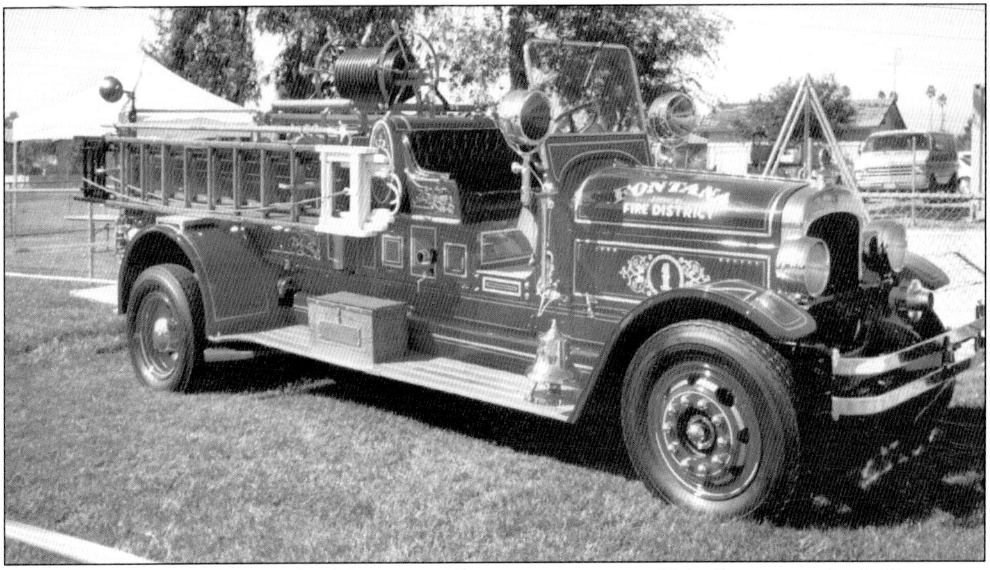

This is the restored fire truck of Fontana. The appointments of Mr. Reeves and Mr. Dreyer as chief and assistant chief, respectively, of the Fontana Fire Department happened on November 28, 1928. The volunteer fireman's organization met for the first time on Tuesday evening, July 23, 1929. Officers and members were Gib Laurie, president; Kirk Sichley, treasurer; Lloyd Martin, secretary; Archie Calkins, vice president; and Archie Moore, Fred W. Alexander, Lawrence Parrish, Paul Endicott, Ralph Setzer, and George Calkins.

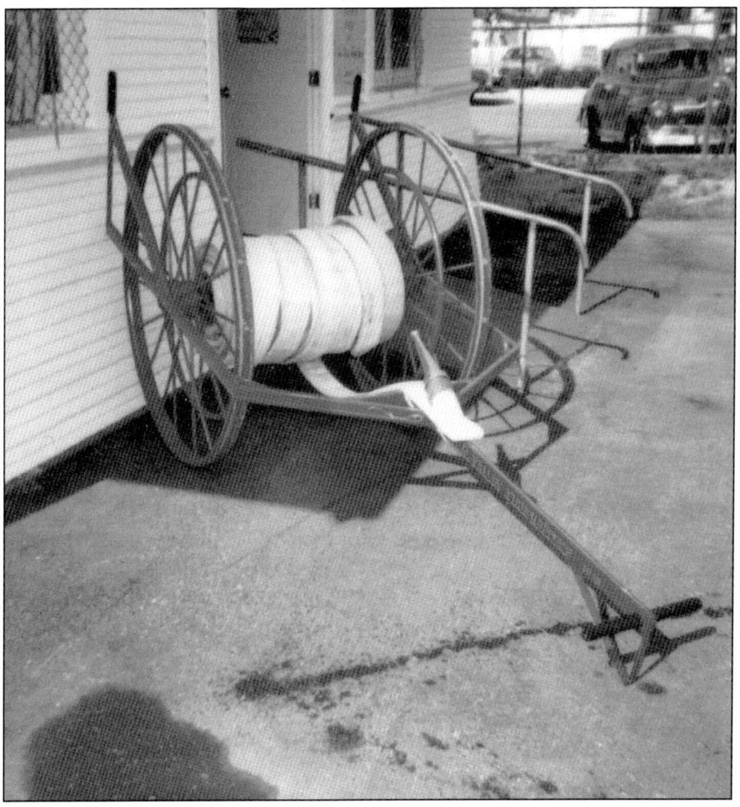

This original hose rig used by the Fontana Farms Company, a volunteer unit, before the new fire station and firemen were put together. In March 1928, residents realized that they did not have a way to save any commercial or residential buildings, so county supervisors voted to create a fire district.

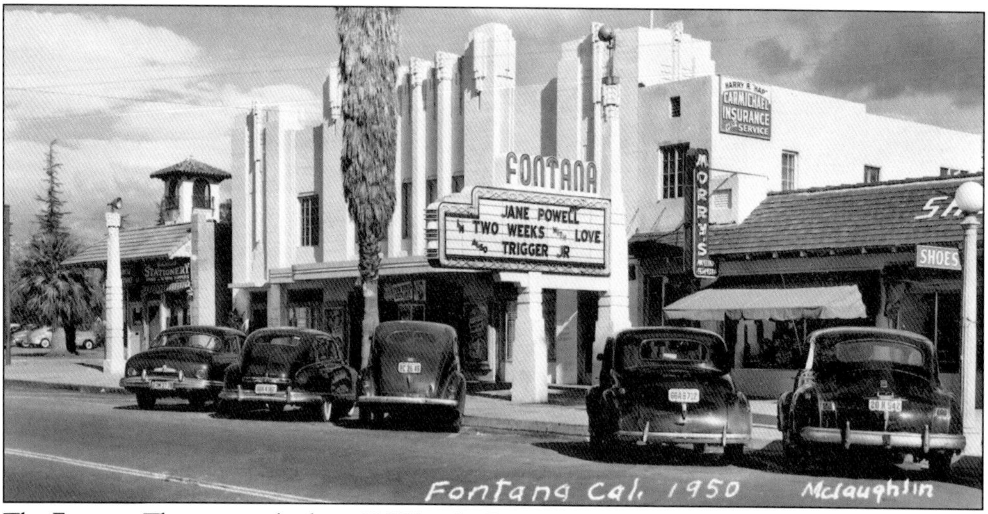

The Fontana Theatre was built in 1937 by the Fontana Farms Company at a cost of $45,000. It was the first true theatre in the area, though movies were shown in the Fontana Woman's Club House previously. General manager R.E. Boyle and Philip Hasbrouck, head of the engineering department, supervised construction. The plans were drawn by Carl H. Boiler of Los Angeles, a leading theatrical architect, to fit 750 people. On the main floor was a large stage that has two rooms of 20 by 20 feet for a store on each side. The theatre sign was separate from the building, which was never done before. The movie sound was piped into the restrooms and baby room on the second floor. It had shatterproof windows upstairs. There was also an apartment upstairs for the owner, Glenn Harper, a renowned theatre owner. The City of Fontana now owns the building and is restoring it to its original appearance.

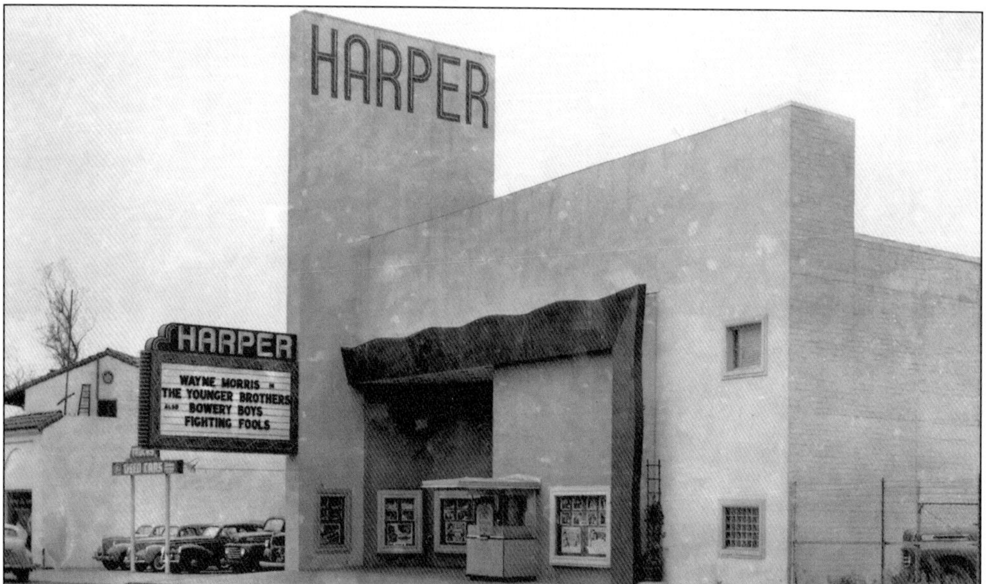

The second theatre in Fontana was the Harper, one block west from the Fontana. It opened November 10, 1948, could seat 700 people, and was constructed at a cost of $100,000. Its "lamella" construction was designed to resist earthquakes and have excellent acoustical qualities. The exterior, designed by S. Charles Lee, included a 50-foot tower and modern marquee. Admission was 50¢ per adult and 20¢ for children. It is now a church.

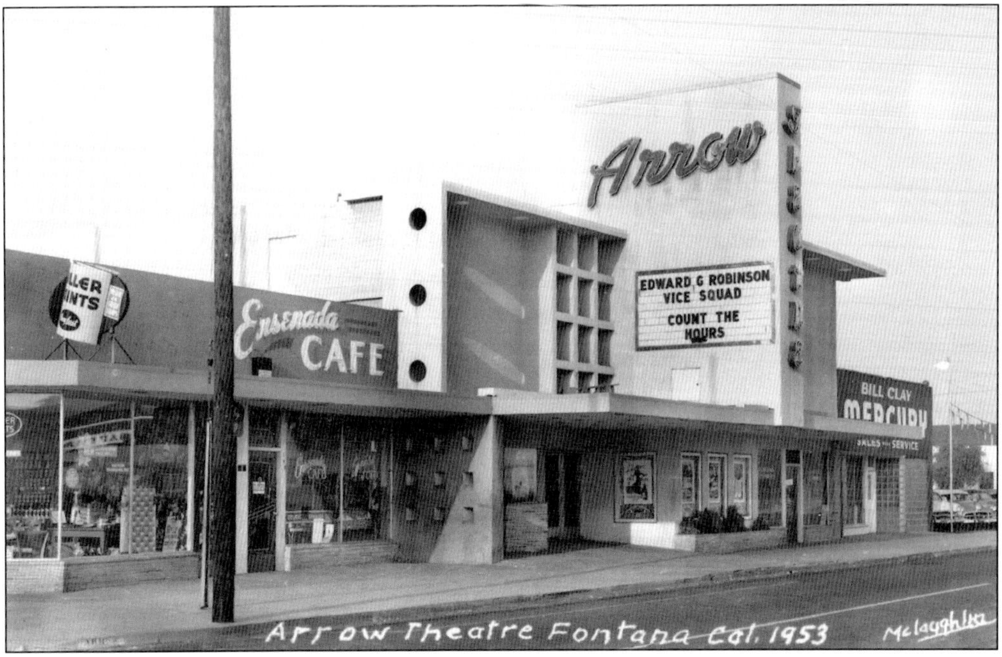

This is a 1953 view of the third theatre in Fontana called the Arrow Theatre, built in 1948. The Arrow has had minimal changes over the years as the flagstone front trim is still there, as well as the ticket booth. It is now a church.

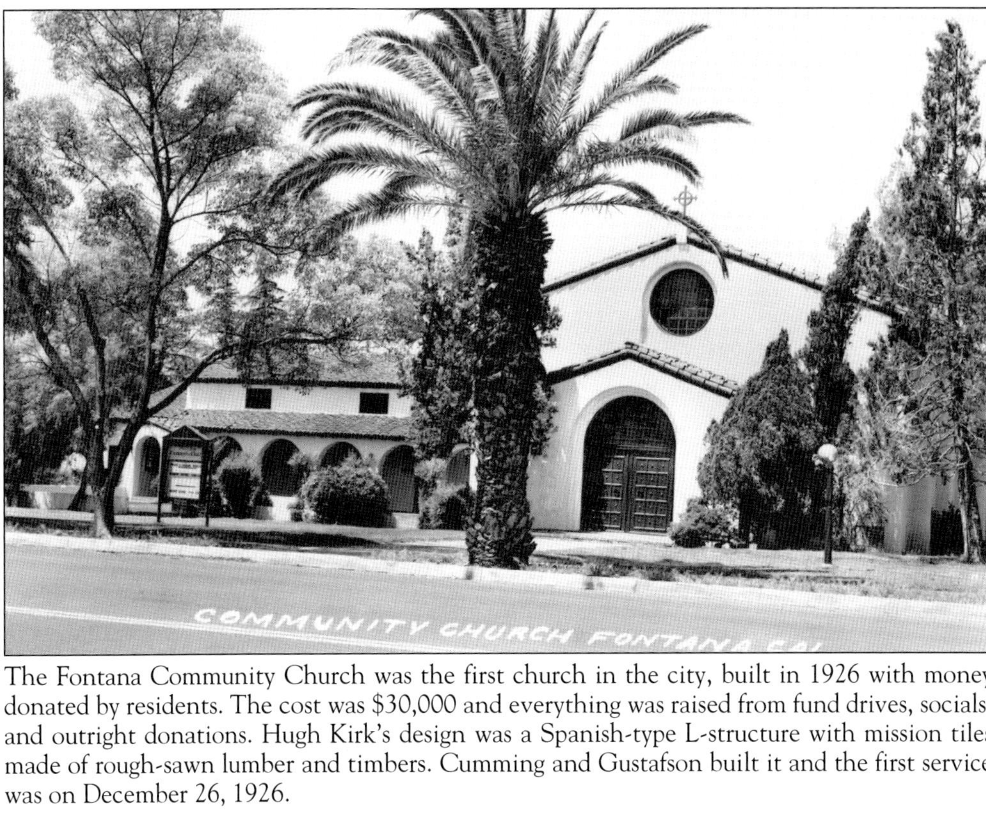

The Fontana Community Church was the first church in the city, built in 1926 with money donated by residents. The cost was $30,000 and everything was raised from fund drives, socials, and outright donations. Hugh Kirk's design was a Spanish-type L-structure with mission tiles made of rough-sawn lumber and timbers. Cumming and Gustafson built it and the first service was on December 26, 1926.

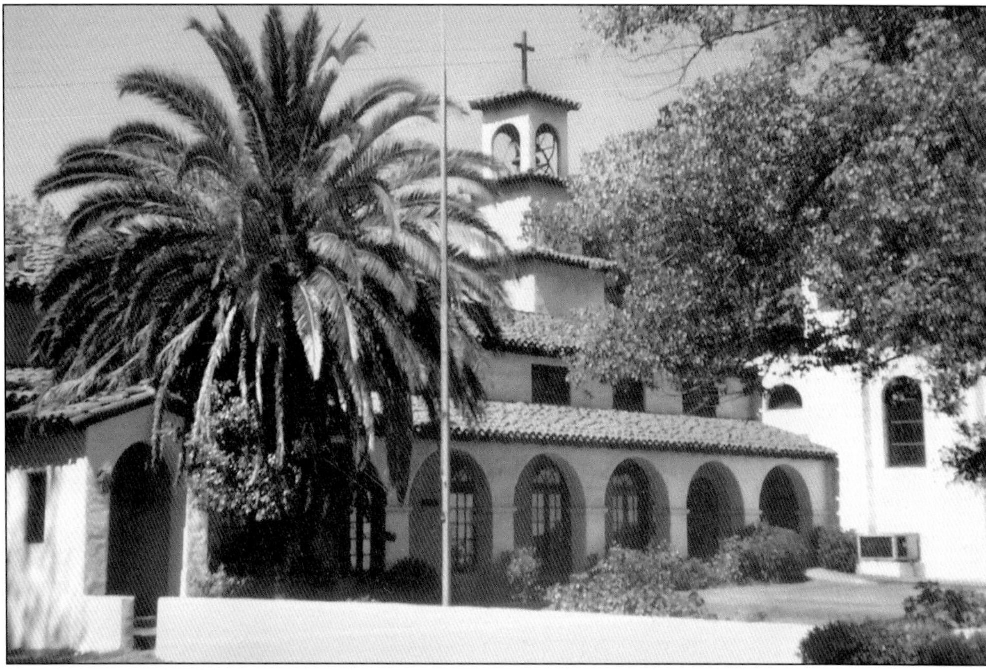

This is an image of the Fontana Community Church with its bell tower. It was donated in 1952 by Judith and Mrs. R.E. Boyle to the church in memory of father and husband, respectively.

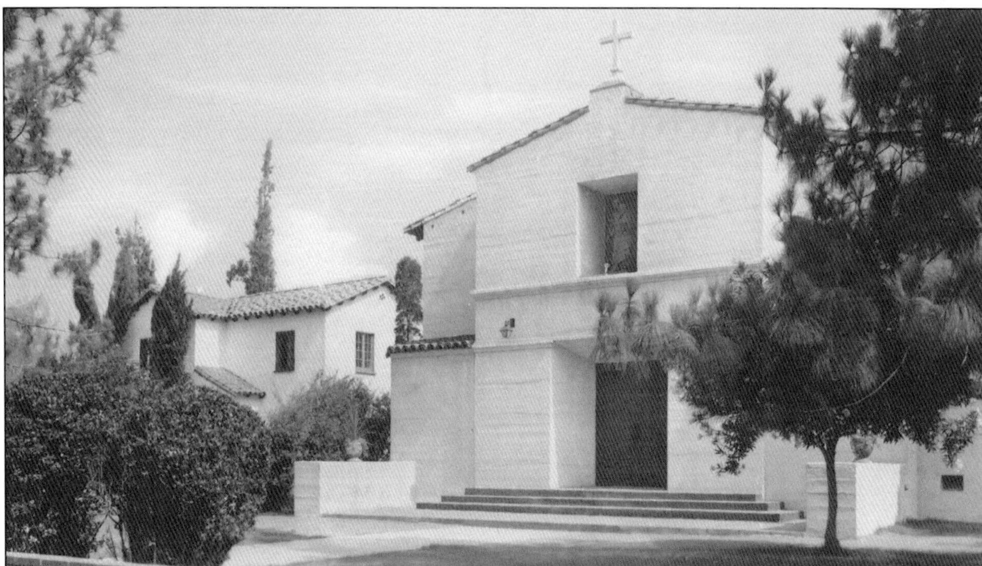

The second church in Fontana, a Catholic edifice for the many citizens who met in homes or at the Woman's Club House, cost $20,000 to build and was located in the heart of the community. It is on the northwest corner of Mango Avenue and Arrow Highway and was designed by M.L. Barker of Los Angeles. Mr. Gustafson built the church as a prominent contractor of Fontana, and the Right Reverend Bishop J.J. Cantwell of Los Angeles dedicated it on May 11, 1930. On October 16, 1931, Reverend Meade was assigned to the Fontana Catholic Church, and on October 23, 1931, the area of Fontana became a parish and was officially named Saint Joseph's Catholic Church.

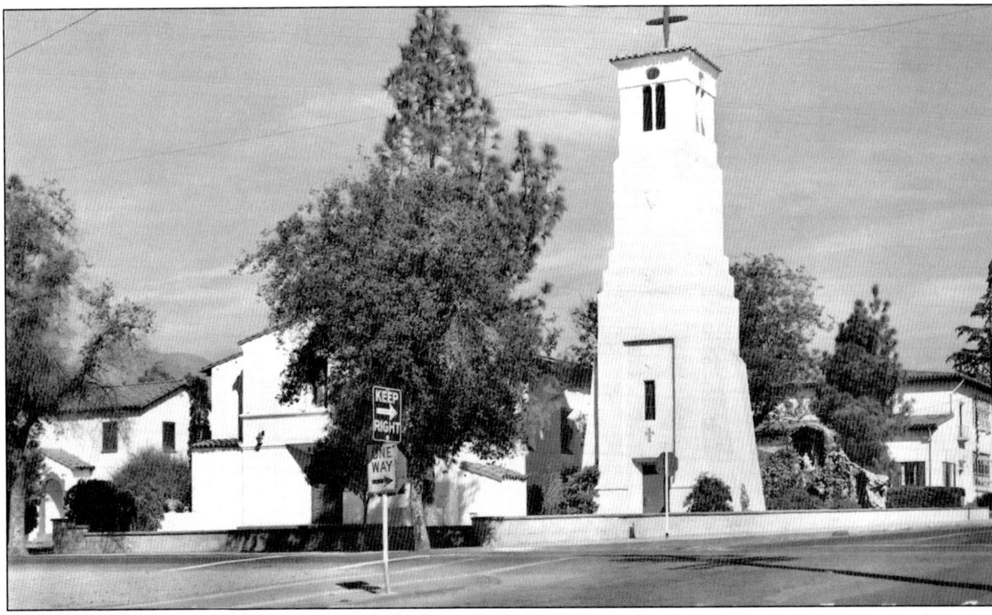

This is an image of the Saint Joseph's Catholic Church. Its bell tower was built after World War II to honor those lost in the war. The rectory is to the left, the elementary school is to the right, and the grotto is behind the tower.

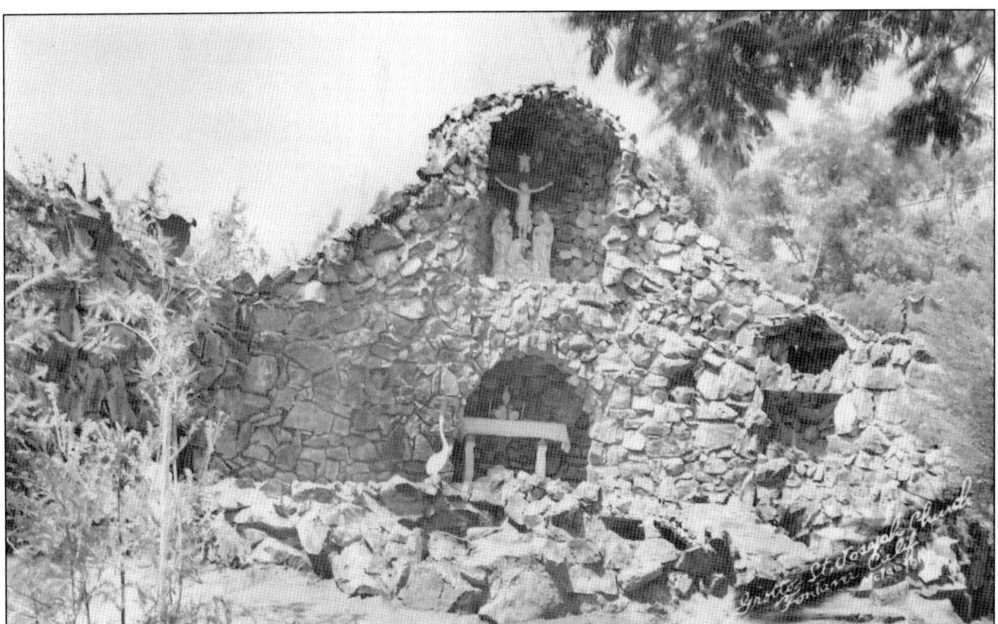

The Blessed Virgin Grotto was made of rock and mortar. Over the years, the vines and plants made the grotto unsafe and it had to be torn down. A new one was built between the church and rectory.

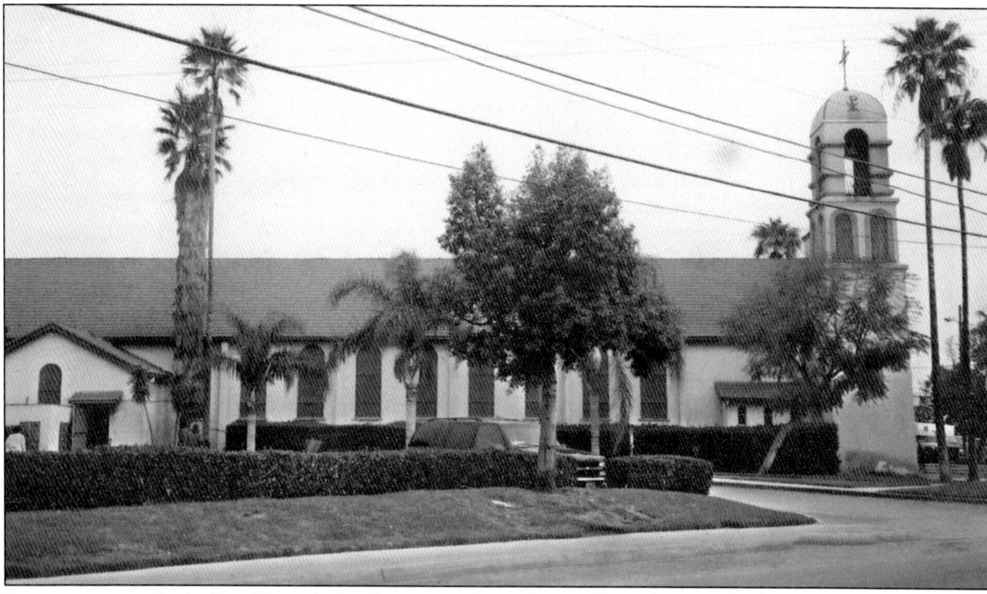

Resurrection Catholic Church broke away from Saint Joseph's Catholic Church because so many Catholics were in the Fontana area. The parish was formed in 1953 and members met in homes around the area. Fr. Albert Kowalczyk was pastor when the present church was constructed in 1957. One of the most attractive qualities is a series of 21 stained-glass windows. He also oversaw the opening of a K–4 parochial school, Resurrection Academy, which has grown to include students through the eighth grade. When the school opened, it was at one of Fontana's private school buildings. Under Fr. Timothy Keppel, a large parish hall was built in 1989, and six years later three classrooms were added.

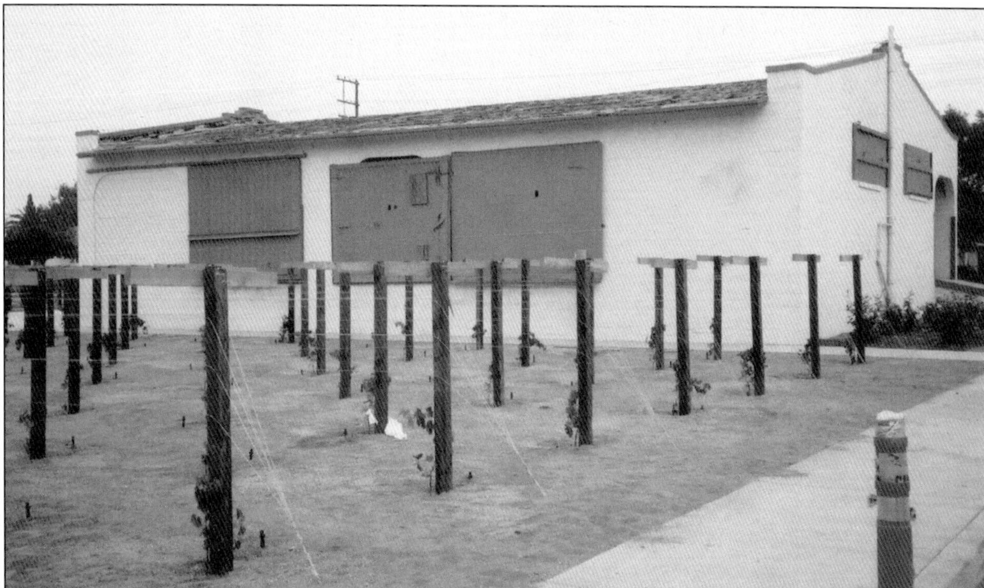

This is the first Pacific Electric station for passengers and freight, built in 1912–1913. It was the First Mercantile Store, then a lumber yard. The structure is part of the new Hazel Putnam Plaza and is being restored by the City, who now owns it

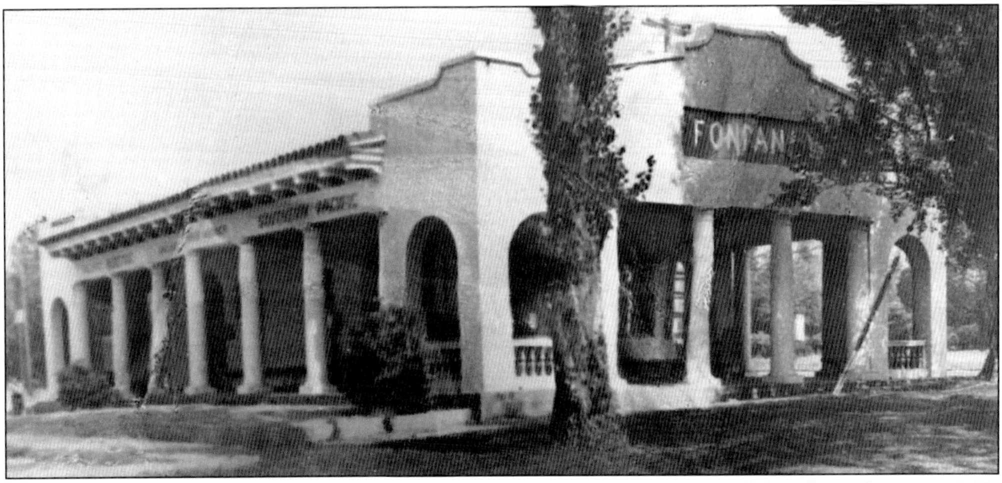

This photo shows the second Pacific Electric depot for passengers and freight, taken in 1949. Built in 1914, the Spanish-style building remained in use until 1974, when it was demolished. This is what caused residents to start the Fontana Historical Society. The first depot is still here, and will be restored soon by the City.

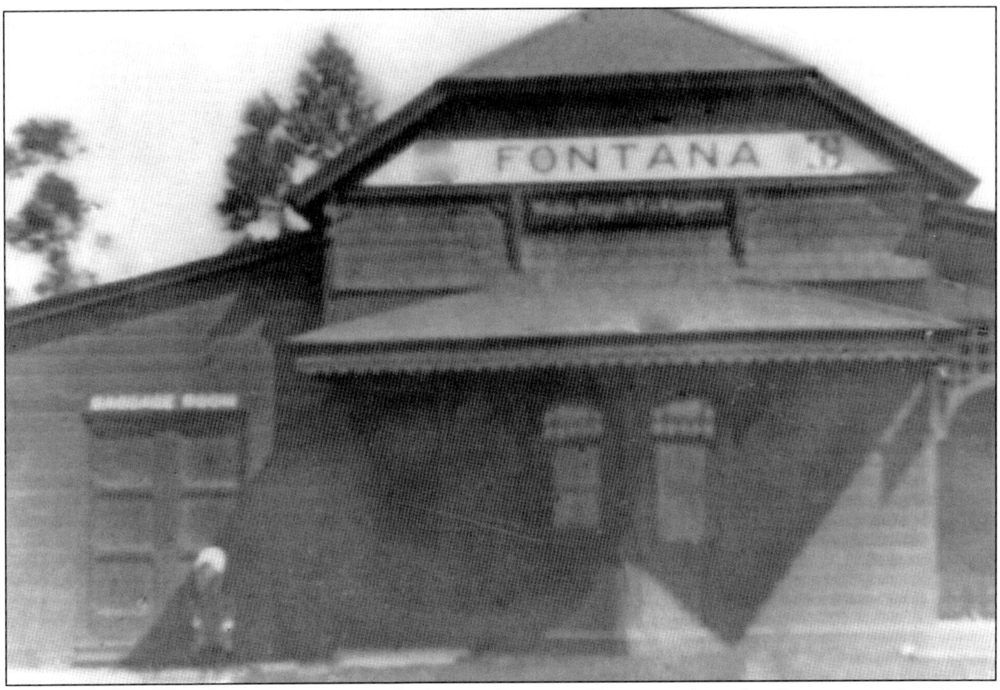

The Santa Fe Railroad Station was the second one in Fontana, but the first was only a lean-to. The building was made of redwood, and had a baggage room on the west side and living quarters on the east. The doorway had latticework over the entrance and a little passenger waiting porch. It was built about 1917 at Ceres and Pepper Streets. When Roy Hilton was appointed to the station, there was just a boxcar where the family lived. Esther Bowen of Riverside was commissioned to do an oil painting of this same photographic view, as part of a series for Fontana's new Mervyn's store. Other paintings in the series are of the Taylor residence in Grapeland, the Perdew schoolhouse in Grapeland, and the Camp No. 1 foreman's Ranch House at the Fontana Farms Company.

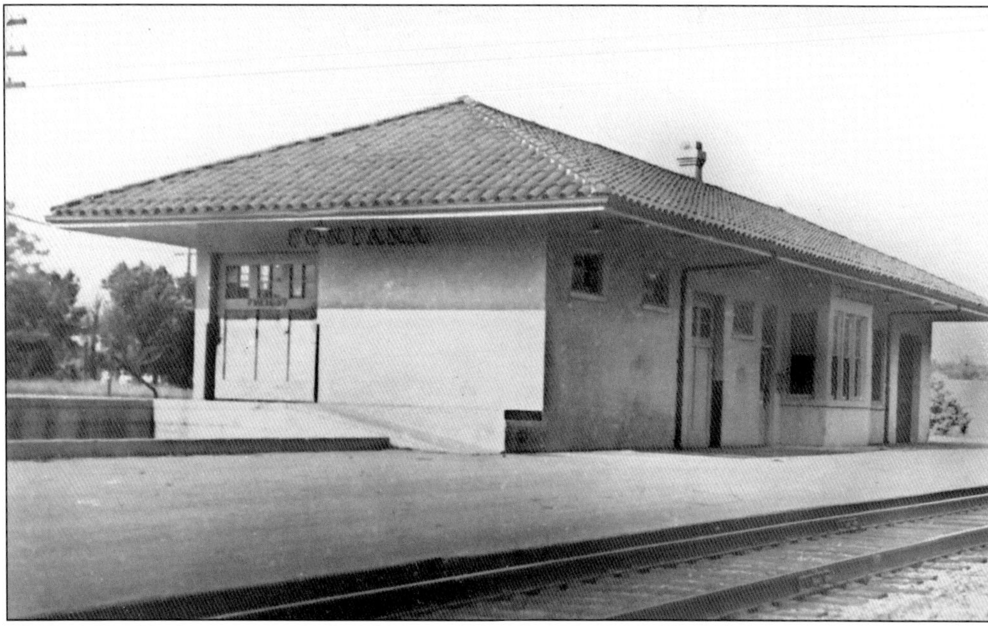

This is the third Santa Fe Railroad Station in Fontana between Juniper and Sierra Avenue, where the Metrolink Station is now, on Orange Way. It was built in 1924, and stationmaster Roy Hilton moved to a home up near Seville Avenue and just worked at the station.

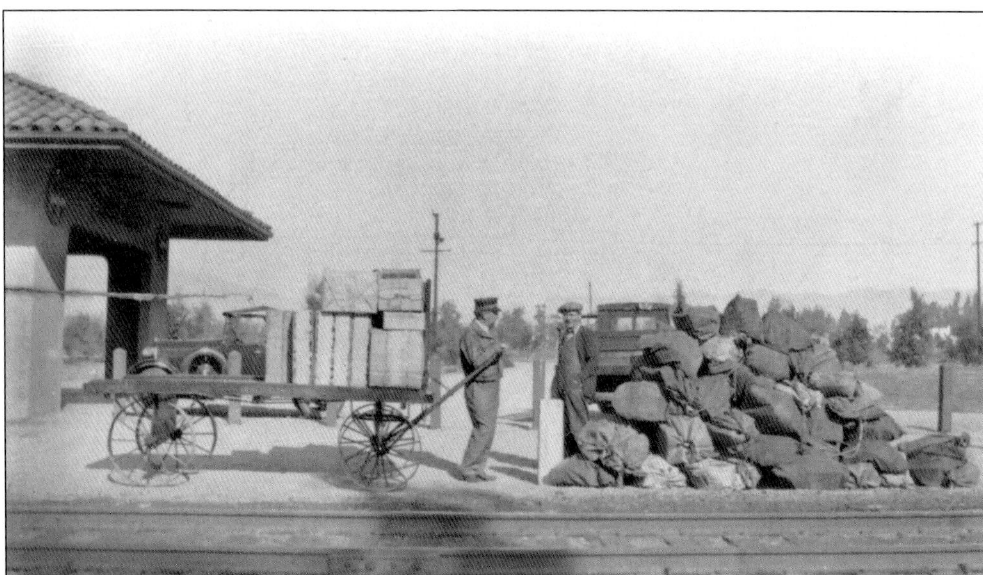

This photo shows stationmaster Roy Hilton working the baggage wagon at the loading area of the Santa Fe Railroad Station. It was torn down in the 1980s.

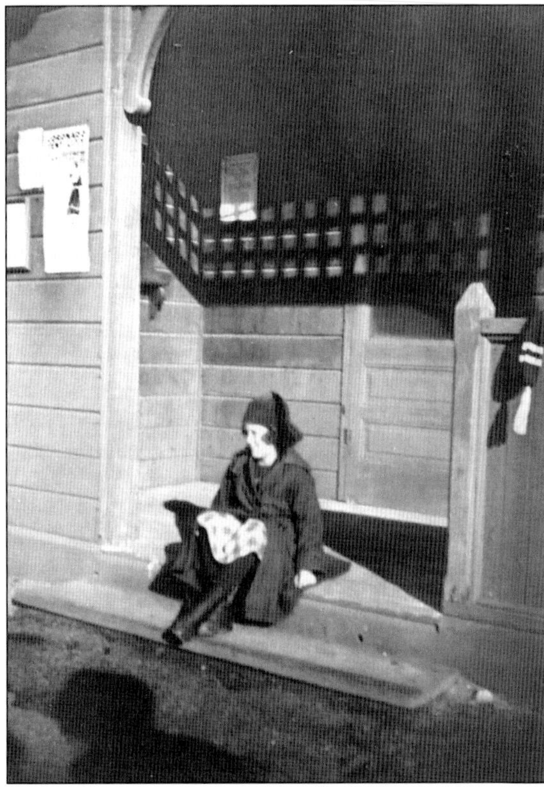

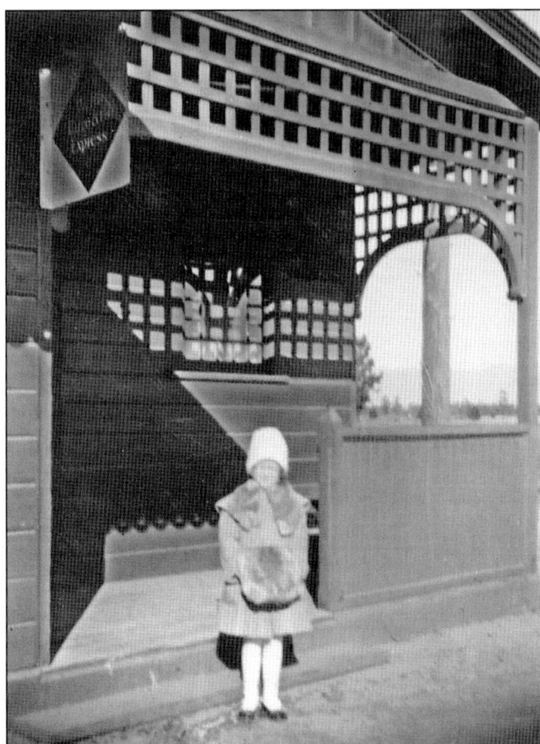

These two photos show Mildred Hilton Crawford as a young girl on two different days. She lived at the Santa Fe Railroad Station as her first home there was a boxcar, it then was the station itself, and finally it became a real home in the town site.

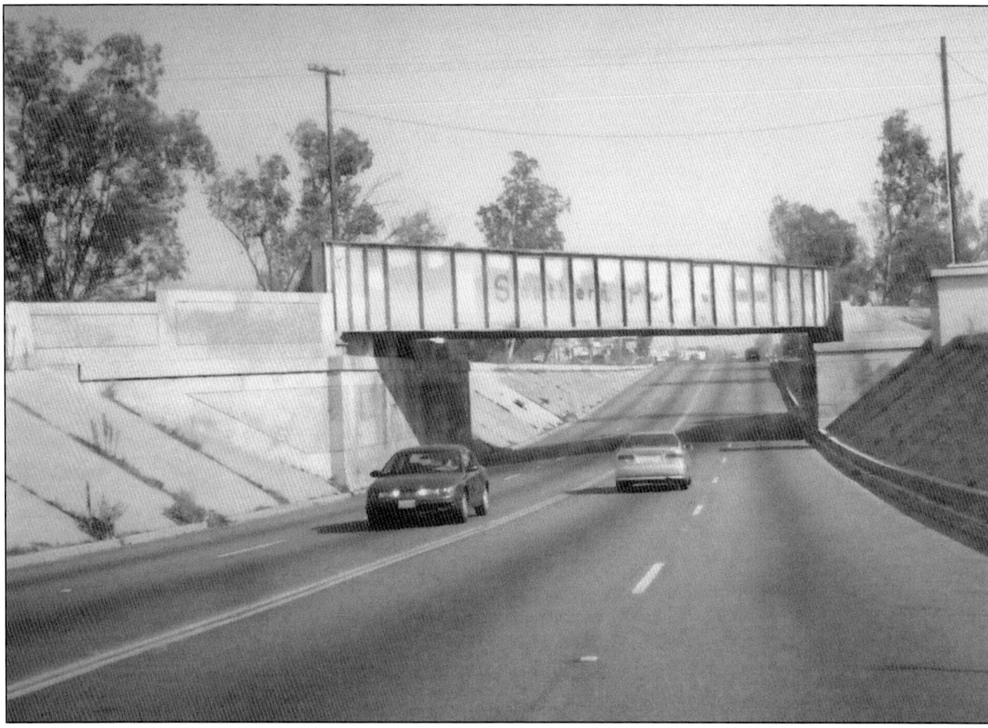

The underpass on Foothill Boulevard, near Almeria Street, was built in 1931 to get the Pacific Electric Railway over Foothill to ease traffic problems. The pump building at the top right keeps the water out of the underpass. It is still in operation today.

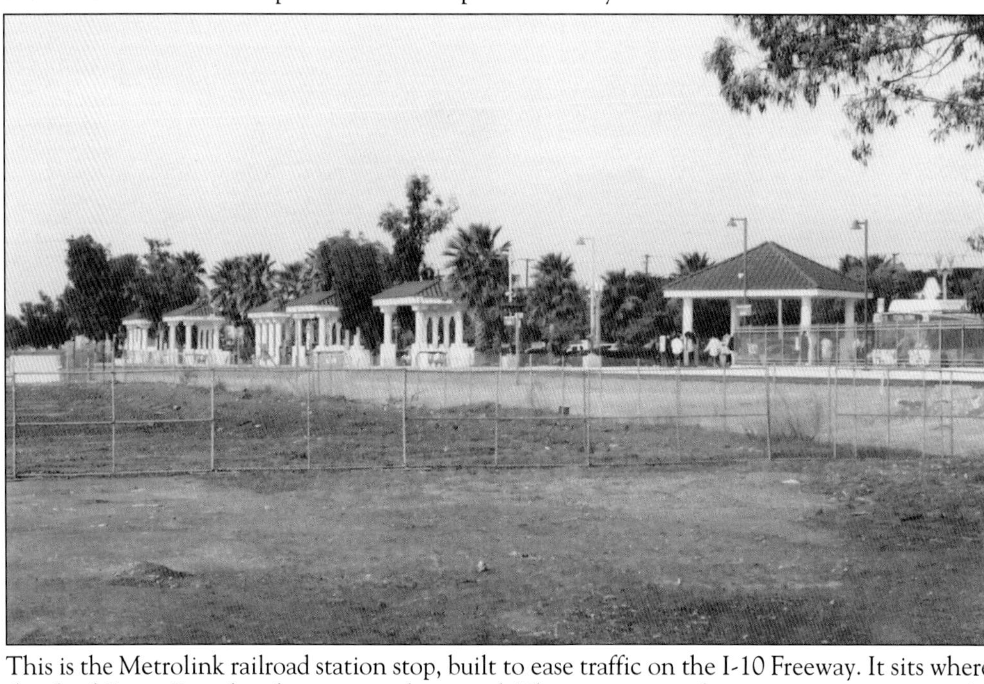

This is the Metrolink railroad station stop, built to ease traffic on the I-10 Freeway. It sits where the third Santa Fe railroad station used to stand. The area now is the transportation center for Fontana and a hub for buses. The new senior center now surrounds it.

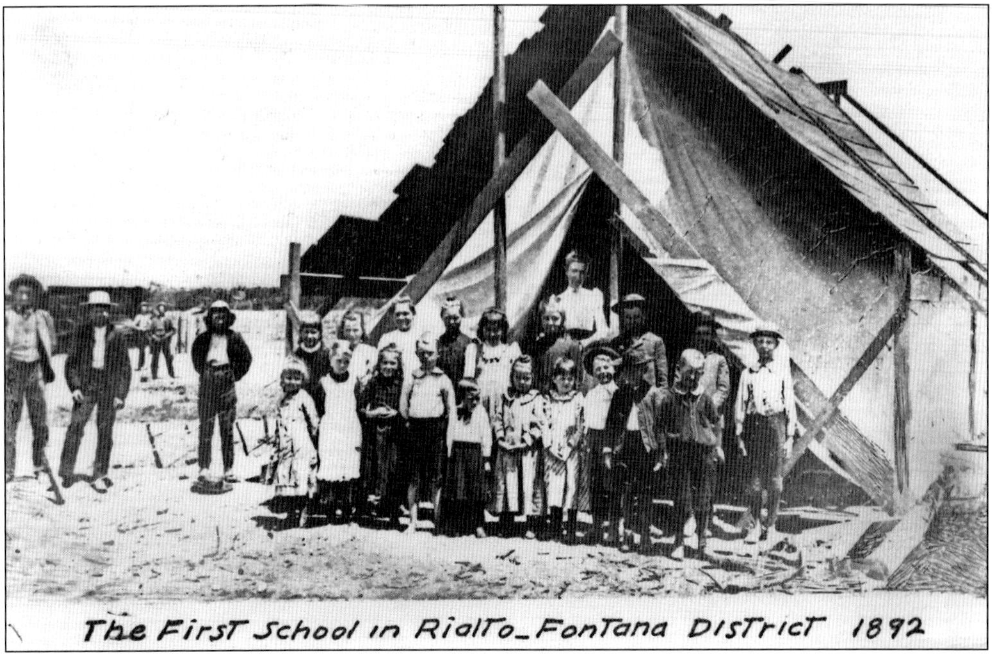

Pictured in 1892 is the first grade school of the Rialto-Fontana district. There were only a few students in the area at the time.

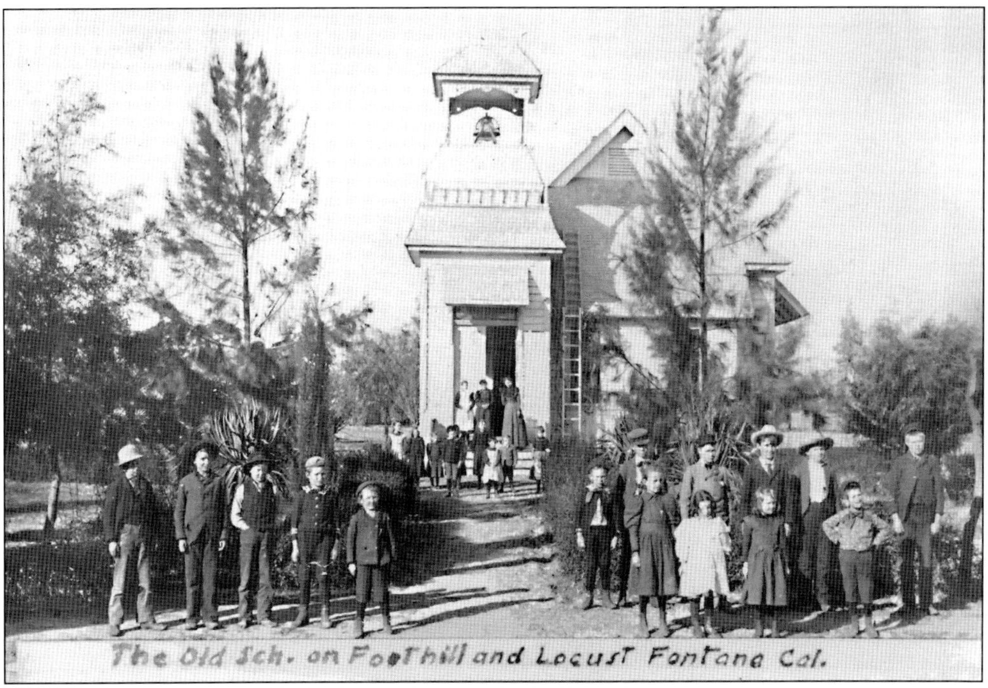

This is a c. 1910 image of the old school on Foothill Boulevard and Locust Avenue.

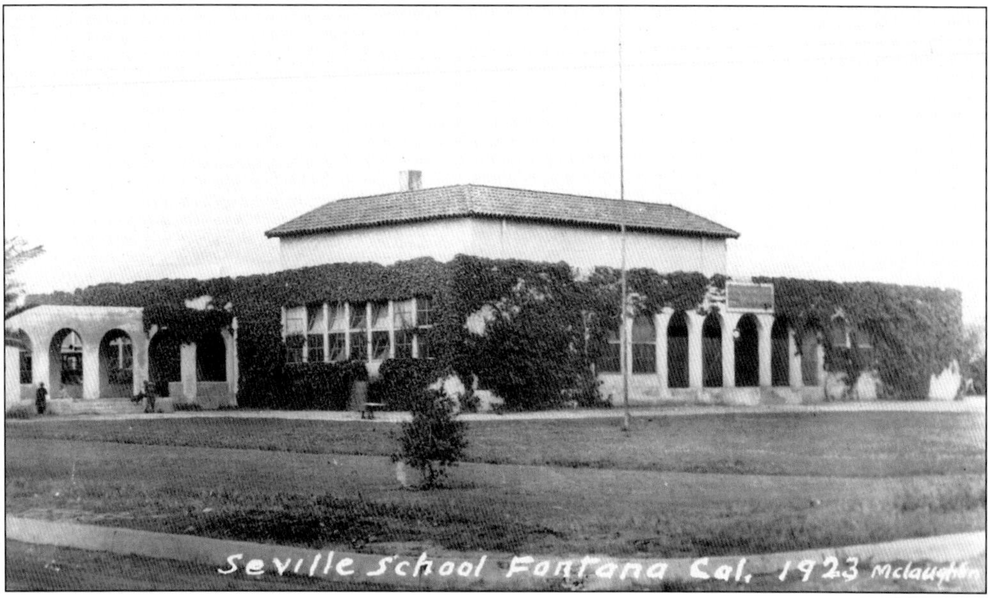

This is a photo of the Sierra-Seville School in 1923, built in 1913–1914 on the corner of Sierra and Seville, northeast above the Pacific Electric Railroad. The design for the school was actually going to be the Pacific Electric Railroad Station, but when A.B. Miller saw the plans he fell in love with them and decided to make use of them for the school. The structure cost $18,000 to build and was one of the first in the town site. The school lasted until the 1960s, but was torn down to make way for the new city hall.

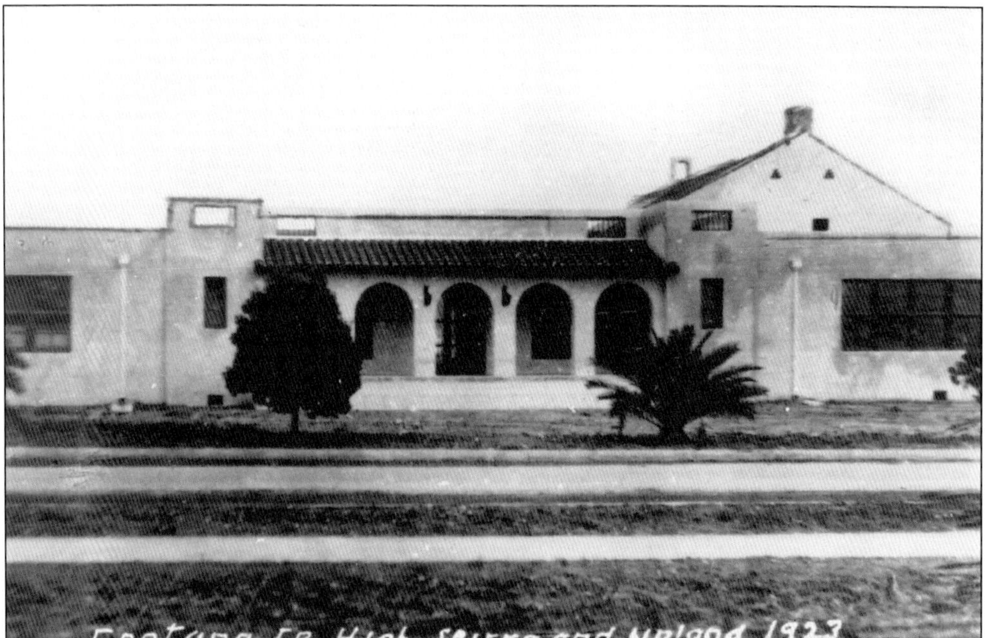

This is a 1923 photograph of Fontana Junior High School on Sierra Avenue and Upland Avenue, where city hall is now.

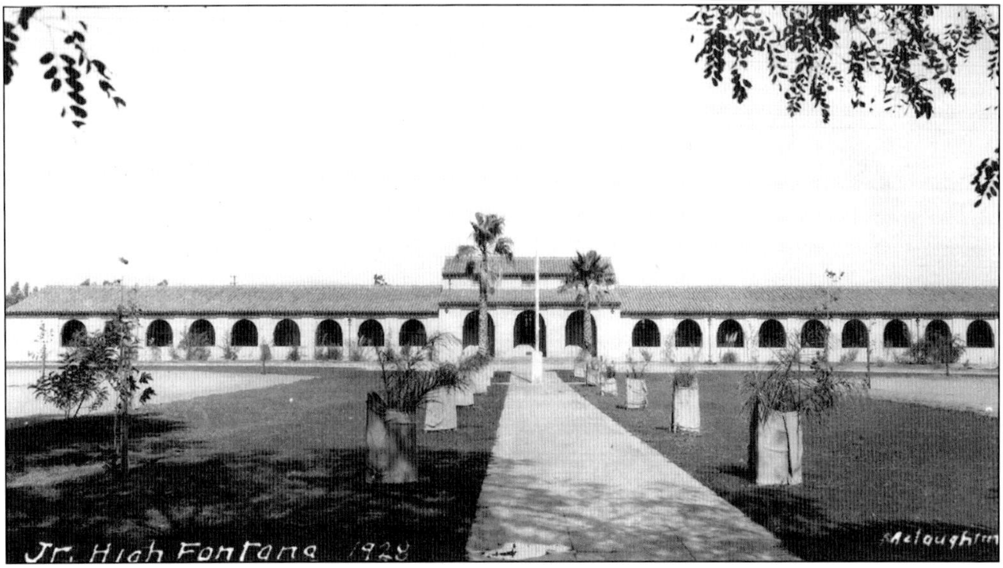

The first unit of the four-part Fontana Junior High School was completed in the spring of 1928 in Fontana with a total cost of $150,000. The first unit was a three-arched center section with two wings of nine arches each. It is located on the northeast corner of Arrow Highway and Mango Avenue. It had a red tile roof with stucco walls and there is more steel in this building than any other in the town site, which gives it greater resistance to earthquake and makes it fireproof. The building is now 76 years old, and some changes have been made as the arched areas have been filled in, and the red tile roof is now shingled, and the trees have grown up as the sycamores and palms are mature now.

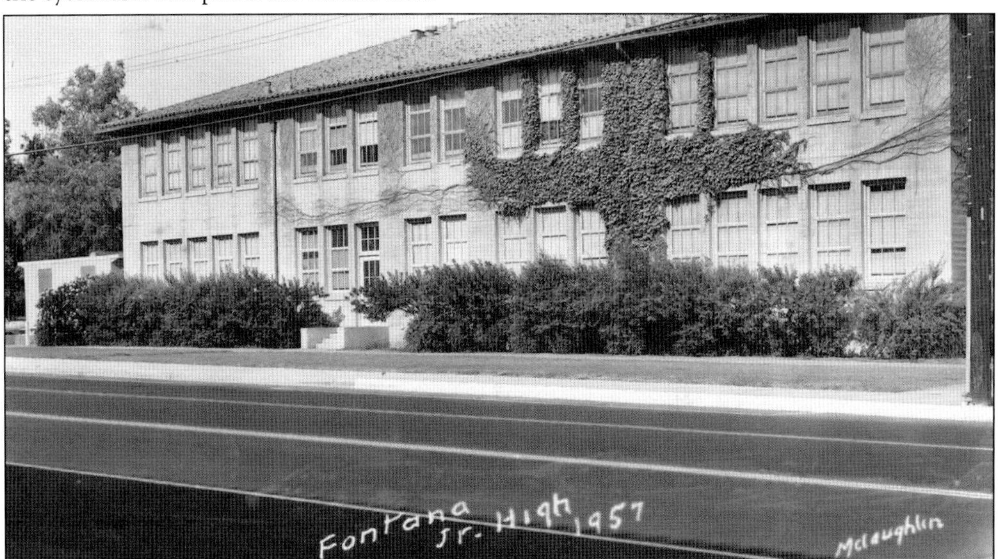

On March 9, 1931, it was announced that the second unit of the complex would be built to the north of the unit built in 1928. Dr. Merton E. Hill felt that the Fontana students should be taught in Fontana and not at Chaffey High in Ontario, as busing at that time cost $16,000 a year. Los Angeles architects Allison & Allison designed the structure, which is still certified by the State and in use today. The windows have been refurbished for more energy efficient use of the glass.

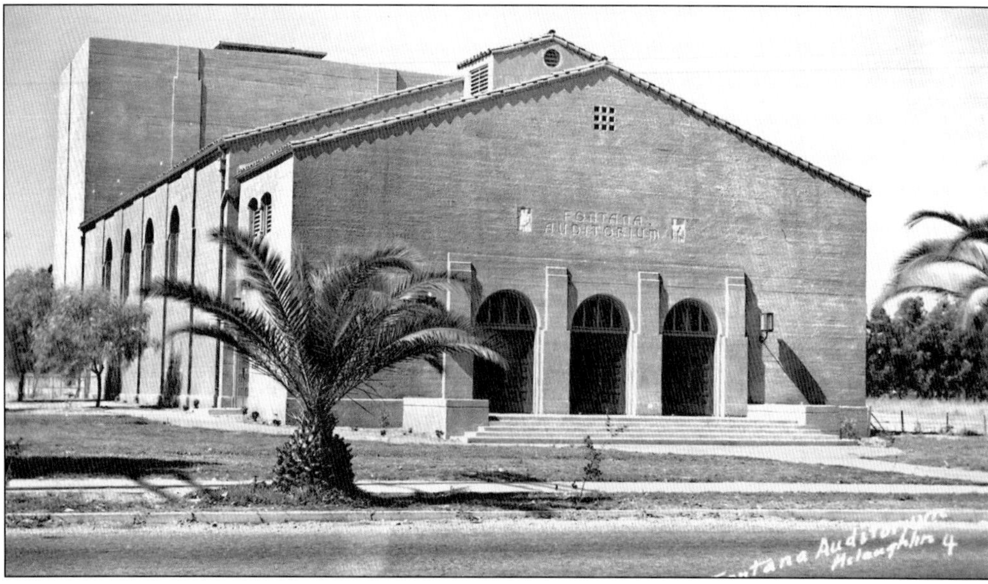

A school auditorium was needed, but letters had to be written to get officials in Washington to okay the project. The news arrived in September 1936 that the president had approved the federal grant of $32,727. F.A. Crawford, president of the school board, called a special session and decided that the architectural firm of Marsh-Smith-Powell of Los Angeles would design it. The walls were made with reinforced concrete to protect against earthquake. The dedication was on November 10, 1937. The fourth structure, which included the gymnasium and shop, was built in 1936 at a cost of $35,000. Also that year, the athletic field was constructed for $43,268 to make the complex the most modern in the valley.

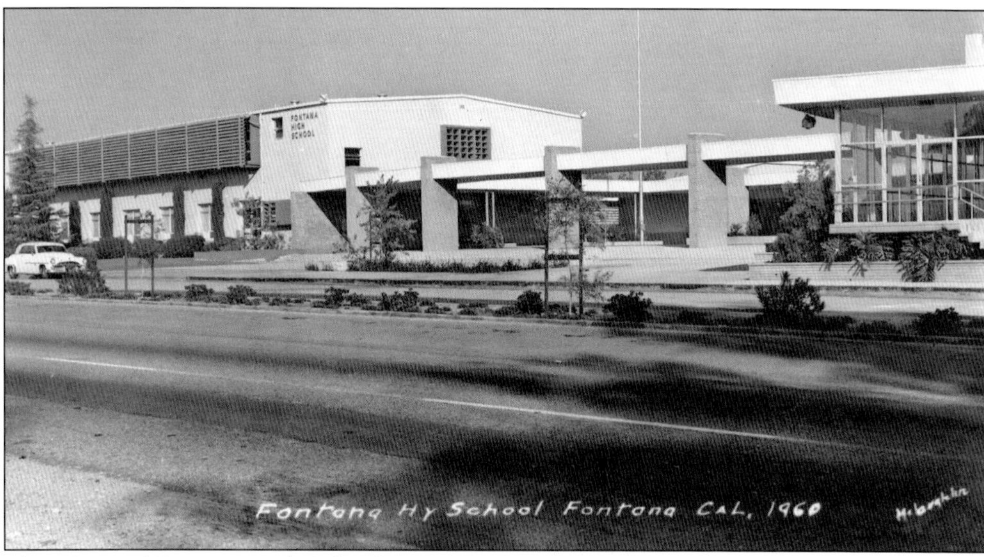

This photo of Fontana High School on Citrus Avenue was taken in 1960, eight years after it was built in 1952. The Chaffey High School District purchased the Fontana land for $31,260, to create Fontana High School, which opened on September 15, 1952. There were 724 members of the student body. In 1956, Fontana High School split from the Chaffey High School District and joined with other schools to form the Fontana Unified School District. The year 2005 is the 50th anniversary of the school.

Seven
Special Events

Some of the following items were of interest during the first years of development in the community:

1915	The "Fontana Girl" citrus label is created.
1923	The Fontana Days celebration begins.
1924	Lady Fontana, the egg-producing hen, dies.
1924	The Orange Show Packing Plant is built by the Fontana Farms Company.
1924	Gold is discovered in July in Lytle Creek.
1925	The Belle of Fontana breaks a record by producing 325 eggs.
1926	Robert Fulton's grandson visits his sister who lives in Fontana.
1926	The Queen of Fontana, a four-year champion egg-producing hen, dies.
1928	Prince Erick and the Princess of Denmark visit the ranch and are especially interested to see the poultry, cattle, rabbit and swine operations.
1940	The U.S. census identifies Fontana as the top agricultural community in the country

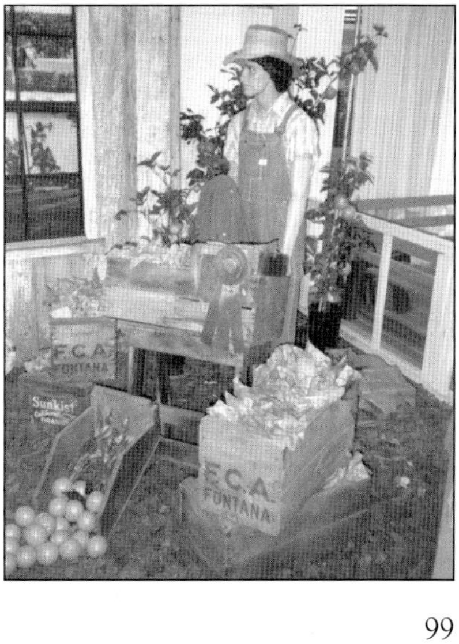

This Fontana Citrus Association display won a first place at the Los Angeles County Fair. All of the crates, stands, and boxes are originals.

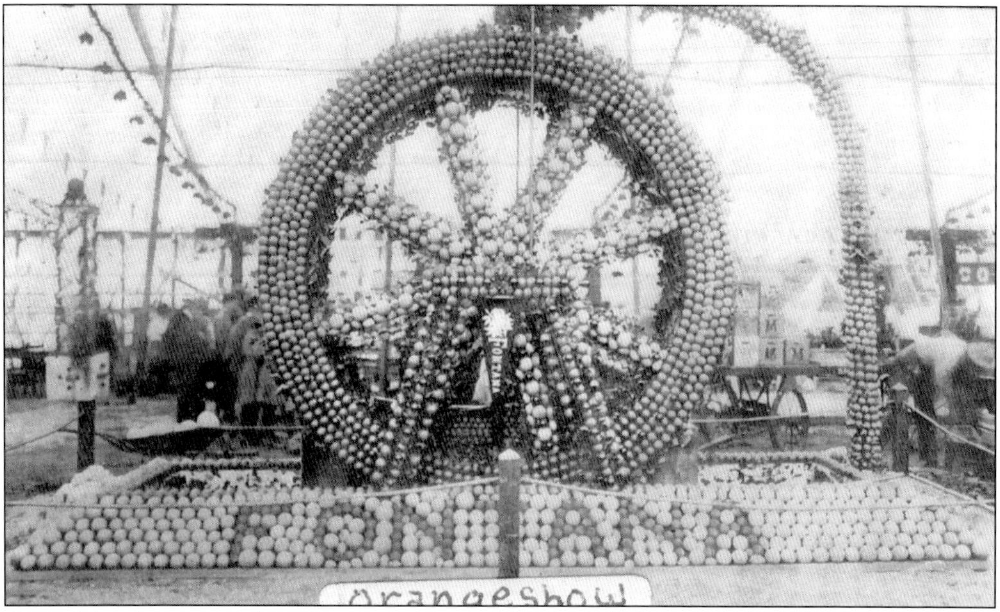

One of the first events that Fontana participated in was the San Bernardino National Orange Show. There used to be big parades of cars and floats that accompanied the show. In February 1930, the parade was a mile long with 500 cars and floats. The stage show of the event was attended by over a 1,000 persons. The displays of oranges were different for each city that raised the fruit, with prizes for the best display.

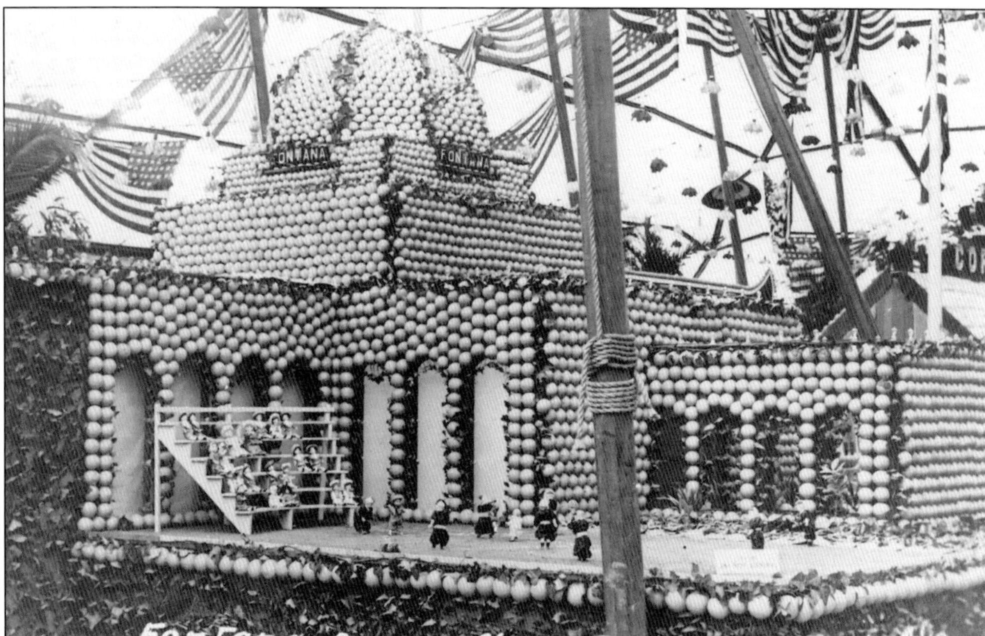

This display is of the Sierra-Seville Elementary School. It is entirely made out of oranges, lemons, and grapefruit. It took top honors in 1915. The displays were in big circus tents until new buildings were constructed.

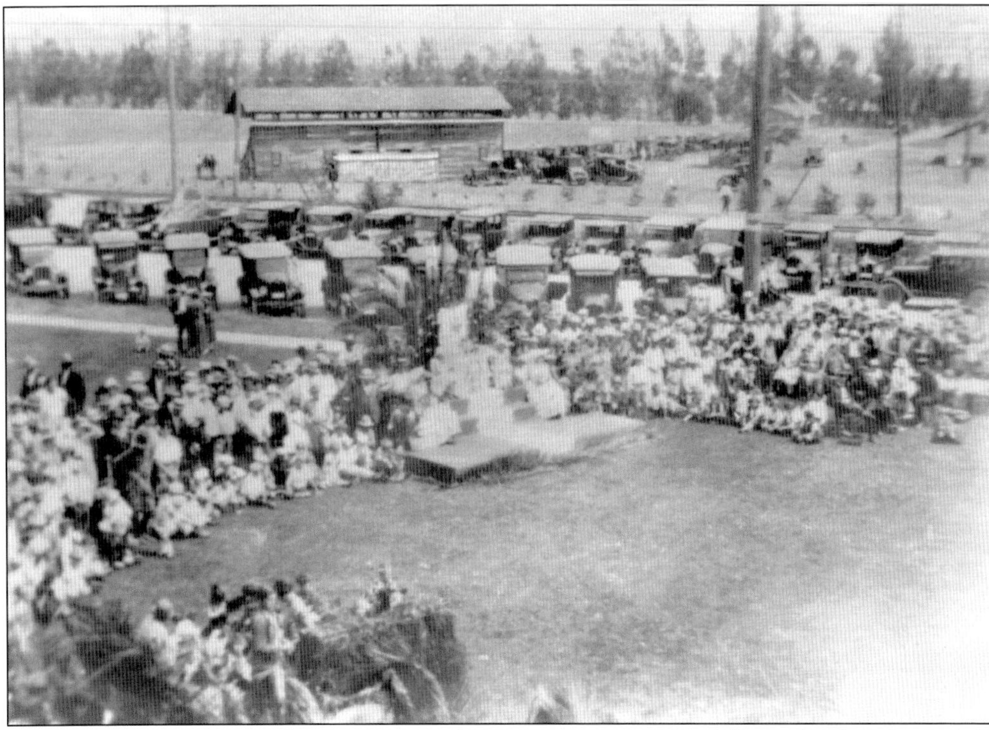

The first major festivity of Fontana started on June 7, 1923, to celebrate the founding of the city and has remained an influential event. The first celebration had a ballgame, electric illumination, fireworks, and a dance in the new garage. It has evolved become a four-day event with a parade, carnival, and car show. Fontana is home to the only "Hen derby" in the world.

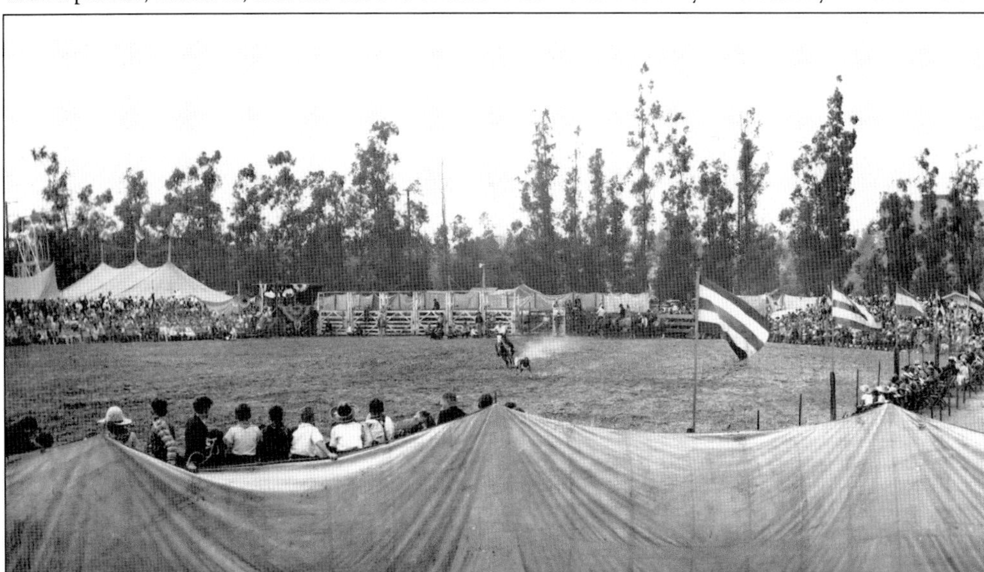

This is a view of the 1938 Fontana Days event on its 25th birthday and silver anniversary celebration. Emmy Lou Williams was the Silver Queen and adorned a special western outfit that has since been donated to the Fontana Historical Society.

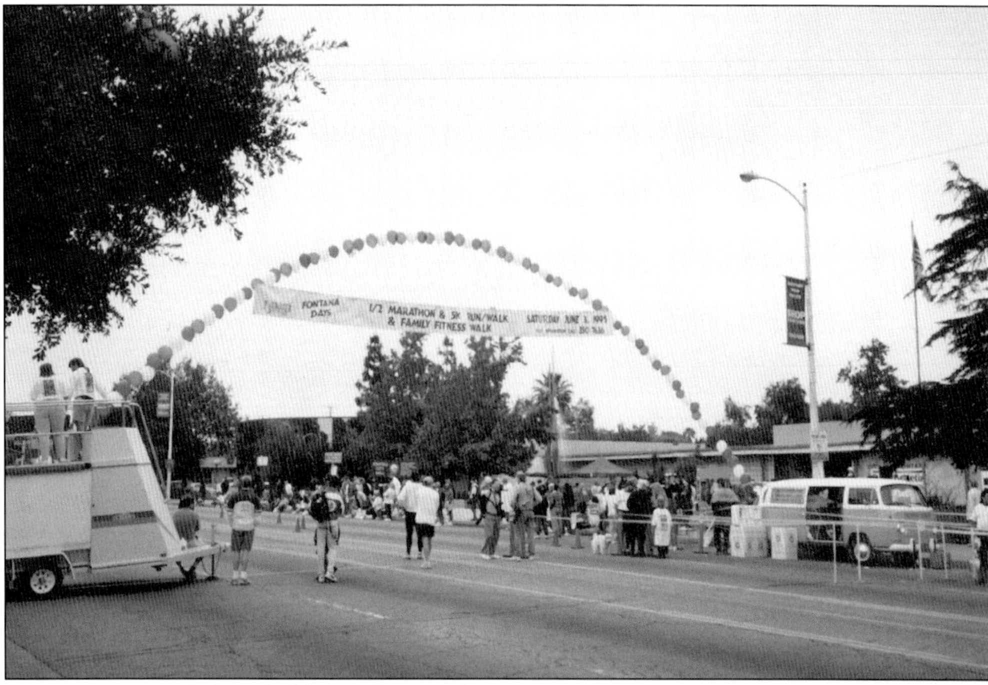

Fontana Days includes a half-marathon and a 5-K race. It starts in Lytle Creek and goes down the mountain to Fontana on Sierra Avenue to City Civic Center, where there are booths with all sorts of racing items and T-shirts for all participants. The balloons mark the finish line for the race. The rotary club offers breakfast to everyone involved.

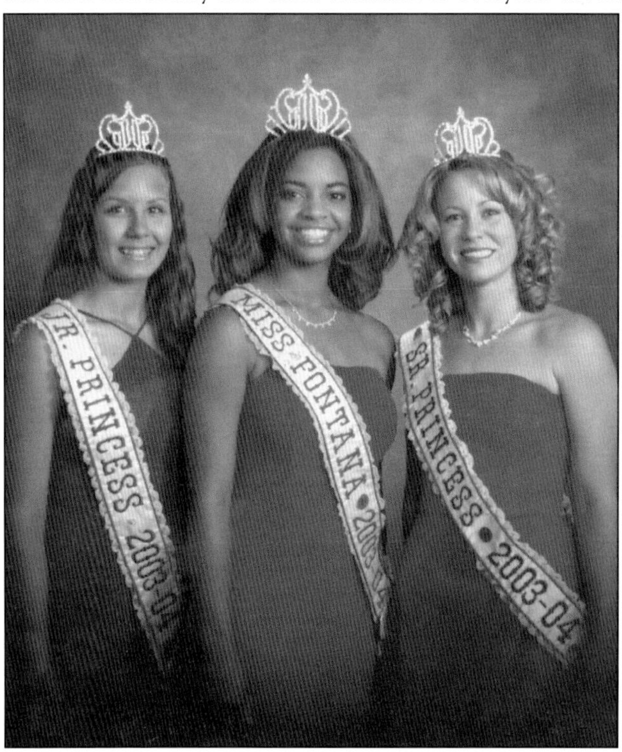

Every spring, Fontana holds a contest to decide the queen of Fontana Days and her court. Winners rule for one year and go to all city functions. The court for 2003–2004, from left to right, was Vanessa Gonzalez, 18, junior princess; Crystal Gray, 21, Miss Fontana; and Anna Krentzer, 21, senior princess. (Courtesy of Richard Burnett Photography.)

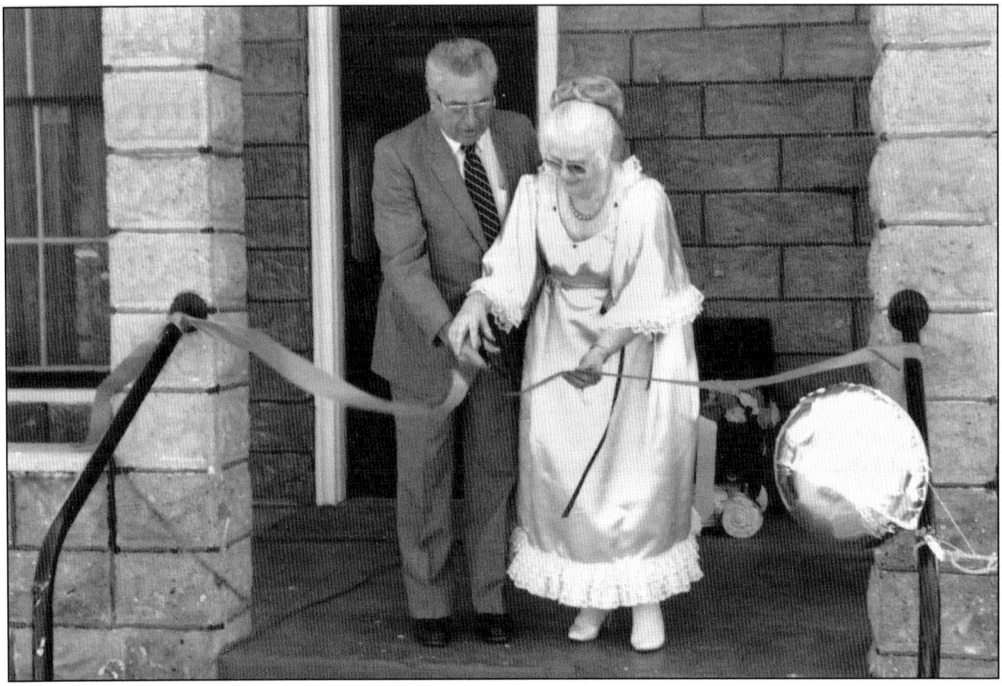

This is the dedication of the Fontana Farms Company, Camp No. 1 foreman's ranch house in 1978. Mayor Nat Simon and Mary Vagle, founder of the Fontana Historical Society, cut the opening ribbon. It took several years to restore the house as a museum. It has a barn and farm equipment with many displays in the house, barn, and on the grounds.

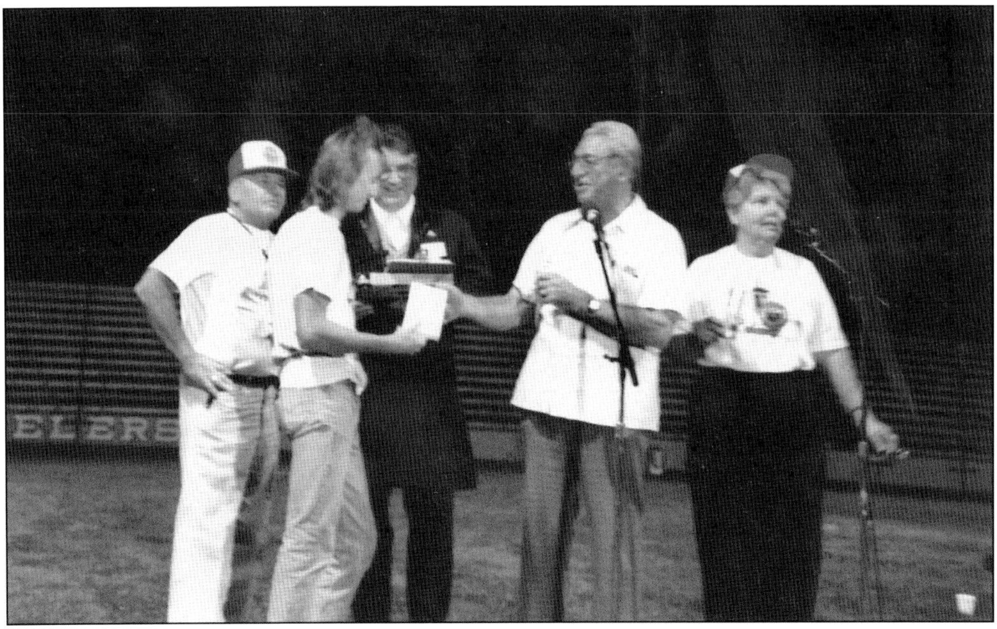

Depicted here is the 1988 celebration of the 75th Anniversary of Fontana that had a week of tours, a parade, a dance, and many other events. There was a real diamond contest with fireworks at the Fontana High School Stadium, the first in many years. The photo shows Mr. Zanella, who won the diamond, John Charles Anicic Jr., Mayor Nat Simon, and Pat (Alexander) Murray.

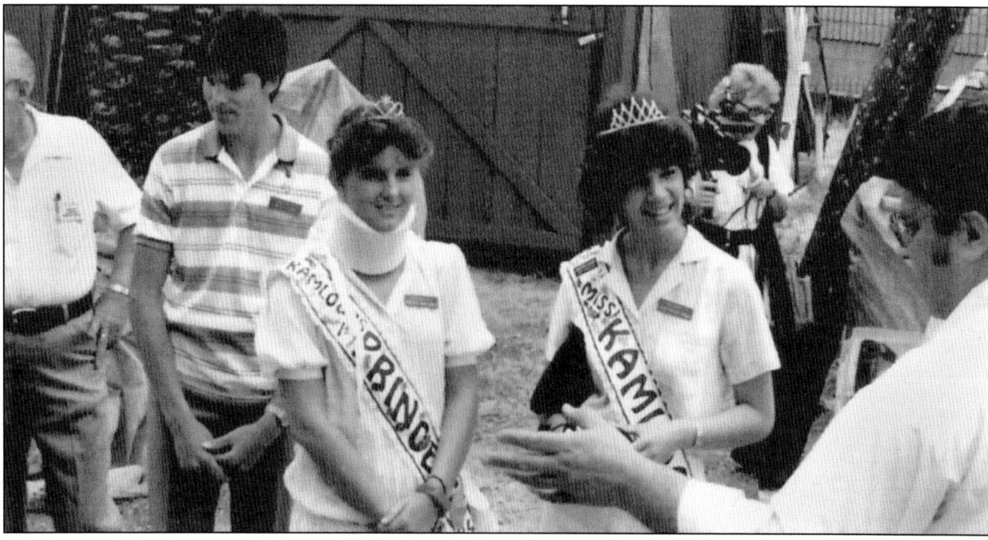

The city of Fontana is a sister city of Kamloops, British Columbia. The chamber of commerce has handled the visits over the years. It was started by A.B. Miller on December 6, 1914, and was incorporated in 1941. They were a driving force in the development of the city over the years. This B.C. group toured the Camp No. 1 ranch house.

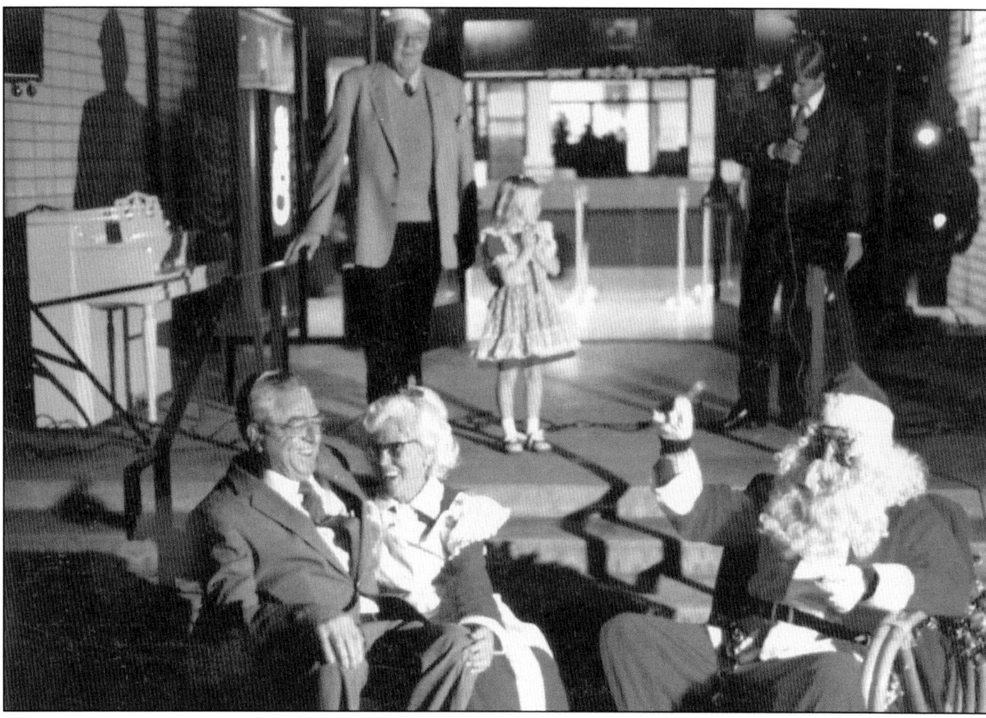

A few years ago at the Christmas parade and city-hall party, Santa and Mrs. Claus came to visit like they did each year. Pictured are Mayor Nat Simon with Mrs. and Mr. Tiegen. The city treasurer, Charles Koehler, is in the background. The tree lighting is also held on this night. The original Christmas tree that the Sierra-Seville students decorated is still alive, but is very large standing in the south city hall parking lot, so they now light a smaller one in front of city hall.

In 1952, Fontana had a visitor from the San Gabriel Mountains—a 500-pound brown bear that wandered into town during the night of June 23. Harry Bonner and his family were sleeping in their backyard to escape the summer, only to be awakened by the barking of their puppy. He spotted the bear prowling along the fence a few feet away, pulled his wife and son into the house, and called deputies at the police substation. They thought he had been drinking, but realized it wasn't a joke and sped to the area at 4:10 a.m. on Monday. The officers reached Merrill and Chantry, where they spotted the bear. Reserve officer William Poteen held a spotlight on the animal so that Deputy Art Linder could take aim. The bear was felled with one shot. The brown bear was in excellent shape. It was the second bear killed in three years.

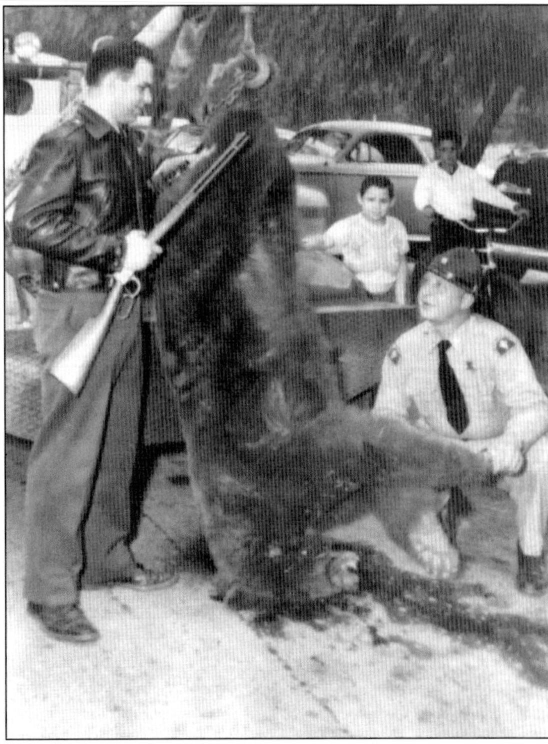

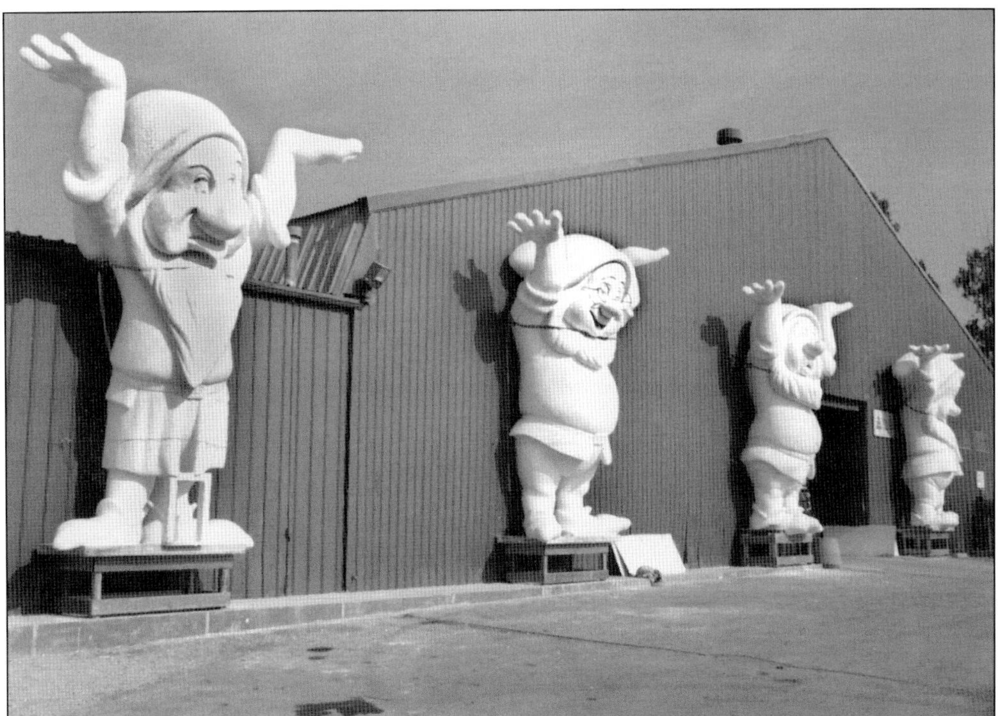

These dwarf statues for the Walt Disney Studio in Burbank are on the top ledge of the building and can be seen from the freeway. They were made in Fontana at the Dura Art Stone Company.

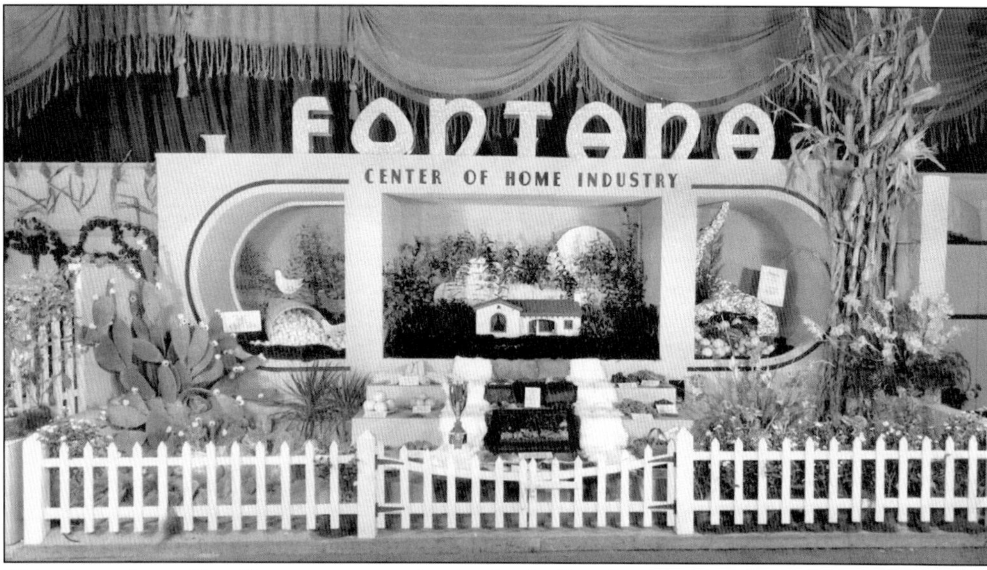

This photo shows Dowd's construction display for the Los Angeles County Fair in Pomona. The little house shown eventually found its way to his daughter's garden in Redlands. Dowd was a leading contractor in the Fontana area. (Courtesy of Eleanor Meyering.)

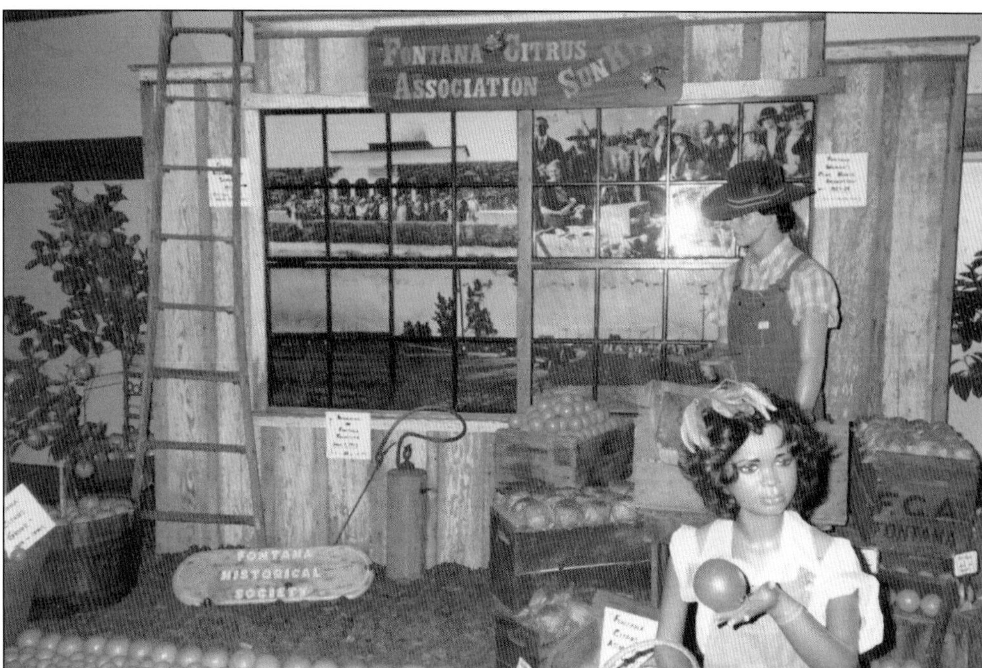

This display by the Fontana Historical Society won s few awards. The artifacts are from the citrus industry in Fontana. The photos on the wooden building model were from the restaurant in South Fontana that were saved by the Ingold Family and donated to the society. The display was also part of the Los Angeles County Fair.

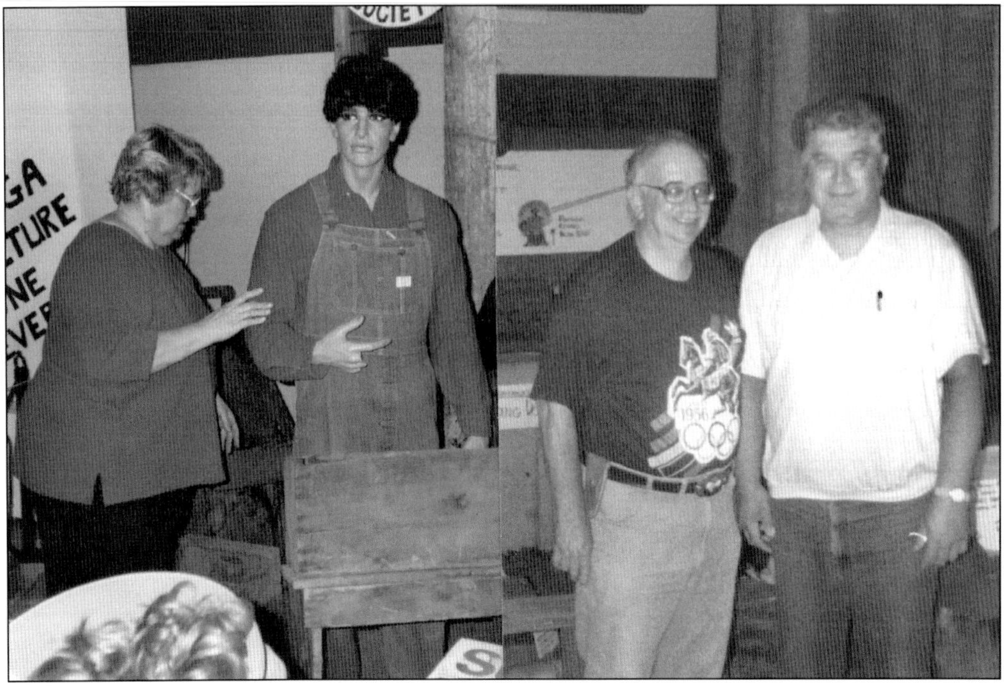

This grouping is of forever-remembered friends of the Fontana Historical Society (Sandy on the left and Ron Rezes standing next to the author). They worked on many displays at the Orange Show and the Los Angeles County Fair. Sandy was secretary for the society, and Ron had been president. They had been on many committees, were always willing to work, and were true volunteers that loved helping the community. They passed away a few years ago and are greatly missed.

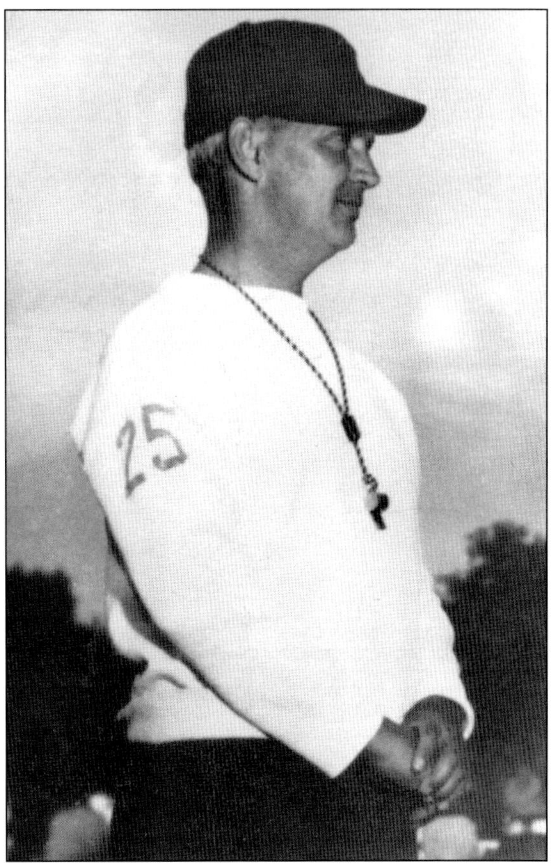

When the city was incorporated, it needed a recreational department. The only place with recreational items was the Miller Community Park, which had a pool and ball field. The tract office was in the park by this time. And it officially became the recreation office for the new City. The person who became director was a Mr. McDermott, who remained with the city for many years. He now has a park area named after him in the Village of Heritage.

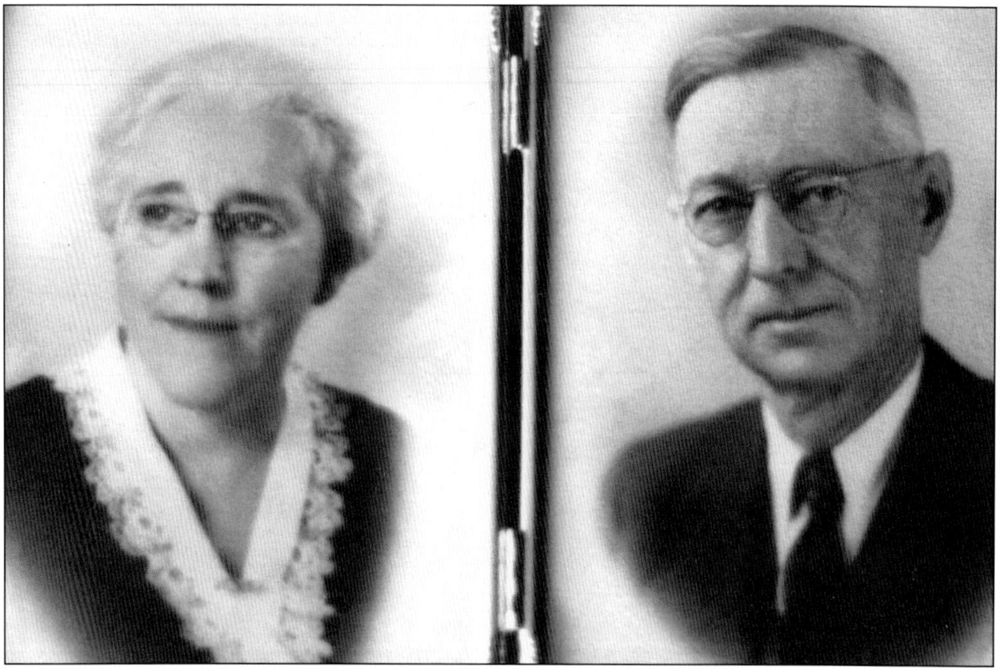

When A.B. Miller died, his right-hand man, Mr. Richard E. Boyle, took his place. He was born in Camp Point, Illinois, on July 15, 1876. He came to California as a young man and settled in Woodland, marrying Catherine S. Gwinn in Woodland in 1898. In 1921, Mr. Miller employed Mr. Boyle as superintendent and ran the Fontana Farms Company for years until Mr. Miller died. Mr. Boyle died on May 1, 1952.

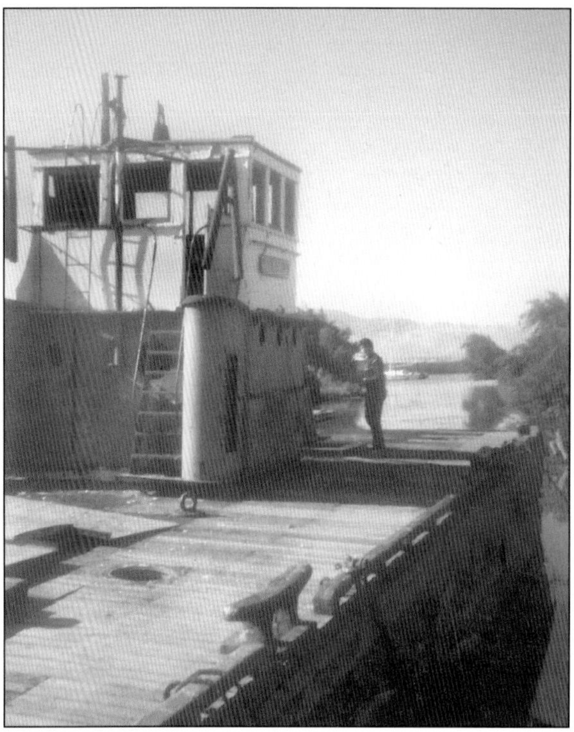

A.B. Miller and Swift owned the Montezuma Ranch. It was a cattle ranch with over 50,000 head cattle in the area around Bird's Landing, near the ranch. The store at Collinsville was built in 1852, and the men from the ranch would shop there. There was an old tug, now half-sunk that the author's son, John Charles Anicic III, climbed out on. He is seen at the front of the tug.

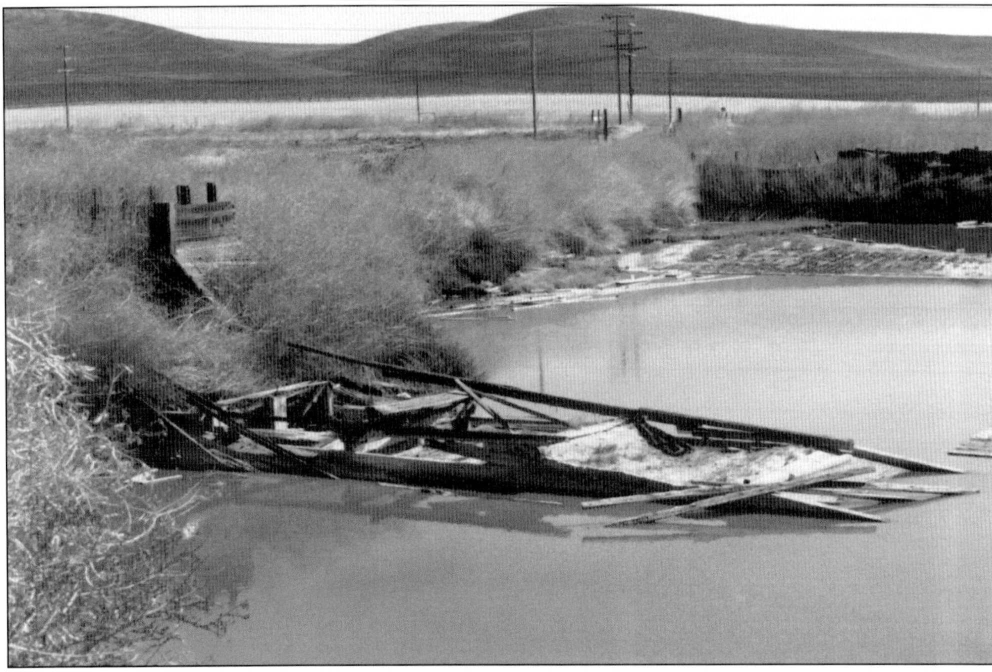

The Montezuma Ranch had barns, corrals, and silos for grain. The silos are the only items still in good shape. The ranch used to ship cattle to market in San Francisco by barges like the one in this photo. The walls of these channels are falling down and the wood that held them up has rotted.

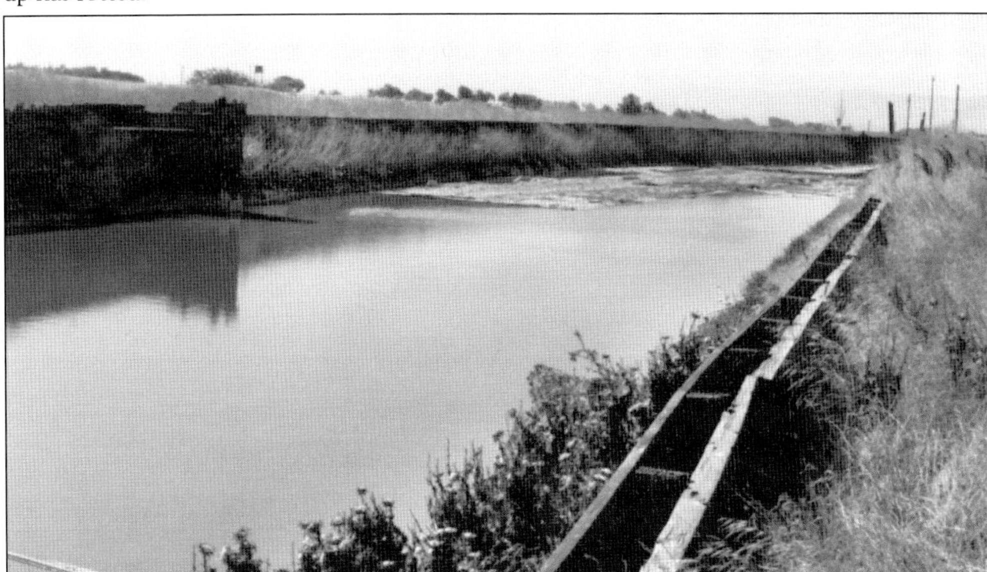

The channel seen here went to the Delta that used to be full of barges and tug boats. Now there is nothing but birds and water plants. After Mr. Richard Boyle closed the ranch, it was sold to the State of California as a bird sanctuary. During the Depression, Mr. Swift left the ranch to go back to Chicago so he wouldn't lose his company there. He left Mr. Miller as the sole owner after the Depression. The 50,000 to 70,000 head of cattle were part of the largest operation in California and the country at the time. It was even larger than the King Ranch in Texas.

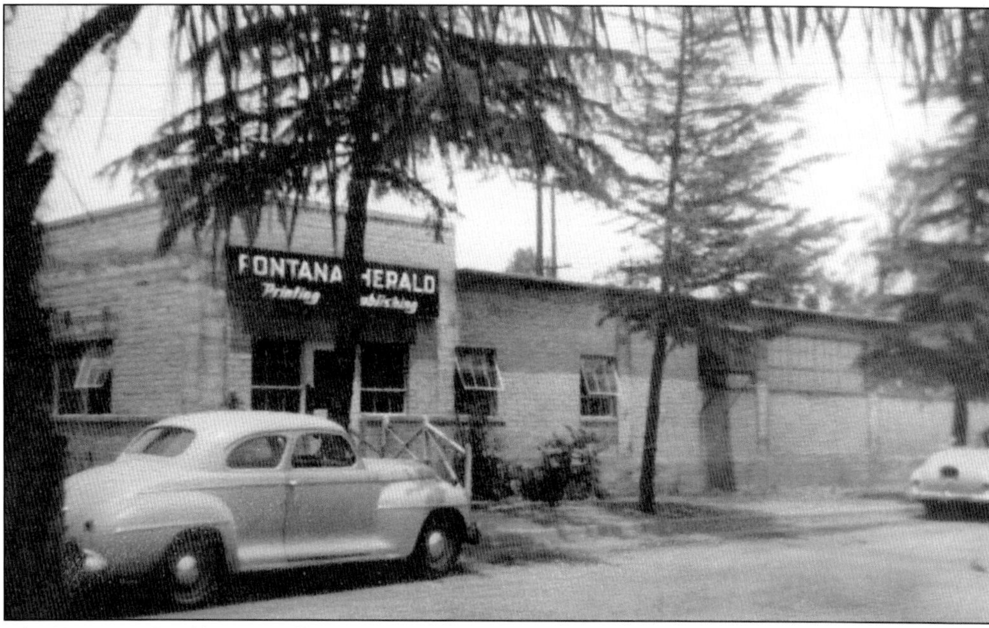

The *Fontana Herald-News* office on Spring Street was the first and only paper in Fontana. The trees seen on the outside are three pines called the "Three Generals" that were planted many years ago. Only one remains. There was also a monument to armed servicemen from Fontana who lost their lives. What happened to the monument is unknown at this time. The newspaper building was built to hold a second story, which was never built. The building is gone now and will be the home to the future library.

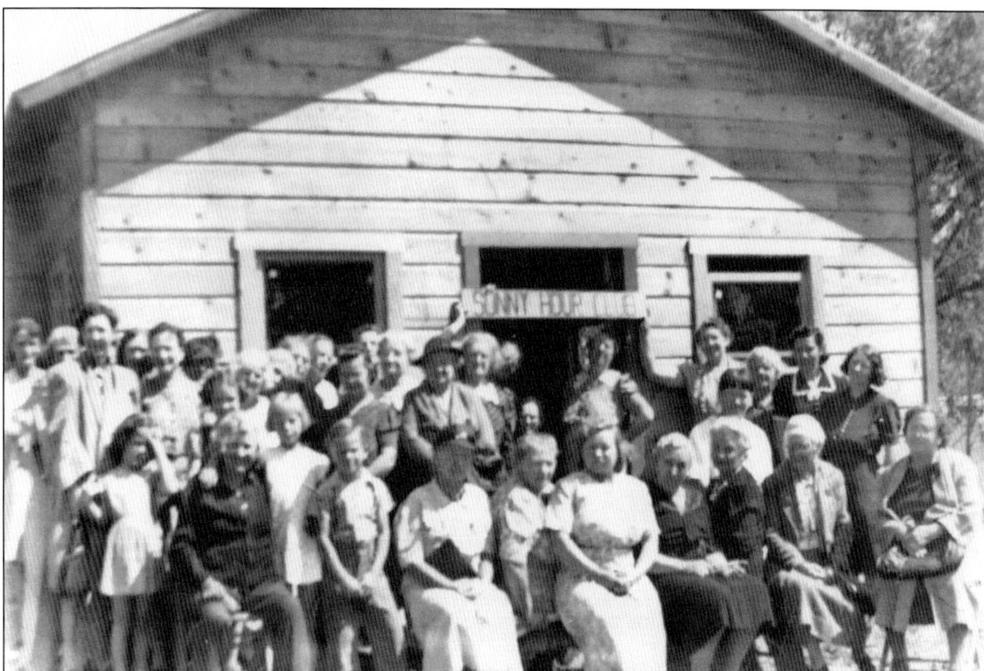

The Sunny Hour Club House was on Boyle Street below the I-10 Freeway. It was a gathering place for ladies in the area. When group membership waned, the building was sold.

This is a shot of the monument to the 75th anniversary of Fontana by a local boy scout Adam Weitzel. He built it as a project for Eagle rank in scouting out of rock from Grapeland and the site of the Scott residence. The plaque reads, "Dedicated June 7, 1988 by Adam Weitzel, Eagle Scout. Fontana 75th Anniversary 1913–1988. Stones gathered from Grapeland—an original home site of Fontana."

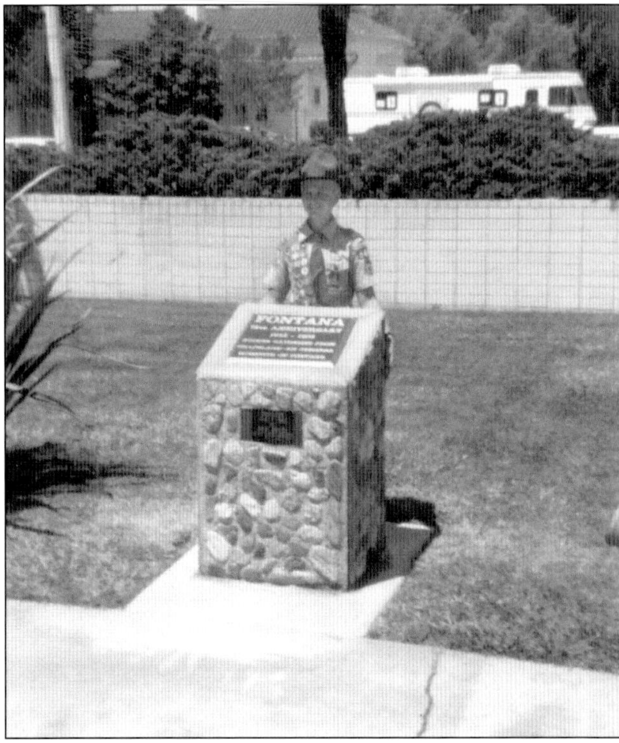

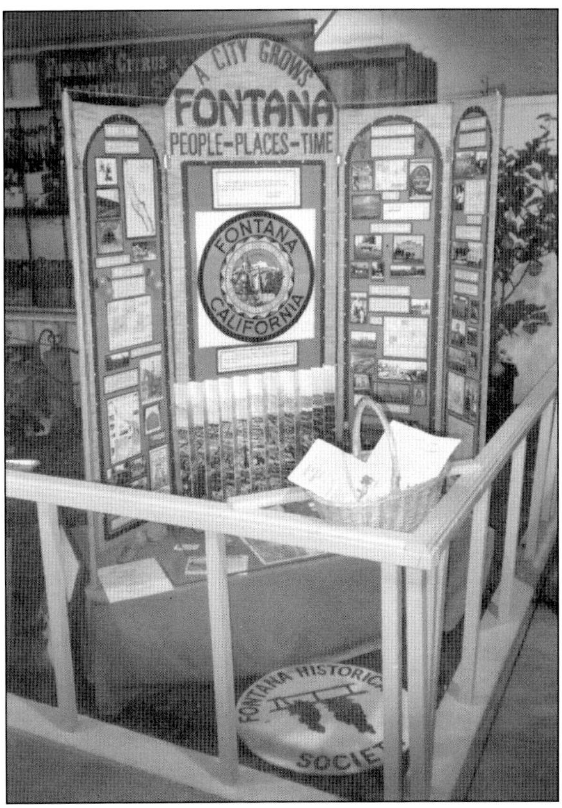

Fontana has very dedicated teachers who help students ready their entries in the yearly History Day contest, and many of them won at state and national contests. One year the display was of Fontana and donated to the historical society. It was displayed at the Los Angeles County Fair, as well as other places. The district is one of the best in the valley in terms of their support of the History Day Contest.

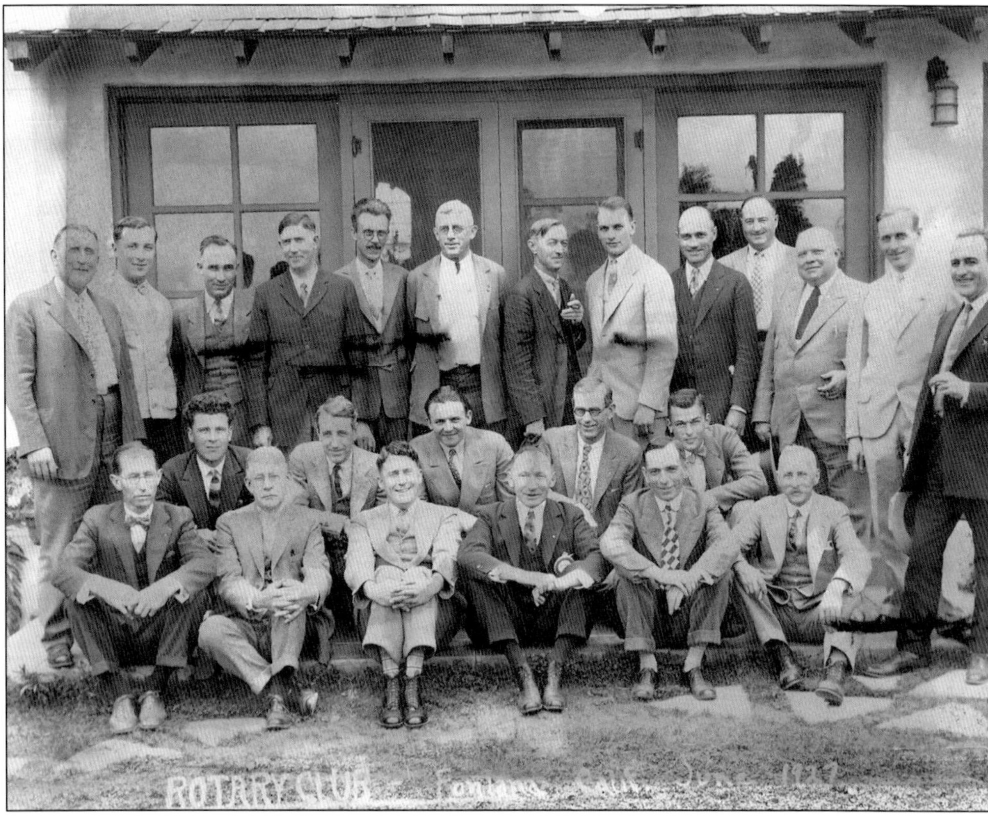

This is an image of the Fontana Rotary Club, organized in 1926, in front of the Fontana Inn. The club is now 89 years old. Pictured, from left to right, are (front row) Frank F. Fanning, Phil Deicker, David Tilt, Douglas Whitehall, Ed Snyder, Bill Caldwell, Cornelius de Bakcsy, George Calkins, Bill Smith, Roland Cox, and Dr. Myron Antel; (back row) an unidentified general contractor, Harry C. Crosley, Charlie Woods, Frank Williams, E.P. Bradbury, Phil Hasbrouck, Richard E. Boyle, Duff Hansen, Dr. P.C. Guyselman, Ed Hauser, Pinky Shaw, Harry Barbee, and Ed Reese. William J. Janka donated this 1927 photo.

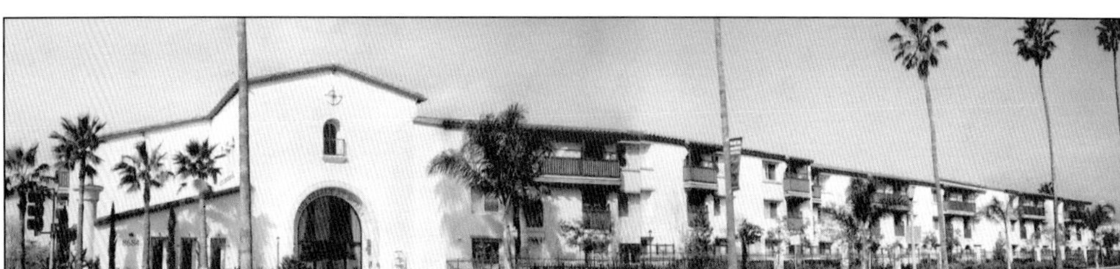

The first unit of the downtown senior center housing was finished in 2004. Two more units are under construction.

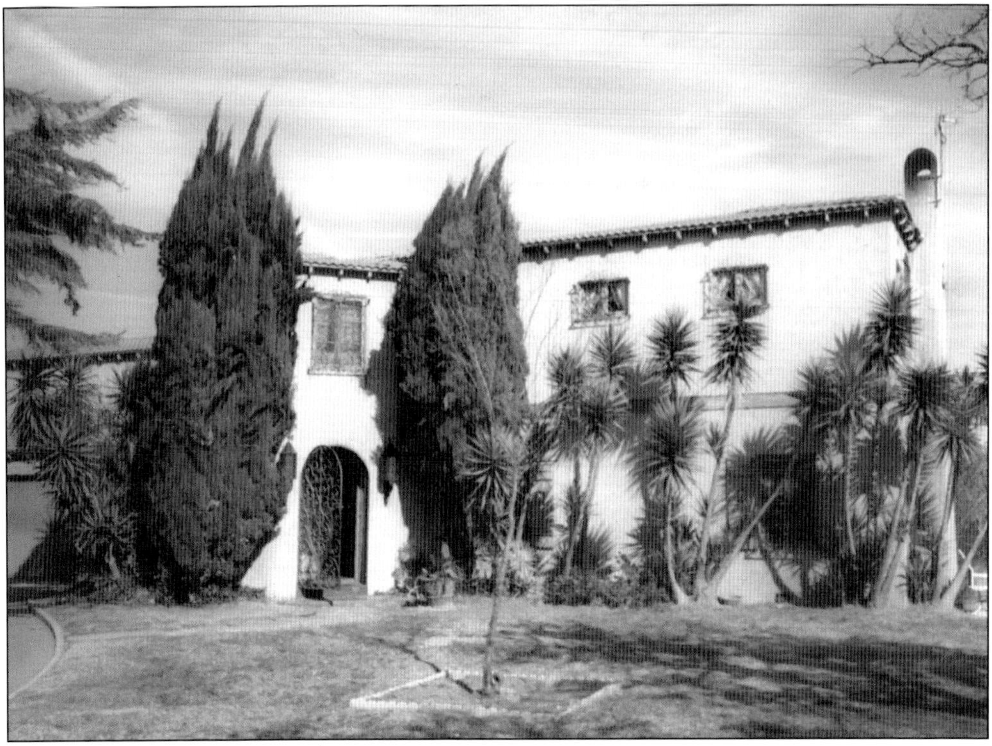

The name of this structure is the "Al Capone" house. It is close to the Santa Fe Railroad tracks, south and east of Palmetto. The section pictured is the main entrance, with the living room to the lower right and the master bedroom/bath on the second floor. The dining room is in the back with French doors. The section to the left is a room over the garage area, as well as a kitchen. There are two chimneys in the house: one for the living room and another in the center of the house. The one in the center is not a working chimney. All rooms on the first floor have exits, and all upstairs rooms have secret exits.

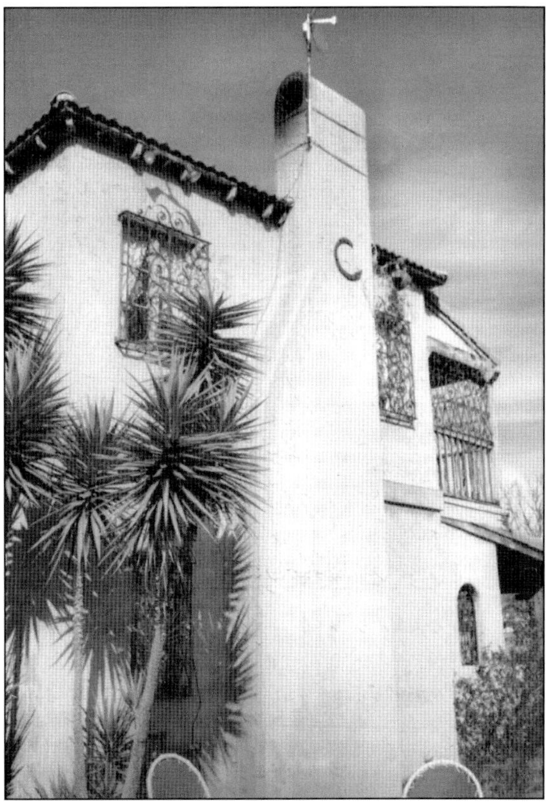

The south chimney for the living room has a "C" on the outside. There is no way anyone can prove that Al Capone was ever there, since he only came to California a few times, but the house was owned by close friends of his in Chicago who did not have a "C" in their names.

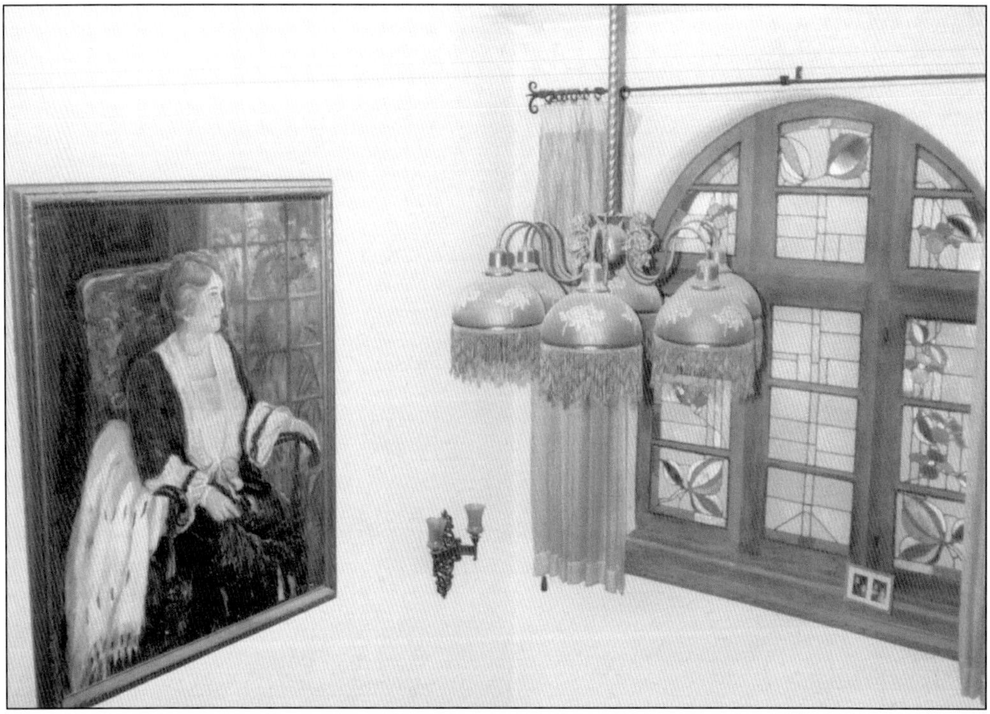

The Al Capone House has a few other mysteries. One of them is the lady in the painting that hangs in the staircase; another is the chandelier. Both items have remained in the house through the years. The windows are also original.

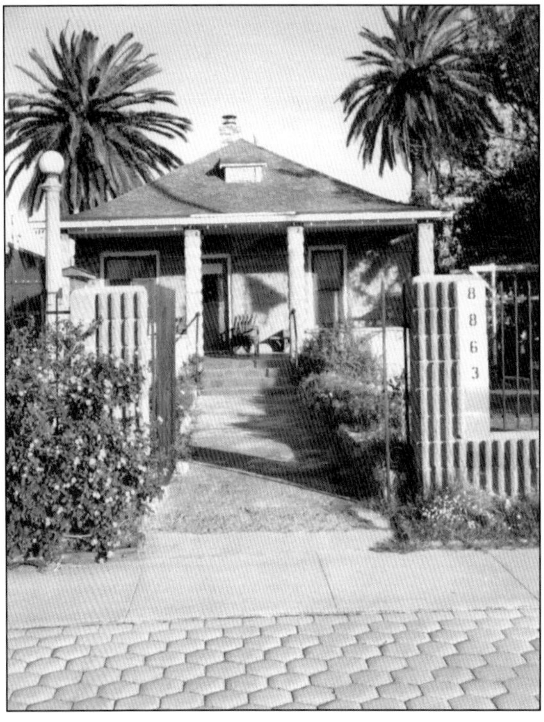

The Fontana Farms Company Camp No. 1 foreman's ranch house at 8863 Pepper Street is Fontana's house museum. The palm trees are from the original plantings around the house. The lamppost is one of three left from when electricity came to Fontana in the 1920s. The Fontana Lions Club donated the block walls and the wrought-iron fencing was from many businesses in Fontana, as well as the cement for the mortar. The cement for the block walls and the driveway and sidewalks was from 4th Street Cement and Rock. The farm equipment came from all over Fontana. The house is mostly original. The grounds in the 1940s had fountains and waterfalls and fishponds on the south side of the house. The Camp No. 1 site derived from the work of the city, citizens of Fontana, and the Conservation Corps of California so the house could open to the public.

This is a 1924 photo of the Olson family. Mr. James Olson was the manager of Camp No. 1 from its beginnings until the 1940s when it closed. He lived in the house with his wife and daughter Lillian. This photo was taken on the south side of the house. The north door was probably used as an office door for the workers to receive their pay.

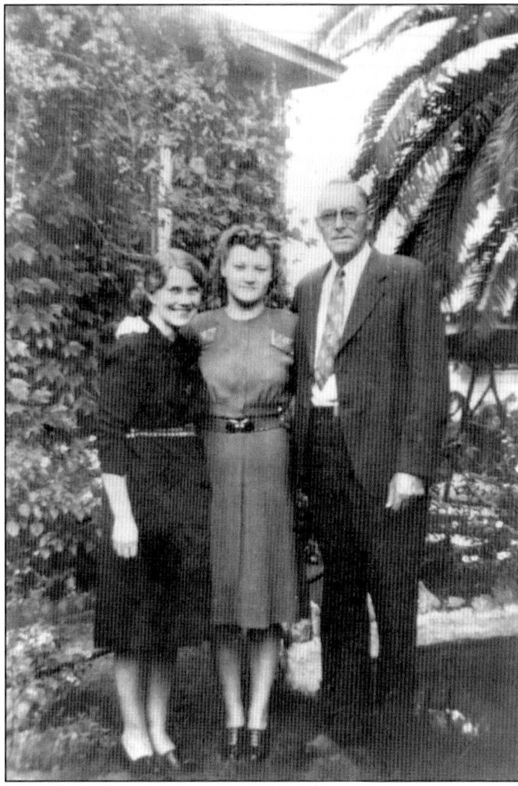

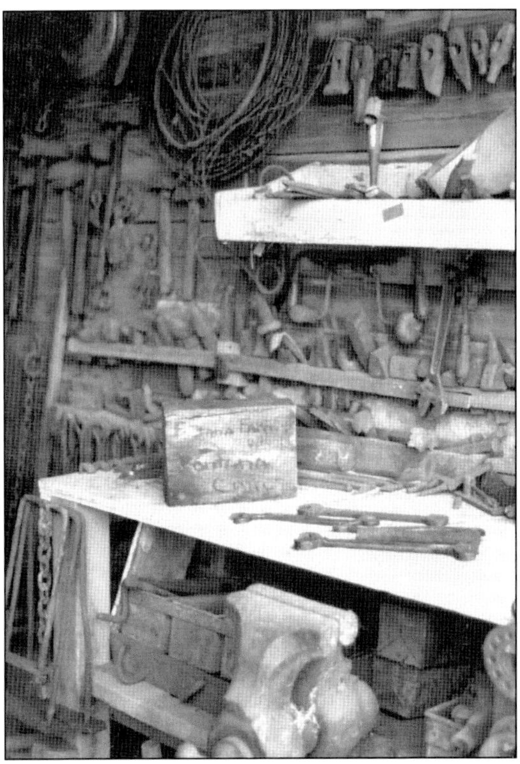

The blacksmith shop was in the barn that was brought piece by piece from Bloomington. It was donated by the Gus Polopolus family along with the trucks, equipment, and much more. In June 1981, the Fontana High School carpentry class dug and formed the concrete floor, then put up the lower frame walls before school was let out for the year. The Fontana Swim Club Fathers finished the framing and put the metal roof back on. Fontana firemen, while fighting a fire, found the blacksmith shop on Slover, in South Fontana.

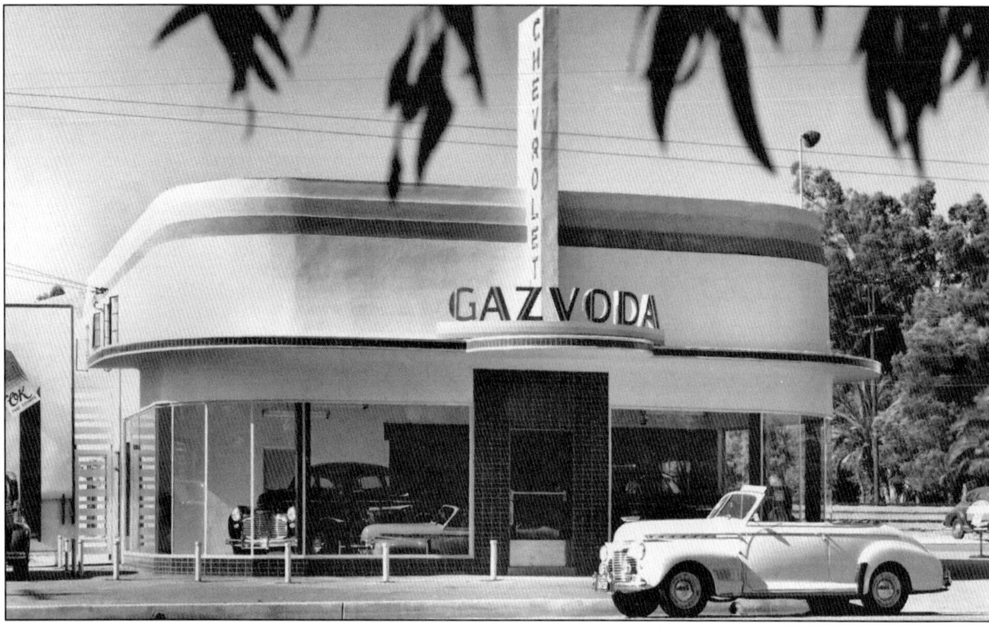

The Spring residence was on the northwest corner of Sierra and Foothill in the 1920s and 1930s. In the 1940s, they sold the corner to Rudy Gazvoda to build a Chevrolet agency and car repair shop and the Spring house and garage were moved to the north. The new building was two stories, so Rudy and his wife could live upstairs with an entrance to Sierra Avenue. It was a modern building that survived for years after Rudy died. It was later sold to build new food places and make the corner more accessible to cars. (Courtesy of Eleanor Meyering.)

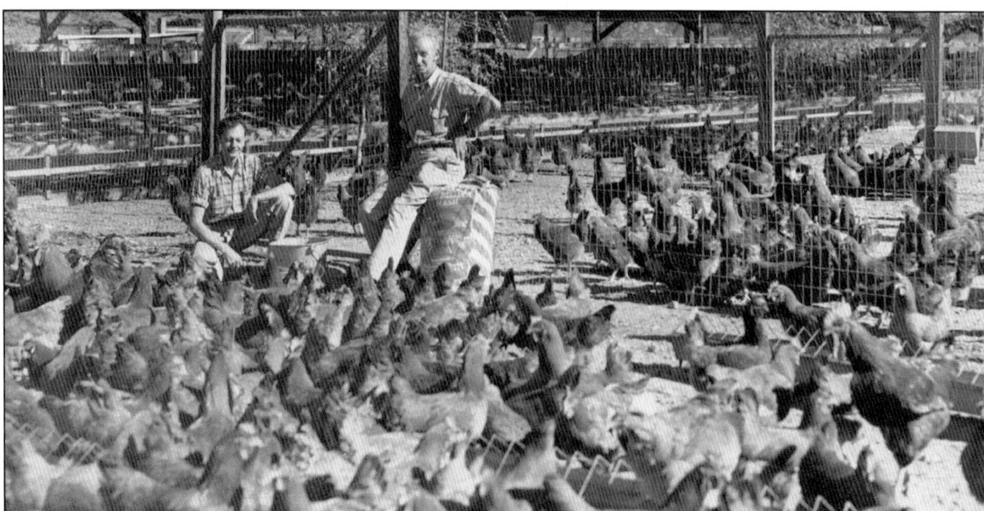

This is a photo of the chickens from the Austin Hatchery on Palmetto Avenue, run by Capt. L.A. Austin. He was retired and living in Fontana after coming to the U.S. from India, where he was an officer. He worked as a consultant on the movie *Gunga Din*, since he lived in India during the time period covered in the movie. He joined the army at age 14 and was part of the Indian 84th Punjabis regiment that fought in World War I, an outfit that was part of the 8th Brahmins, a fighting group founded in the 1770s. (Courtesy of L.A. Austin's daughter.)

Eight

Ailea, San Sevaine, Declez, Declezville, and South Fontana 1888–Present

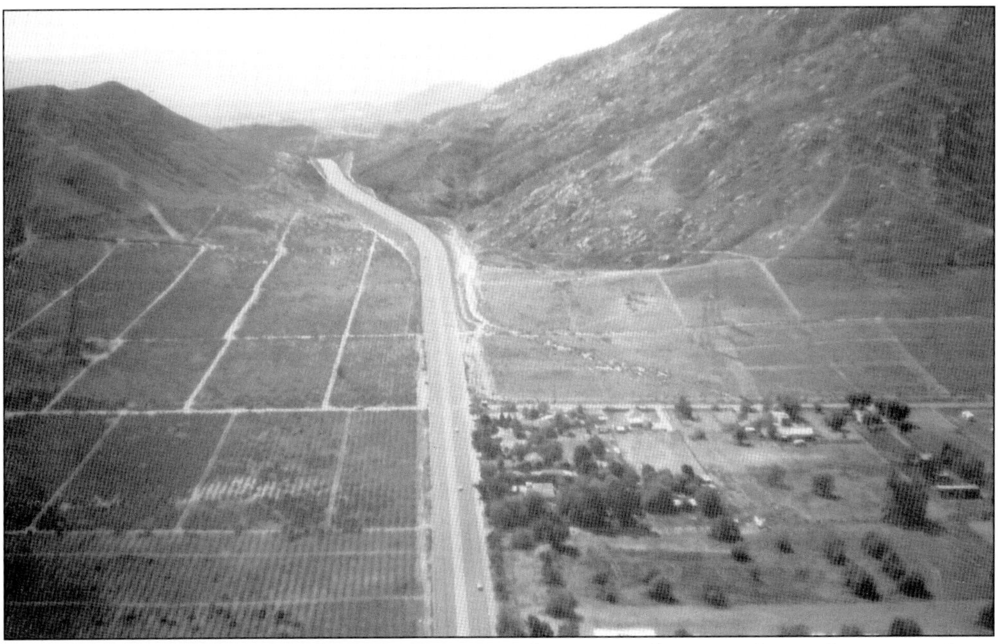

The area now known as South Fontana was much more in the way of a settlement, with its railroad stops along the Southern Pacific Railroad Tracks called Ailea and San Sevaine. Declez was also a railroad stop with another settlement a mile south on a spur line called Declezville, a quarry town. Both of these towns were named for William Declez, who had owned the quarry and settled the area years before. One of the earliest Los Angeles skyscrapers, the Brison block at 3rd and Spring, was of the quarry rock found in Declez. Other structures as far as San Francisco and many public buildings and residents were also built with the material. In 1910, cement replaced rock, which is now used only for trim. By 1911, the Southern Pacific became owners of the Declezville Quarry, who used the quarry in 1912 for the San Pedro Breakwater and Santa Monica Wharf. In 1938, after floods and the ocean wore down the breakwater, the quarry was reopened, but it is not being used today.

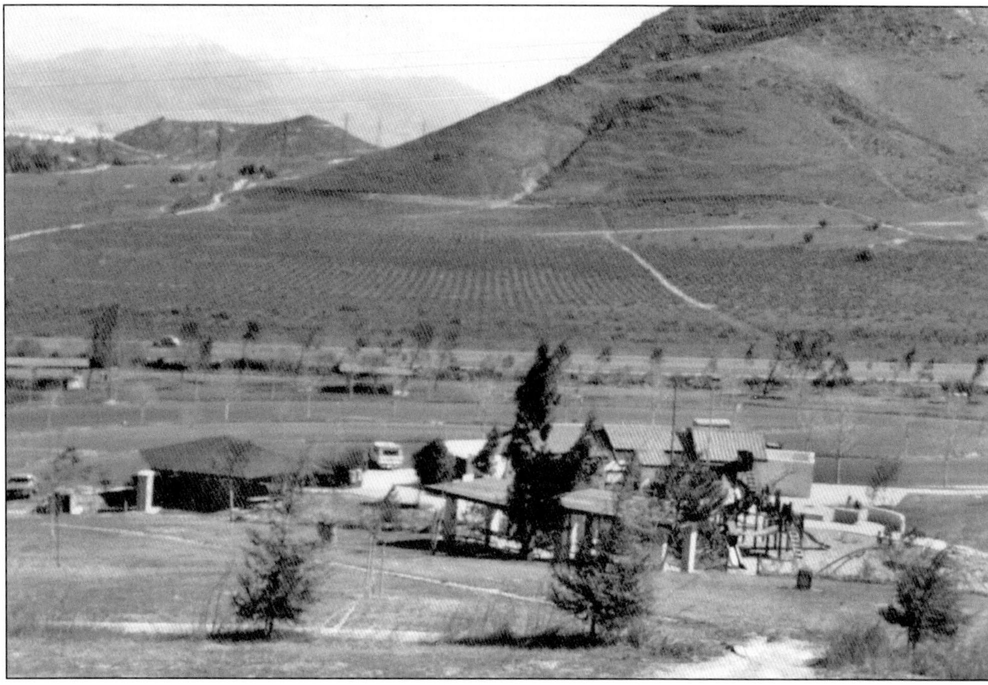

This is an aerial view of a section of South Fontana with Sierra Avenue going over the Jurupa Hills to Riverside County. The Santa Fe Winery and Ranch is over the hill to the left. The mountaintop to the right is part of the Mount Jurupa range. The area to the right of Sierra Avenue was the Family Vineyards. The vineyards of the Tudor Family have become the Martin Tudor Regional Park. This view is looking east.

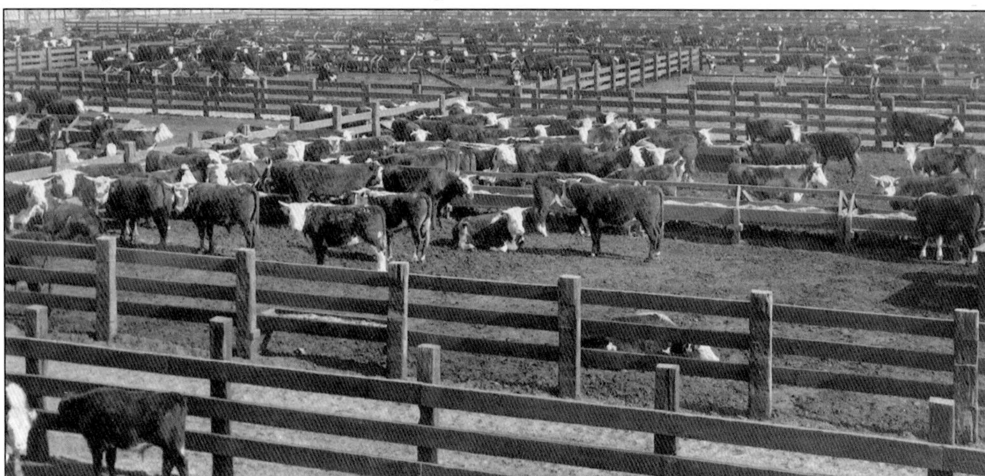

The B.B. Company was incorporated in 1929 in Declez and called at that time "Baby Beef." There were over 2,500 cattle and 5,000 sheep. L.F. Swift of Chicago and A.B. Miller of Fontana owned it. In 1932, Miller acquired all of B.B. Company, which now owns 14,000 acres in Collinsville, California and 385 acres near Chino, California, with more than 14,000 total head of cattle. After the company was sold, Mr. Boyle also sold the Collinsville Ranch to the State of California as a bird sanctuary, which it still is today. (Photo courtesy of Judith Boyle McOmie.)

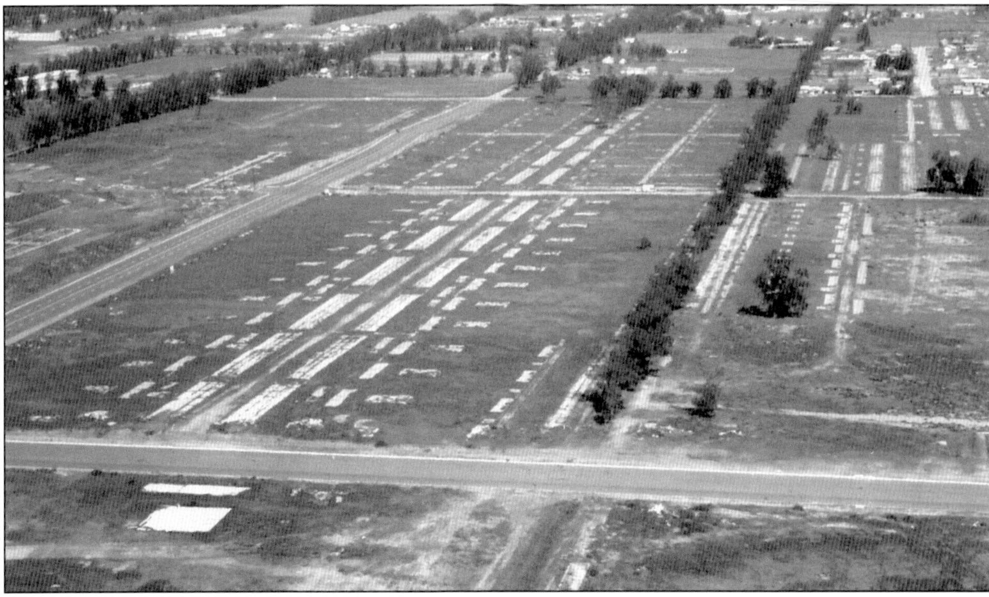

The Fontana Farms Company hog ranch was started in Declez in 1920. In 1921, the company signed a contract with the City of Los Angeles for the wet garbage that was shipped to Declez in special rail cars and dumped into the pens directly. The foreman's office and camp was at the corner of Slover and Live Oak Avenues and was known as the Hoffman Camp. In 1922, Mr. William Ezekiel Minner sold his livestock business in Colorado and shipped his Poland and Duroc swine to the Fontana Farms Company for breeding purposes. In 1924, A.B. Miller hired Mr. Minner to be superintendent of the Diamond Bar Hog Ranch. A short time later he became superintendent of the Declez and Wade Hog Ranches. He stayed with the company until he died in 1948 at the age of 69. The hog ranch photo only shows the pads of the pens and rail lines. They are mostly gone now due to development.

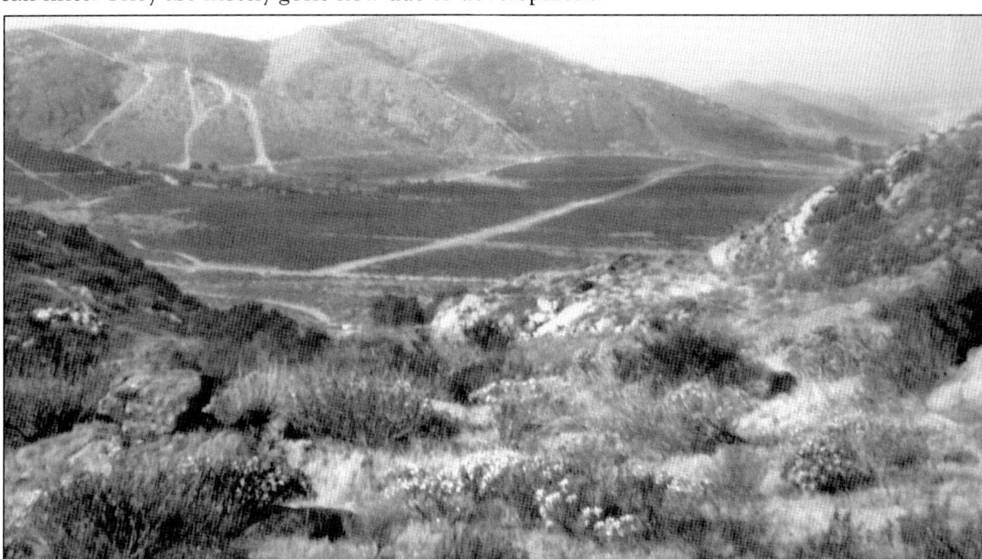

This view of the Declez Valley covered in vineyards looks east from the top of Declez Quarry, where there was a beautiful valley ridge with Indian signs all around. The spot is now a water tank, and the valley below a housing tract.

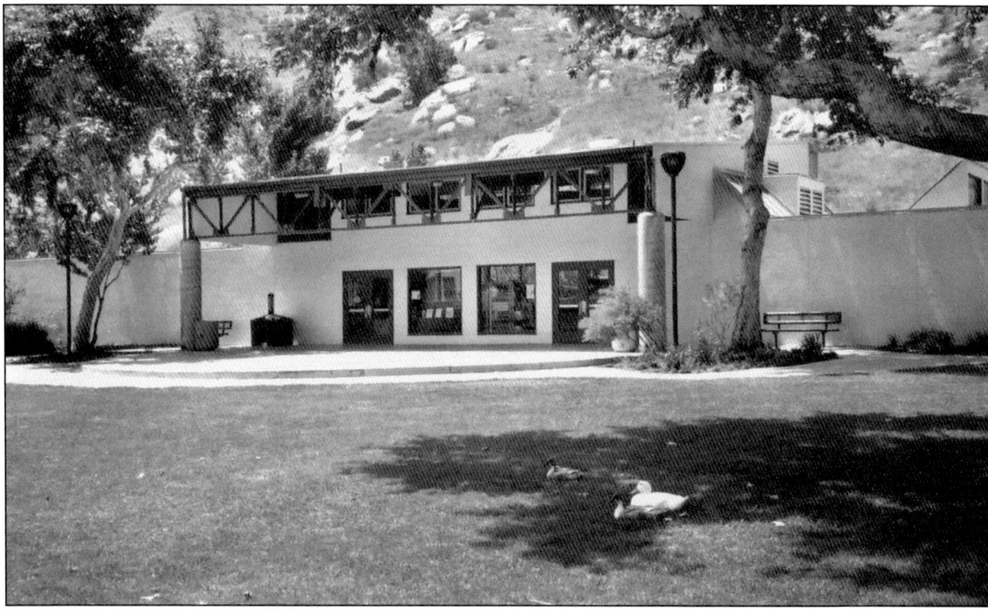

The Mary Vagle Science and Nature Center has a wide range of environmental education activities, which include a reptile viewing area, displays, diorama, and a nature classroom. After school there was a science adventure club as well as a summer science day camp with programs and classes on the environment. Many volunteers help run the center, which is on South Cypress at the foot of the Jurupa Mountains.

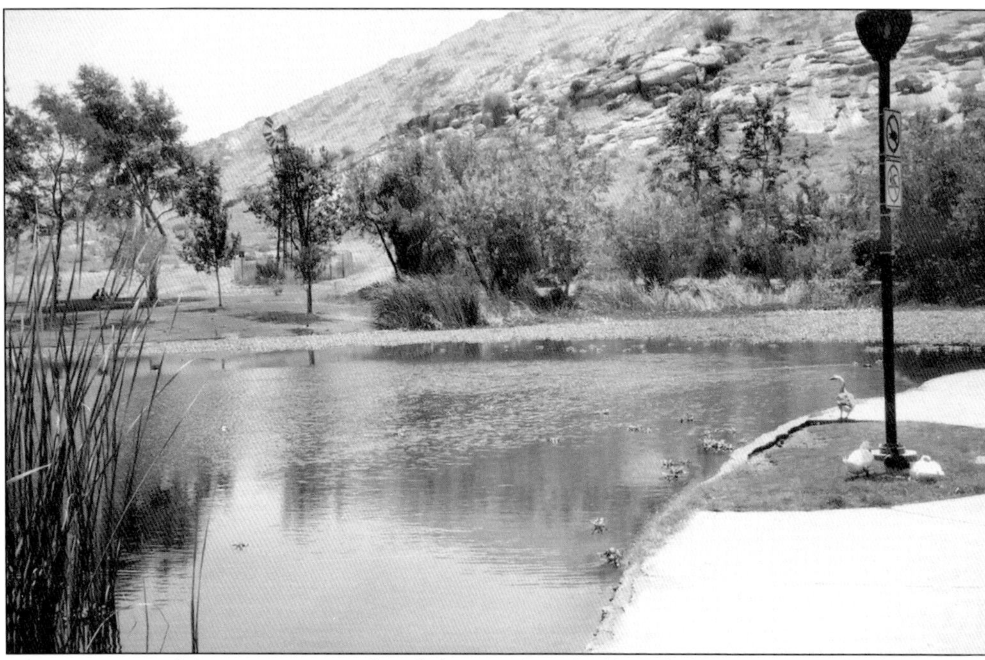

This is a view of the one-acre pond and three miles of self-guided hiking trails (and the ninth significance petroglyph site in the State of California). Hawks, rabbits, deer, rattlesnakes, coyote, and bobcats thrive in this protected habitat. The windmill and winery is at the foot of the foot of the rock.

The La Vesu residence at the foot of the Declez Quarry is now gone due to development of Southridge. The La Vesu family acquired land and planted vineyards. There were two quarries in Declezville; the main one and the old family quarry on the border of Riverside County and San Bernardino County. It sits on the north (facing) side of the mountain at the canyon of Declezville. The workings of the 1888 period are still visible.

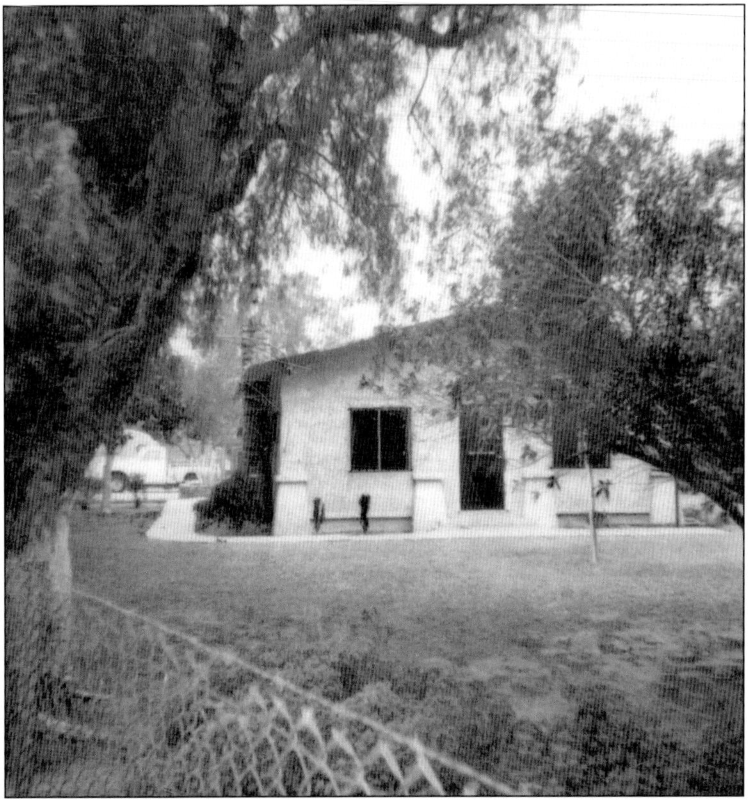

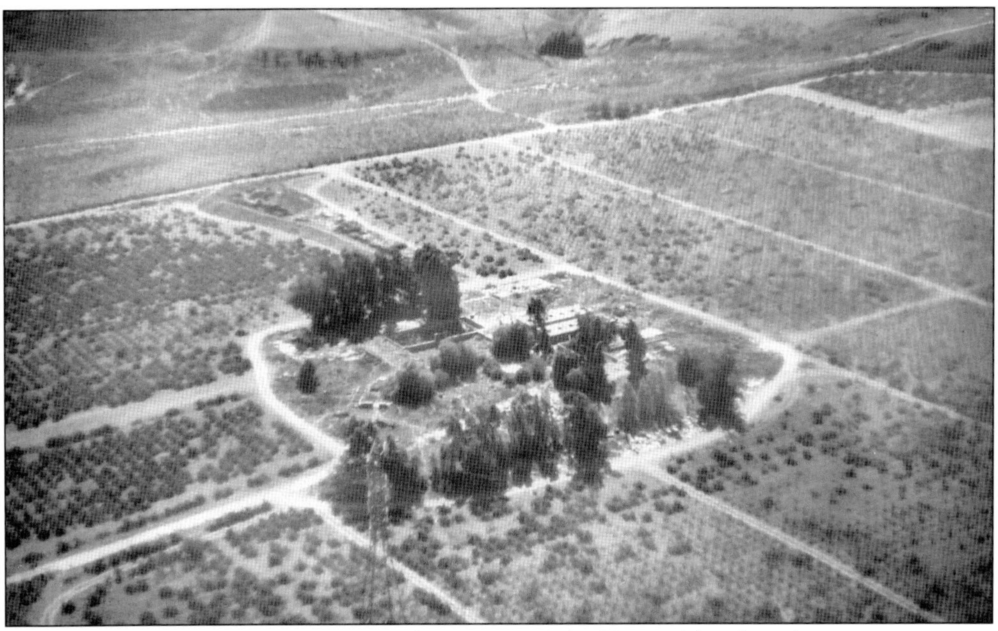

This aerial view of the La Vesu Winery shows its size. It had beautiful rockwork in its construction and storage vats for storing wine that were half out of the ground with a covering over the top. The road at the top of photo goes to the family quarry, and the vineyards were all over this area. The Filippi Winery was a few miles away.

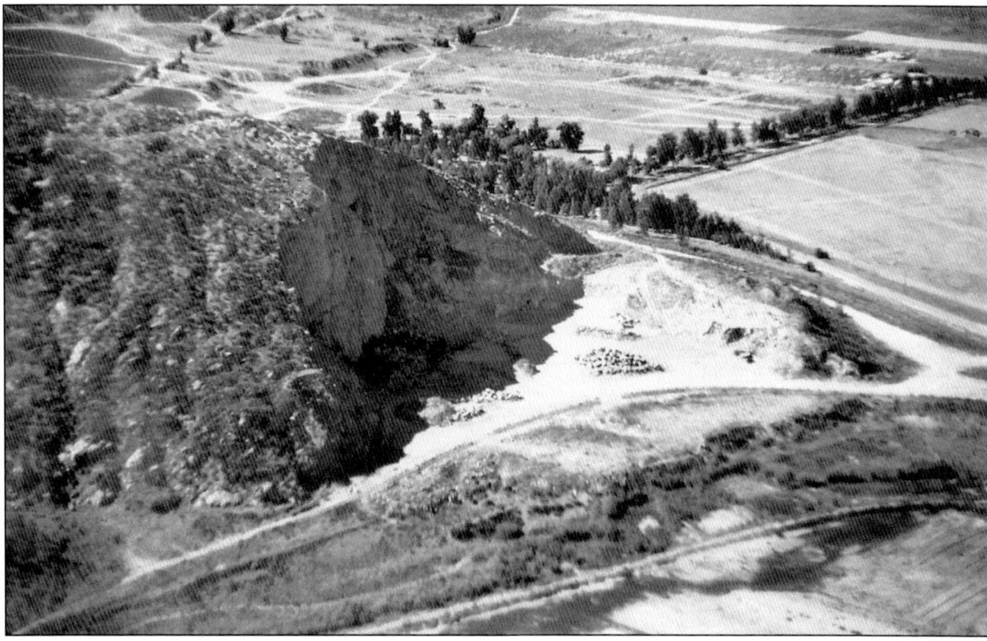

This view of the Declezville Quarry is looking southwest. The original settlement was at the foot of the quarry and the spur tacks used to come in from the right. The street to the left of the trees is Live Oak and underneath them was the Bird Farm. The small trees at the upper left are where the worker's cabins were located and the shrubbery going to the right represent the La Vesu Winery area. The foreground area was the city's sewer plant area, vineyards of the Pagliuso Family, and the chapel area.

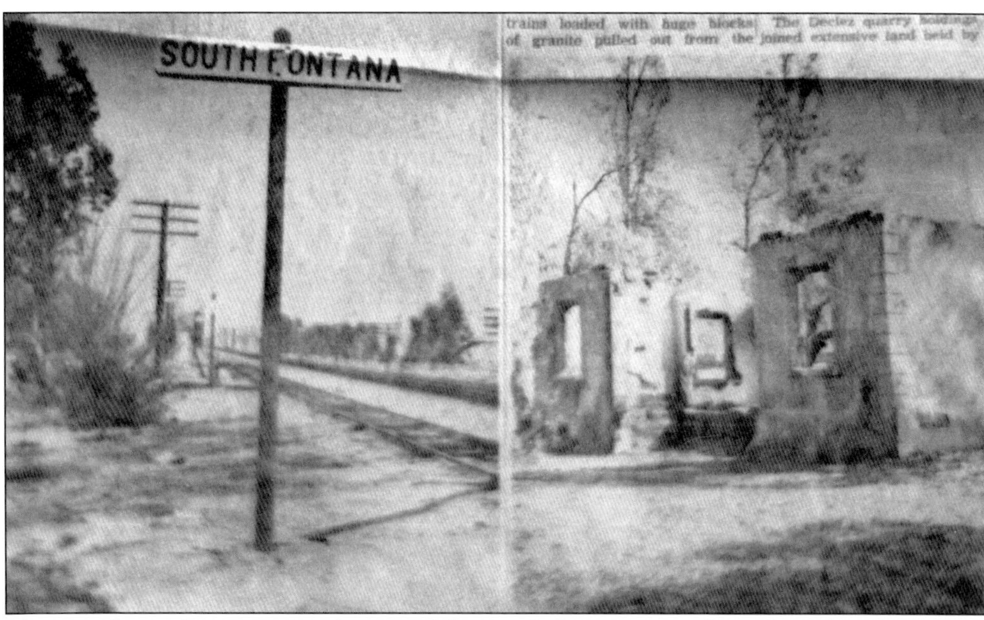

This is a photo of a newspaper clipping of the South Fontana sign along the railroad tracks and the ruins of the Declezville Post Office, now both gone.

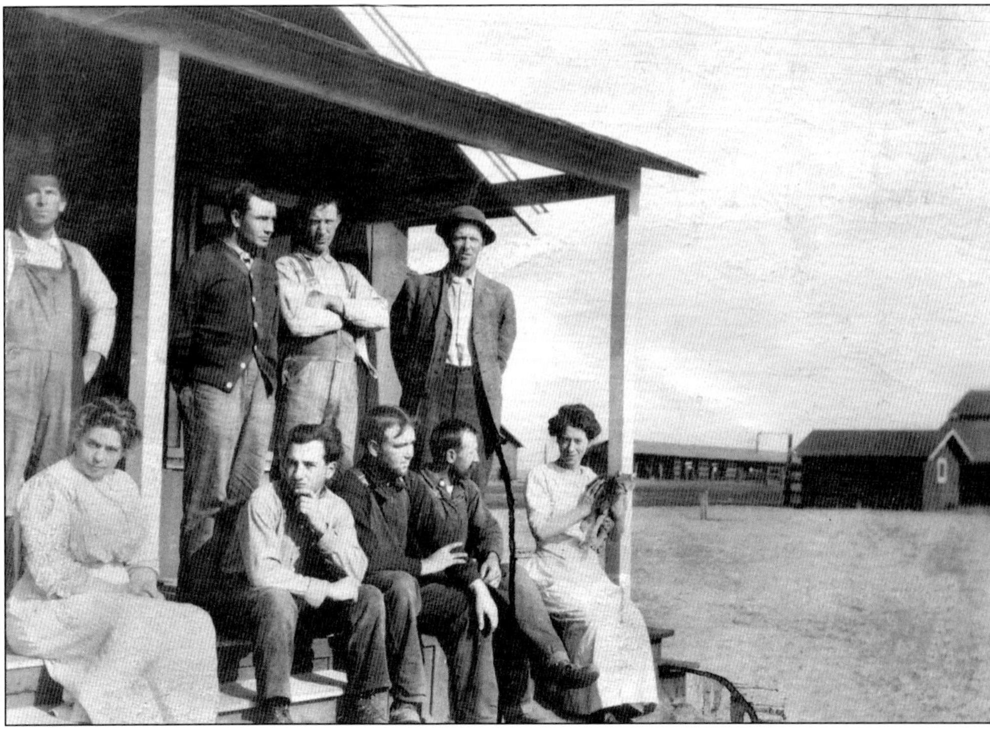

These two views are of the Fontana Farms Company hog ranch when it was at Declez from 1910 to 1912. They show the warehouses, the foreman's ranch house (that is still in the area), and some of the men's barracks. It was the center of the swine plant in Declez from 1921. In December 1925, the census count of the huge hog ranch showed 44,244 pigs of various size, age, color, and sex. It was the largest swine plant in the world. The camp headquarters was at Slover and Live Oak Avenues and operated until the 1940s.

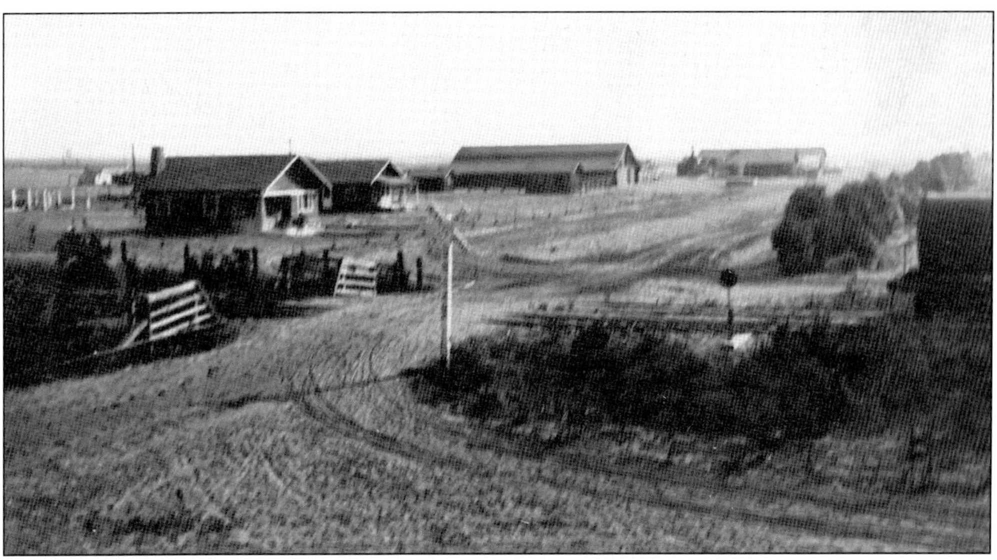

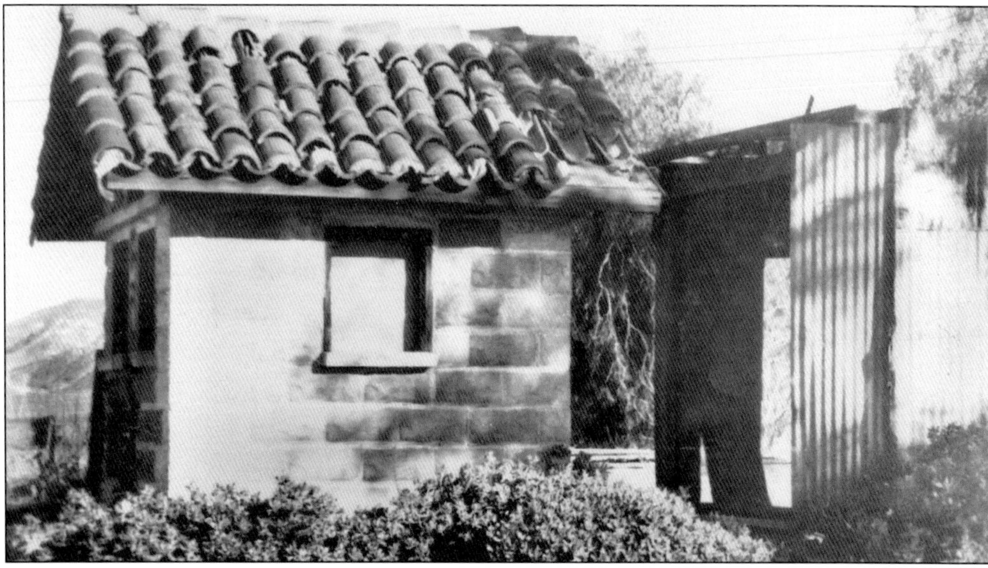

The Felice Pagliuso Chapel was built in 1925. Felice wanted to be a priest in Italy, but his brothers convinced him to come to America. The concrete block and clay bricks were from the Colton/Bloomington area. It stood at the highest point of the property facing the hills. The pitched roof was of Spanish tiles and formed over the knee, by hand, in Corona, California. A cement cross topped St. Anthony's, named by Felice. Father Russo, an Italian priest from Italy, blessed the church/chapel. Felice prayed often at the chapel until his death in 1936. The family kept the chapel in his memory and it now has been moved to the center of downtown Fontana by the Pacific Electric Station. There is now a vineyard planted around it and it is part of the Hazel Putnam Plaza.

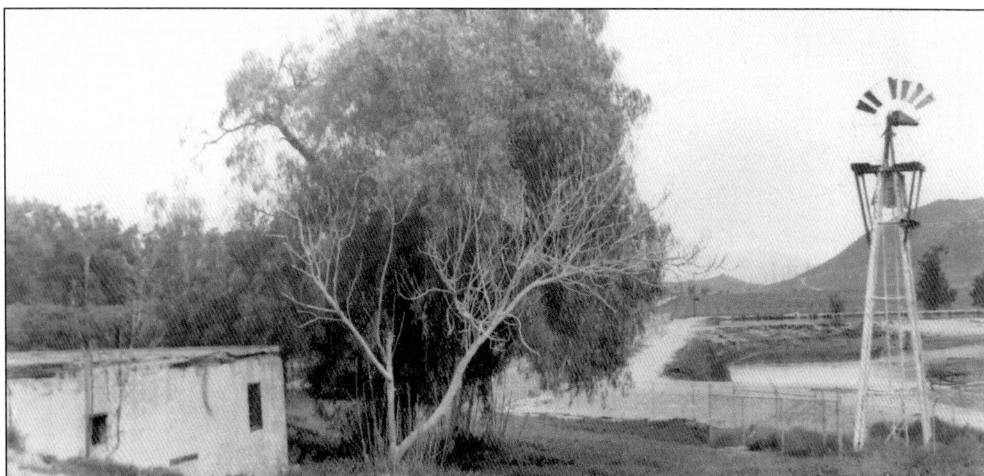

The Pagliuso Brothers settled the land across and north of the Declez Quarry in the 1890s. In exchange for clearing and planting vines on 60 acres, they were deeded 30 acres of gently sloping land at the foot of the Jurupa Hills by William Declez. They worked at the quarry for a $1 a day, 11 hours a day before going home to clear their land. They lived in a crude hut and had to hide several times from marauding Indians. They used their guns to scare them away. They planted, by hand, Mission Grape cuttings on their land and watered each plant with barrels from Pedley and the Santa Ana Rivers.

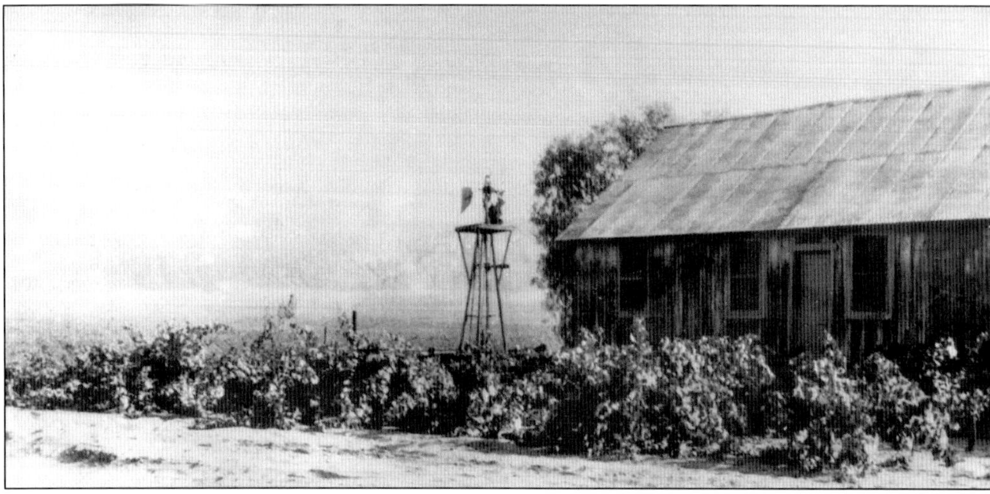

The winery and windmill were in South Fontana on property owned by the Chino Basin Municipal Water District. They leased the property to the Fontana Historical Society in 1979. Vandals burned down the house on top of the winery in 1974, with all the furnishings destroyed to the concrete floor of the winery basement. Felice lived in the house and took care of the buildings and vineyards. Margaret and Guiseppi then moved to Mill Creek and homesteaded 240 acres, planting vineyards and grain crops. Guiseppi worked for the Electric Power Plant. They later pioneered a homestead in Riverside of 40 acres, which was lost to development in 1979.

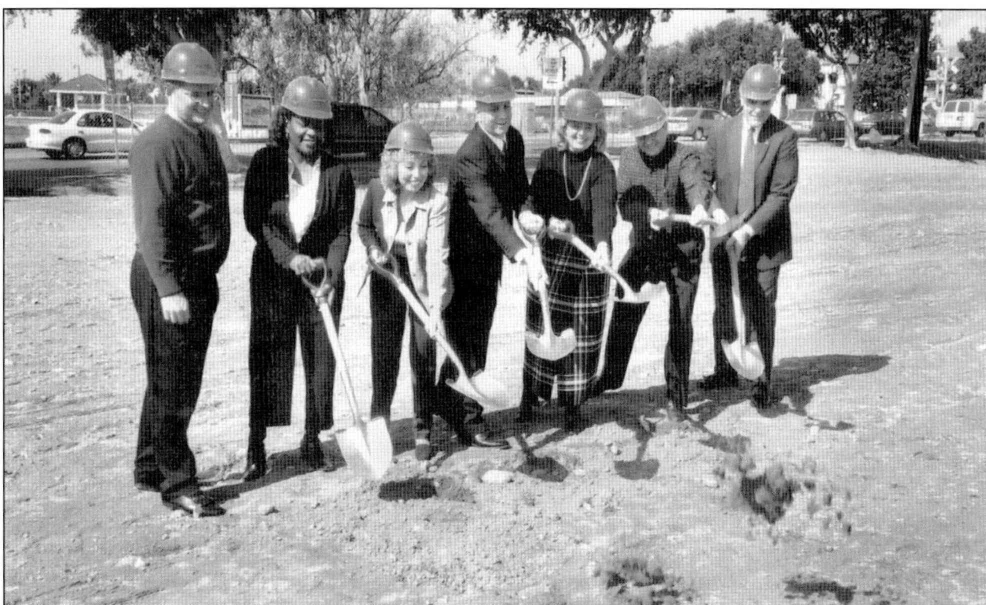

This 2004 photo shows the groundbreaking of the second senior citizen's center, looking northwest toward the Metrolink station, the Santa Fe tracks, and Sierra Avenue. The third senior citizen's center will be ready by the fall of 2005. The city council includes Ken Hunt, city manager; Acquanetta Warren, councilmember; Josie Gonzales, councilmember (now the supervisor's fifth district representative); Mark N. Nuaimi, mayor; Janice Rutherford, councilmember; John Roberts, councilmember; and David R. Edgar, director of Department of Housing and Business Development.

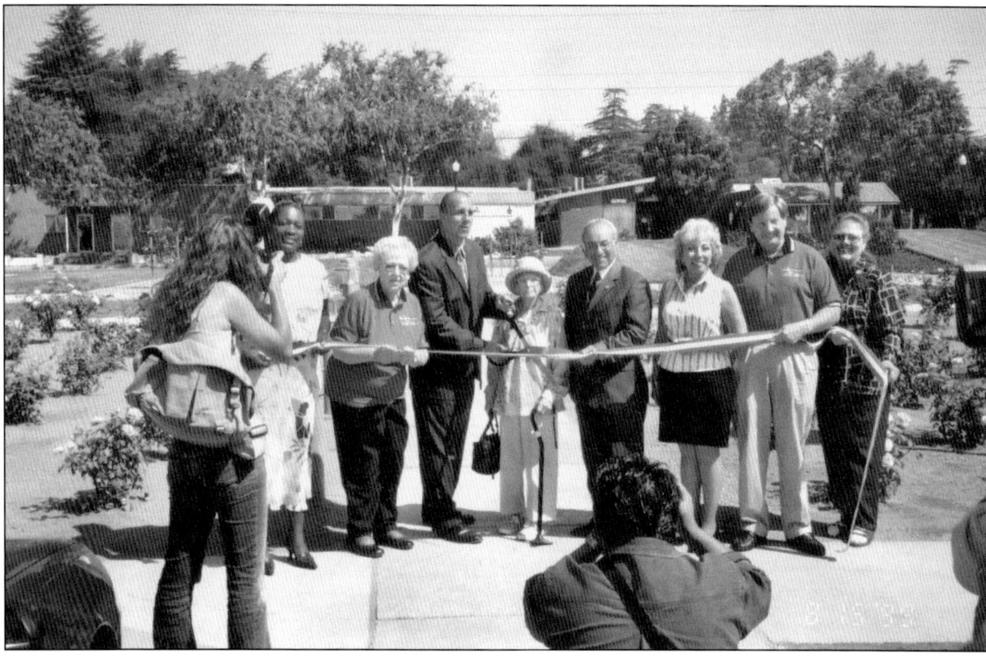

Pictured in this 2004 photo of the dedication of the new Hazel Putnam Plaza, from left to right, are Acquanetta Warren, Beatrice Watson, Mark N. Nuaimi, Hazel Putnam, Rep. Joe Baca Sr., Josie Gonzales, John Roberts, and Janet Koehler-Brooks. The plaza is located downtown on the Pacific Electric Trail, between Seville and Spring Streets, west of Sierra Avenue. The Plaza contains the *c.* 1912 Fontana Farms Company tract office, the Fontana Historical Society office, the 1912 Pacific Electric station, and the Felice Pagliuso St. Anthony's Chapel.

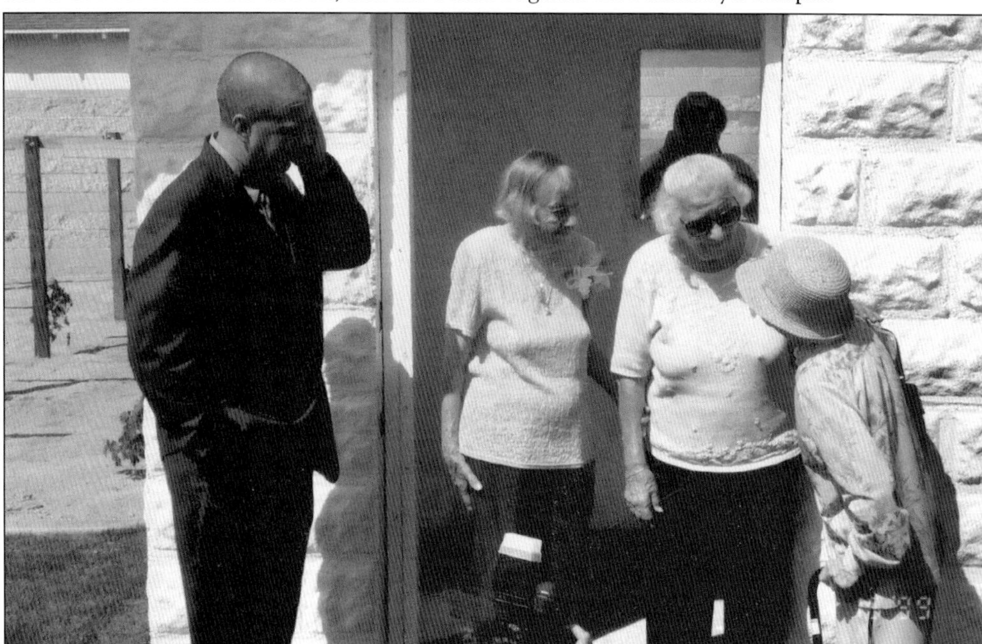

Pictured at the dedication are, from left to right, Mayor Mark Nuaimi, the Pagluiso daughters, and Hazel Putnam.

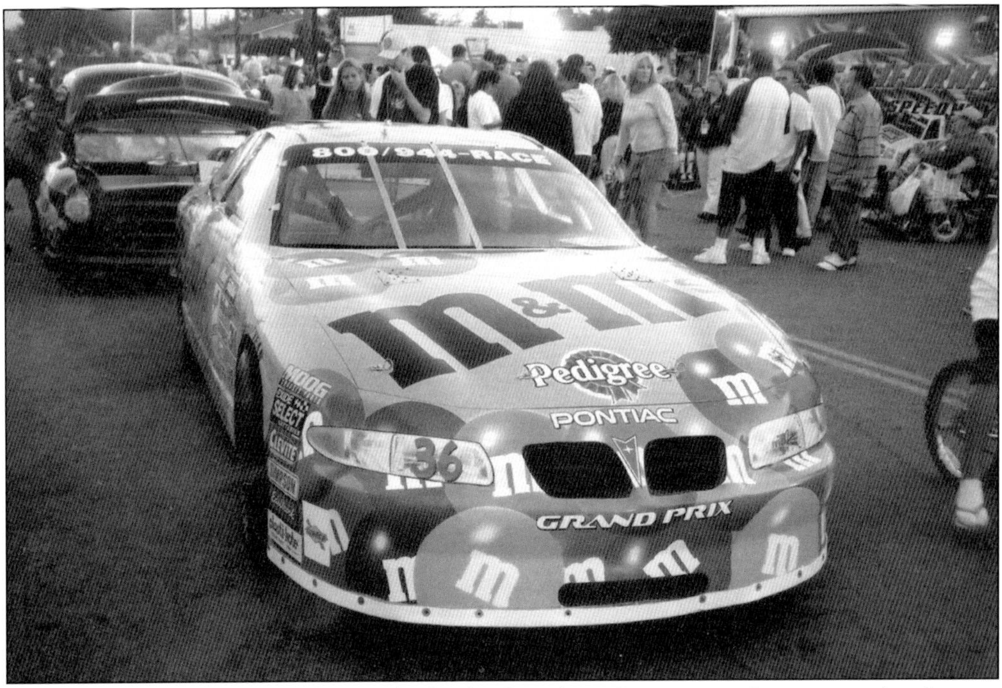

The monthly Cruise and Market Night for the Speedway Connection features a wide selection of cars on display, drivers signing autographs, and plenty of music and food. The event is held on the first Friday of each month on Nuevo Avenue, between Arrow Highway and Valencia Avenue.

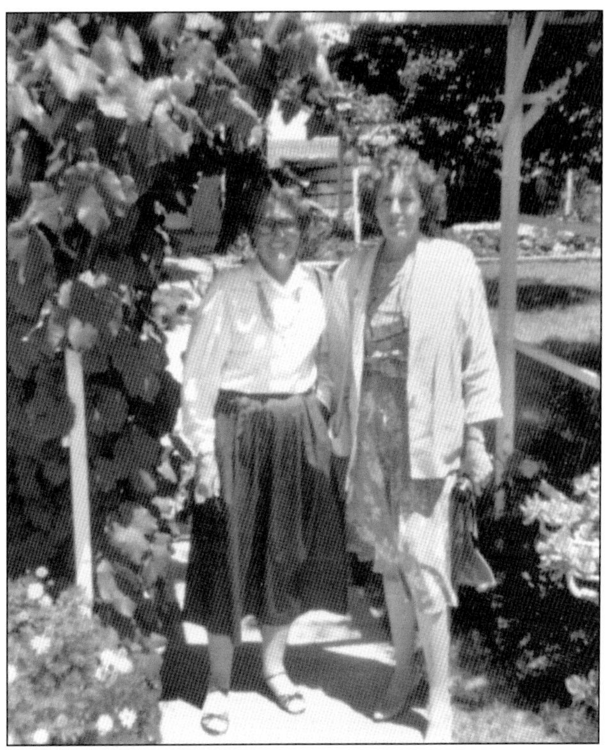

Pictured under the trellis at the foreman's ranch house of Camp No. 1 are Dorthea Newport and Constance Crawford, the grandnieces of A.B. Miller.

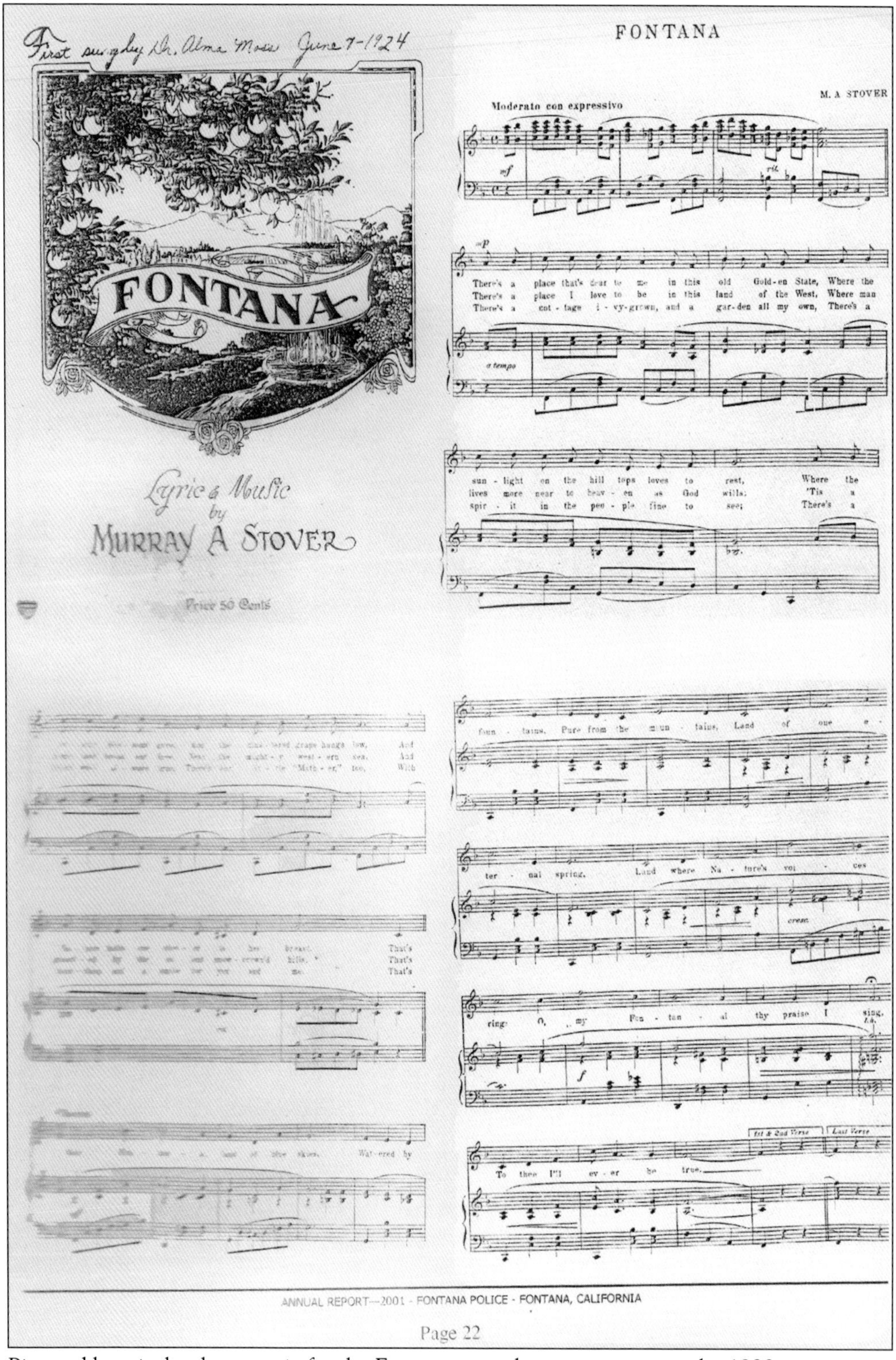

Pictured here is the sheet music for the Fontana song that was written in the 1920s.